Shell Games

The Life and Times of Pearl McGill,
Industrial Spy and Pioneer Labor Activist

Shell Games

The Life and Times of Pearl McGill,
Industrial Spy and Pioneer Labor Activist

by

Jeffrey S. Copeland

PARAGON HOUSE

First Edition 2012

Published in the United States by
Paragon House
1925 Oakcrest Avenue
St. Paul, MN 55113

Photo acknowledgements:

For photos of Pearl McGill we gratefully acknowledge Jean Burns.

We also thank the Musser Public Library for their kind assistance in locating and providing photos of the period from the Graham Collection, the Oscar Grossheim Collection, and the Arnold Miller Collection.

Cover buttons photo and "Mississippi Harvest" on page 344 by Douglas Hartley.

Library of Congress Cataloging-in-Publication Data

Copeland, Jeffrey S. (Jeffrey Scott), 1953-
 Shell games : the life and times of Pearl McGill, industrial spy and
pioneer labor activist / by Jeffrey S. Copeland. -- 1st ed.
   p. cm.
 Summary: "Describes life in the Mississippi river town of Muscatine, Iowa
and the pearl button industry through the eyes of a young woman working to
create safe working conditions and fair pay for factory workers and looks at
the controversy of labor union development from the viewpoint of the owners
and workers"--Provided by publisher.
 ISBN 978-1-55778-899-3 (pbk. : alk. paper)
 1. McGill, Pearl. 2. Women labor union members--Iowa--Muscatine--History.
3. Labor movement--Iowa--Muscatine--History. 4. Pearl button
industry--Iowa--Muscatine--History. I. Title.
 HD6079.2.U52M87 2012
 331.88'1878--dc23
 [B]
                                        2011048011

Manufactured in the United States of America
10 9 8 7 6 5 4 3 2 1

For current information about all releases from Paragon House,
visit the web site at http://www.paragonhouse.com

For my wife,
Linda

Author's Note

THE RELATIONSHIP BETWEEN BUSINESS OWNERS and the labor force has always been an unsettled one characterized by the necessity of give and take on both sides, with change often mediated by the representative unions. However, from an all-time high during World War II with unions representing 35% of the nonagricultural labor force in this country, union membership has declined to less than 12% today, roughly the same level as when Pearl McGill began her work.

Pearl McGill and the other champions of workers' rights gave their hearts, their souls, and in some cases even their very lives to make possible the improvements in working conditions we take for granted today. I hope all those who read of her life and legacy will be inspired to look, as she did, to the possibilities of the future and, at the same time, remember the sacrifices of those who came before us.

....

The time period involved herein was compressed to allow the story to unfold as presented. Also, for obvious reasons, some of the names have been changed, and other characters are composites of several.

—JSC

February 5, 1924, 8:27 P.M., St. Louis, Missouri

ANNA TOLIVAR HAD ALWAYS ENJOYED *a brisk walk after her evening meal and was looking forward to it even more so on this day than she had in several months' time. She was in high spirits, having just received a letter in the afternoon mail inform-ing her that a mid-level secretarial position was being held for her in a printing company just across the Mississippi River in East St. Louis. Anna had been out of work now for nearly ten weeks and was keeping her head above water financially only through a siz-able savings she had been able to accrue before being discharged from her last position. She badly needed this job not just for the money but for the emotional stability a regular job provides. Over the past two years she had secured, and was then asked to leave, positions in five different companies, all because, in each case, her past eventually managed to catch up with her. This topsy-turvy life was taking its toll, and she was tired of it. Bone tired.*

Anna had once been, in the crude vernacular of industry, a "mole patsy," a person who took entry level jobs in companies in order to report to the governing unions such things as the safety of working conditions, wage inequities, and all other ways own-ers might be taking advantage of workers. She had been good at her job, relishing the cloak of secrecy and the "game" of stalking the lords of the companies she joined. After obtaining the informa-tion in each location, she would quietly resign from her position, report her findings to the union, and then vanish, like a ghost flit-ting away into the night. The details she provided often served as the ammunition the union needed to go on the attack and allow it a toe-hold for negotiation with those in power.

Ultimately, however, she played the game too long. Her undo-ing had come just over two years before when she had unwittingly taken a position in a dress manufacturing plant operated by the same family who owned a large woolen mill she had infiltrated the previous year. While at the mill, she passed along information to the union that led to almost immediate change, change that had helped improve the lives of many workers but that had cost the owners nearly a fourth of their profit margin in the process. In the aftermath, several workers from the woolen mill had been given a choice: relocate to the dress plant and remain employed at a reduced salary or stay and face likely elimination of their current positions. Jobs were scarce, so most grudgingly made the move, leaving long-time homes, and in some cases family members, behind. Before Anna left the woolen mill, several of the line workers had finally guessed what she was up to, but they kept their mouths shut and did not inform the owners. Some of her co-workers were even supportive and provided her with specific, personal examples of how ownership had been taking advantage of them. Little did they know, this same information would eventually come full circle and lead to their forced relocation. Two of these workers in particular put full blame for their situations on Anna's shoulders, so when they recognized her one morning at the dress plant, they wasted little time informing the plant manager there was a spy in their midst.

That same afternoon the plant manager had called Anna to his office just as her shift was ending. As soon as she entered his office and the door closed behind her, a man to her right grabbed her while another pulled a sheet tightly over her head and clamped a hand over her mouth. She struggled mightily, but a sudden and brutal blow to her forehead was the last thing she remembered until waking up tied to a cot in a room she did not recognize. A grimy oil lamp provided just enough light for her to see three men sitting around her. Her forehead throbbed, and her wrists and ankles ached from the tightness of the rope around them. When the men saw she had regained consciousness, a tall, shadowy figure suddenly appeared behind them and told her she was going to be allowed to live so that she could spread word to other patsies that they would be dealt with severely if they kept to their spying. They didn't give Anna a chance to respond. In an instant, the sheet was over her head again as they took turns kicking and beating her until sweet unconsciousness overtook her once more.

Her days as a patsy were done. She was then officially black-listed, and her name and photograph were sent out to a wide network of industries and businesses across the country. Initially, even the unions she worked for turned their backs on her and dis-avowed any knowledge of her work so as not to fan the fires of their strained, combative relationship with ownership groups. Anna was now alone. Her only hope for future employment would rest in finding positions at companies that hadn't yet been sent informa-tion about her past. It always seemed just a matter of time before she was found out. Five positions in the past two years spoke vol-umes to this.

Thus, on this brisk February night she once again wore a broad smile as she walked along and thought of the new position waiting for her at the printing company. Maybe this time would be differ-ent. Plus, if she could last in this job long enough, another oppor-tunity, one more suited to her, might be just on the horizon. As she strolled along the sidewalk on Grand Avenue, she reached into her purse and pulled out a letter that had come the week before from a woman she had worked with just over a dozen years before in the button manufacturing industry in Muscatine, Iowa. The carefully worded language in the letter let Anna know that she and several of her old friends were going to be contacted by a new branch of a national union to "Pick up the good fight again." And this time, the letter went on to say, they would finally receive the financial compensation they deserved and had not been provided in the past for their efforts. Anna was warned that this news should be kept in absolute secrecy.

As she slowed her pace and turned to the next page of the let-ter, a large man walking toward her suddenly grabbed her arm. She was so stunned she found herself pulled halfway down a deserted alleyway by two men before she even attempted to scream.

The scream never came....

....

The larger of the two, a burly man wearing a new skimmer straw hat, slowly stepped forward and kicked the body forcefully just below the rib cage near the small of the back. There was a dull thud—but no other sound or movement. "She's dead, all right," he said, flatly. "Dead as a bag of hammers."

The short man nodded, stood next to the body, and said, "She won't be poking her nose in other people's business anymore. Wonder what she thinks of her labor union rights now?"

The larger man pulled a thin, curved knife from a sheath tucked in his sleeve. "Time for the message," he said, kneeling down and grasping the body's right hand.

In one swift and sure motion he severed the index finger, wrapped it tightly in his handkerchief, and placed it in his coat pocket. "There will be no more finger pointing," he said with a thin smile.

"You enjoy your work too much," the short one said.

"It's a living," the larger man responded, shrugging his shoulders.

Both men stepped around the body and disappeared into the darkness of the alley behind them.

....

April 3, 1924, 12:15 A.M., Chicago, Illinois

RUTH ANN EVANS HATED THE *three to twelve shift, but it paid ten cents more per hour, and she was glad to have the extra income. After years of scrimping and saving, she was close to having enough money to place a down payment on one of the small homes she adored in the south side of the city.*

For nearly ten years she had moved from one city and town to another while working as a patsy for so many labor unions she wasn't sure she could name them all now. She was proud of the work she had done and proud of the changes that had resulted.

The fight had been worth it, but the physical and emotional toll of living a double life for so long had worn her down. She was only twenty-eight years old, but the deep lines on her face and dark circles under her eyes made new acquaintances guess her to be in her late thirties or early forties. She also felt the toll of standing for long hours at dozens of workstations in the various factories where she'd worked.

Her current job was line supervisor for a cardboard box making plant. She got the job by falsifying her work background on her application for employment and listing as references other patsies who provided her with superior recommendations. Ruth Ann had done this so many times that the process was now almost second nature. She had taken the position in the box plant to investigate whether stories of widespread safety violations there were true. For the first time in her many years of infiltrating a company, she discovered the rumors were unfounded. This left her in a very unusual position. She loved her job, and it was the first time in her life she was in a company that actually cared about the safety and welfare of its employees.

Upon discovering this, she was almost upset at first. On the one hand, she had wasted all that time in a place where her special talents would be of no use to anyone. On the other hand, because the conditions at the company were so good, she knew it presented an opportunity for her to finally settle down, to give up her nomadic existence and plant the roots she so desperately wanted. And, as a bonus, she loved her work as a supervisor and could see herself continuing in that position for years to come. She doubted anyone at the company would ever find out about her past if she kept a low profile.

After work each evening, she could walk the short distance to the streetcar stop and then be home in about twenty minutes. However, the streetcar ride cost ten cents each way, and over the course of the week, that added up and was money, as far as she was concerned, thrown right out the window. That same money could be saved and applied to the down payment, which would get her into her new home that much sooner. So, instead of taking the streetcar, she often chose to walk just to the south of the plant through a long stretch of trees known to the locals as Miller's Woods, cross a rickety bridge over a mud creek, continue through an abandoned cow pasture, and soon be on 11th Street, just ten minutes from home.

On this clear and cool April night, Ruth Ann was calculating how much of her current week's wages she'd be able to place into savings as she came to the rickety bridge. As she reached for the handrail, she noticed a small man standing, hands in his pockets, several feet into the bridge. At the same time, she heard the footsteps of someone rushing quickly toward her from behind.

The small man smiled at her and shrugged his shoulders.

Ruth Ann dropped her savings book. It hit the edge of the bridge and bounced off into the mud below. In the confusion of sudden terror, she started to reach for it.

It was her last conscious movement.

....

The larger man peered down at the body and said, "I sure hate using a hammer. It's so messy."

"Makes me sick to look at it," the short man said, "but it does make a statement, and that's the point, right?"

The larger man didn't answer. He just stood there and shook his head as he wiped his fingerprints from the hammer and flung it roughly into the trees to his left.

The short man squatted near the body and said, "This one isn't bad to look at. Shame. Rotten shame."

The larger man replied, "Her mouth was too big for the rest of her," he said, shaking his head again. He then added, flatly, "Message time. She won't be tattle-taling now to the unions."

He knelt next to the body and inched to the side to avoid the spreading blood. With his left hand he pulled out his curved knife. With his right hand he pried open the mouth and tried to grasp the tongue.

"Slippery as a damn eel," he said, while trying again and again to get a firm grip.

"What's taking so long?" the short man asked. "You trying to make a career out of it?"

"You ever try to cut one out before? It's not easy as it looks. If you think you can do better, get yourself down here and try."

"No," the short man replied. "I lost my glasses somewhere. Besides, the boss wouldn't like it. It's your job. Just hurry up."

"There—done," the larger man finally said, placing the tongue firmly in the body's right hand.

"I don't know why you're doing that," the short man said, sternly. "Throw it away. Get rid of it. The newspapers around here are pro-union, so they'll never print it."

"You're right, but the people who need to know will get the message."

Then, standing and cleaning his knife, the larger man continued, "Well, that's two. Boss said there's one more to go. Out in some one-dog, whistle-stop town in Iowa. I hate the country. Hate it. Makes me sneeze and cough. Probably catch my death there. After that, it could be the last of the bonus money, too. If it is, I'm going to miss that."

The short man said, "Aw, I wouldn't worry about that too much. You know that old expression: 'There's a squealer in every barn.' It's true as rain. You should know that by now. That's the way of the world. There'll always be a need for us."

They stood a minute in silence, studying the body. The larger man finally spoke. "Yeah, you're probably right again. But you'd think people would finally learn to keep their mouths shut."

"People sure are dumb, aren't they?" the short man said, laughing softly.

"Most aren't smart, like us," the larger man added, sarcastically, rolling his eyes.

The small man started to reply but stopped. He just looked up, smiled weakly, and then said, "We can catch that ballgame tomorrow if we hurry. Ready to go?"

The larger man took one long, last look at the body and said, "You say Donovan's pitching? He's really good. I admire that. A man should be good at his work. You agree?"

After taking his own last look at the body, the short man responded, quickly. "Completely."

They both walked slowly across the bridge and into the moonless night.

....

Chapter 1

Saturday, July 9, 1910

THE TRAIN RIDE ALONG THE rolling banks of the Mississippi River from Grandview, Iowa, to Muscatine, Iowa, was just under two hours, but it was taking me worlds away. I was born and raised in Grandview, and other than a journey to the capital city of Des Moines for the State Fair three years before, I had never been this far away from home. I wasn't frightened to be leaving Grandview. I was excited for what I dreamed the future could hold.

For as long as I could remember, I had wanted to become a teacher like my sister, Anne. I had seen what her teaching certificate had done for her, and I desperately wanted the same. It had been her ticket to new towns, new friends, and new adventures. Life in Grandview wasn't terrible for me. I was surrounded by a wonderful group of family and friends, and life was, well, secure if nothing else. I just wanted more. I *needed* more. I wanted the same opportunities Anne had earned. I wanted to see the country, the world.

I had just completed my high school education, but in order to be qualified to hold either a Rural or County teaching certificate, I had to pursue college studies, and this was expensive. There were precious few jobs available for young women in Grandview, so to raise the money for my schooling I had to go where the opportunities were. Muscatine was the largest button manufacturing center in the entire country, and I had a position waiting for me at the Blanton Button Company, which was, by reputation, one of the best in the entire region.

The job was secured for me by my uncle, Sam Henry McGill. Sam Henry owned and operated the McGill Button Company, a button blank cutting business just outside the town limits of Grandview. The button blanks he produced, the raw, round pieces cut from mussel shells found in the nearby Mississippi, were shipped to companies in Muscatine where they were processed into finished buttons of all manner and variety. Because of how highly regarded he was in the manufacturing community, he was able to find this employment for me, and I appreciated it. He provided the opportunity. Now it was up to me to succeed. And succeed I would. Nothing was going to keep me from my dreams. Nothing.

My mother also helped by finding a place for me to live in Muscatine. Her best friend from her own school days, Flora Reed, had a daughter, Mattie, just a year older than I. Mattie had moved to Muscatine the previous year to work in the button-manufacturing industry, and had taken rooms above a jewelry store in the main downtown business district. Now, thanks to my mother, I was going to be sharing these with her. I had played with Mattie regularly when we were small children at the times when our mothers would get together to visit and relive old times, but I didn't know her all that well. What I recalled most was she couldn't have kept still even if her bottom had been glued to the floor. She was always one blur of constant motion, and I could never keep up with her, no matter what game we played. Living with her and sharing expenses was going to help me save money, which was my most important goal at present. At the same time, I had a sneaking suspicion living with Mattie was going to be anything but dull.

I had hoped she would meet me at the station and help me get to our rooms and settled in, but I had received a postcard from her earlier in the week informing me she and my other new roommate, a girl I didn't know at all, would be out of town the day of my arrival. She would leave a key under a flowerpot on the windowsill outside the door and I was to make myself to home. She ended the note by saying she would return to Muscatine by the end of the weekend. The note was short and precise, and she gave no explanation for her absence.

··· ··· ···

I had never, ever, experienced anything like it before.

The smell hung like a thick fog in the heavy, mid-summer July air, and I was one good sniff or cough away from throwing up.

I clamped my hand tightly over my nose so I could use my glove as a filter, but even that didn't offer protection.

"Heaven, help us!" I shouted to no one in particular as the porter took my arm and led me carefully down the steps of the train when we finally reached the depot in Muscatine. "What *is* that smell?"

Smiling smugly as he picked up his suitcase and inched slowly past me while trying to make his way through the crowded plat-form, a skinny middle-aged man wearing a straw hat tilted jaun-tily sideways first snorted like a pig and then replied, "Welcome to Muscatine, Iowa, Miss. Must be your first time here."

I started to respond, but when I removed my hand from my nose and took another breath, I started to feel dizzy and faint.

A shoeshine boy to my left looked up, laughing, and added, "Lady, 'round here they call that smell 'money in the bank.'" He turned away from me, leaned farther down and, specifically for my benefit, dramatically pretended he was vomiting. He fol-lowed this by sprawling out on the ground, kicking his legs vio-lently several times, and then shouting, "I'm dying. I can't take the smell no more. Take me, Lord!"

The crowd around us on the platform burst into laughter. The shoeshine boy, obviously pleased with himself, jumped right up and bowed deeply, holding out his cap at the same time in case anyone cared to toss him a coin or two for his performance. Several did just that, the coins clinking one after the other.

The sight of him heaving so dramatically just about set me off, had me right on the edge. To repay him for his performance and helping put me into this state, I stepped as heavily as I could on his left foot with the heel of my shoe and pressed down with all my might. He yelped and jumped back, a shocked expression spreading quickly across his young face. The crowd again burst into laughter, and a tall gentleman to our right then tossed *me* a dime.

"Why, you're better than he is, and that's saying something," the tall gentleman said, smiling.

"Thanks a lot," I said as sarcastically as I could. "Throw me another one and I'll use them to plug up my nostrils."

"You'll get used to it," the dime-thrower replied, flipping over another. "Now, let's see it. I want to see you plug your nose with those. Or, are you all talk?"

Several in the crowd inched closer.

"I think he needs it more than I do. Let's try *his* nose," I said, quickly grabbing the shoeshine boy's ragged vest and pulling him toward me. He flailed his arms wildly and kicked again, this time trying to get away from me. His arms somehow got twisted up in the strap of my new handbag, and we crashed together, nearly tumbling to the ground. By this time, a crowd had assembled around us. Everyone howled.

"Oh, hold still," I said, spinning the boy around to face me. "Here, take this money and buy a new act. And then buy some soap and go take a bath. Go on now. Scoot!"

As soon as I let go, he darted away like he was being chased by the devil himself. The crowd roared its approval. I gave an exaggerated curtsy to all and said, "We appear twice daily for your viewing pleasure. Next show at six. Be sure to tell all your friends."

The porter, who had stopped his work to join the onlookers,

stepped forward and said, "Show's over folks. Step over there and get your luggage. Time to go on your way. Keep moving."

Then, turning toward me, he said, gently, "The boy meant no harm, Miss. And he's actually right. Some do call it 'money in the bank,' but if that's true, I've never seen any of it. Heck, most of us around here haven't. No, if you ask me, this town should have a big sign here at the depot that says: 'Welcome to Muscatine: The Outhouse of the West.' That's more the truth of the matter."

As the crowd began to disperse, several close by and within earshot responded a terse "Amen" and "That's for sure" to support the porter's opinion.

I was more confused than ever.

"Money in the bank?" I asked.

The porter didn't answer my question. Instead, he looked more serious and handed me a small glass bottle he plucked from his inside vest pocket.

"Here. Take this," he said. "Keep it. Dab some of this under your nose a couple times a day for, oh, I'd say about a week. Double up on that every time the wind blows up from the south. It'll help."

"What is it?" I asked, pulling the cork and raising the bottle to my nose. Instantly, I could smell the sweet odor of Surprise Rose like we grew back home along the main fencerow up by the road.

"It'll be your salvation if you want to live here," he said, moving away to supervise the unloading of the rest of the baggage. Then, turning one last time and bowing slightly toward me, he added, "Good luck to you, Miss. Keep your head low, breathe through your mouth, and never stand facing the wind. Never." He turned and disappeared into the crowd.

I just stood there, speechless, now more confused than before, which I thought an impossibility.

"He's right," an elderly woman next to me nodded while searching the platform for her suitcase. "My child, keep your head low and your chin on your chest. Took me a good six months, but I finally figured it out."

Then she added, laughing softly, "Only thing, though—we look like a pack of hunchbacks. Take a look around."

I scanned the platform and was stunned to see she was right. Men, women, and children stooped over and looked as if they were carrying invisible loads on their backs.

"What have I gotten myself into?" I said aloud to myself, suddenly very unsure of the wisdom of my travel to what already seemed to be an incredibly strange town.

I stood there for a minute, lowered my glove from my face, and tried as hard as I could to place the smell. Rotting fish was my first thought. Then, after a few seconds, I changed my mind. It was more like the local sewers had overflowed from the rain that had pelted down the past several weeks in this corner of the state.

I placed my glove firmly against my nose and tried not to gag. Then, as quickly as I could, I held my breath, opened the vial given to me by the porter, and smeared the oily liquid under my nose and just in the nick of time.

As my stomach finally settled and I waited for my turn at the luggage carts, I tried to ask others around me about the smell. Most just laughed and turned away. One older man wearing new bib overalls asked me, "What smell? I don't smell anything."

His nose must have been dead.

Finally, someone behind tapped me gently on the shoulder. I turned to see the dime-thrower smiling broadly at me. "What you're experiencing," he began, "is a burden all of us here learn to tolerate. That is the grim odor of industry, which is a financial blessing for this community and, as you've already discovered, a curse of epic proportions. You're smelling the clamming indus- try, the heart and soul and life-blood of this whole area. Without it and the jobs that come from it, this whole town would just dry up and blow away."

Here he paused, motioned to the bench on our right, and continued, "By the way, my name is James. They still haven't unloaded all the bags, and take a look at that crowd. We're going to be here a while, so we might as well make the best of it and get comfortable. Please, let's sit a minute. While we do, I'll do my best to take that terrified look off your face."

"Terrified look? Do I look that awful?" I asked, reaching for the mirror in my handbag to see for myself.

It was then, in one cold, breath-catching moment, I realized my handbag was gone.

I was too stunned to stand and call out for help. Instead, I raised my hands, turned my palms upward, and said, calmly and matter of factly, "I've been robbed. Robbed. What kind of place *is* this?"

"What did you say?" my new acquaintance asked, leaning close, trying to catch my words through the sea of sounds around us on the platform.

"I said I've been robbed!" I repeated again, this time sternly, forcefully. "My travelling money, my favorite jewelry—all in my handbag. It's all gone."

"Gone?" he asked, his smile suddenly evaporating.

When he realized I wasn't kidding, he jumped up and starting searching the platform around us. "Maybe you just lost it. Try to stay calm—we'll find it. I'll find it if I have to tear this place apart board by board."

Still in a state of disbelief, I stood and began searching around and behind the bench when it suddenly dawned on me. As clearly as if I were watching a slow-motion nickelodeon reel, I saw the shoeshine boy tangled up in the strap. When he and I had tussled earlier, I had dropped my arms, allowing the handbag to fall to the platform, where it got wrapped around his feet. When the shoeshine boy finally made his escape from me, he had reached down to grab his shine box…and then my handbag!

"You can stop looking now," I said in exasperation. "It was the shoeshine boy. Why that little…."

I seldom swore. I didn't believe in it. My father always said swearing was "lazy language," and I agreed with him. Well, most of the time. The words that were now coming out of my mouth as I described that shoeshine boy shocked James so badly he sat back down on the bench and took off his hat to fan himself. He started to cut in, to stop the flow of my words that were suddenly just as vile as the air around us, but all he could do was stutter and shake his head.

"Whoa!" he finally managed to call out. "Let's try to get a grip—try to compose ourselves a tad. Slow down a minute."

"Compose ourselves!" I shouted back at him. "I'll show you composure!"

A new crowd, horrified and with mouths gaping wide open, started assembling around us. James quickly stood up, turned to the group, and said calmly, reassuringly, while putting his arm around me, "It's ok, folks. She's new here, and the smell's gotten to her. She's just in shock. I'll take care of her. Go on about your business."

Most immediately let out sighs of relief, nodded knowingly, and started walking away as if they had seen this sort of thing at the station many times before. No big deal.

I tried to wriggle away from him, but he pulled me closer and said, this time sternly, "And I thought you weren't ready for Muscatine. Turns out, I'm not sure Muscatine is ready for you!"

His grip was firm, solid, so I stopped struggling and went limp. As I did, my head fell to his shoulder, and he held me close just for an instant before stepping back. "That's more like it," he said. "Calm down. We'll get your bag back. Really we will."

I stood motionless in front of him, unsure of what I should do next—unsure of what I *could* do next. He smiled again and said, gently, "Please, let's sit back down. Please."

We sat quietly a few minutes as we gathered our thoughts. The platform was still crowded, and an older woman wad-dling from side to side while trying to balance two large suit-cases accidentally whacked James mightily, square on the side of his left knee. He let out a high-pitched "Yow!" but the woman never looked back, never broke her waddle. When James looked my direction for sympathy, I couldn't help myself. I burst into laughter and rocked back on the bench. First he looked angry, but a smile soon appeared, and we both ended up laughing to the point of tears. The tension had been broken.

"That's what you get for throwing dimes at me," I said, playfully. "Serves you right."

"Very funny—and very ladylike on your part to make fun of me," he replied in mock seriousness.

We laughed again before settling back to catch our breath. Finally, after a few minutes, I broke the silence, "Shouldn't we try to find a policeman? We need to find that boy. I *need* that purse."

"Wouldn't do any good," James responded. "He's long gone by now, but if you're sure it was the boy, I think I know how to find him."

"How? This is a big town. Where would you look?"

James replied, "I saw a large, red '7' on the side of his shine box. All the shine boys have a district or area they patrol. It's an unwritten rule in that line of work that others don't wander into territory belonging to other shiners. Call it mutual respect—or survival or whatever. He's in area 7, which is obviously around here somewhere close, so he'll be back. I'll put out the word. We'll find him." He looked at me, saw the disbelief on my face, and continued before I could ask any questions, "I was once a shine boy myself. We all have to start somewhere. And I don't mind saying I was pretty good at it, too."

From the smile on his face I could tell he was getting pretty full of himself, so I couldn't resist. "You're truly amazing," I said. "If I had to be robbed, I'm glad I ended up with someone like you here to help me out. Rescuer of damsels in distress, former shoeshine boy, dime thrower. Is there anything you can't do? Yes, if I had to be robbed...."

"You *are* funny," he replied, rolling his eyes and coughing. "But just you wait. I'll find that purse. I'd bet money on it."

"And I pray you do," I said.

Then, turning serious again, I added, "Sincerely, thank you. Thank you for being so kind to me. You don't even know me, and you're still being so kind."

"That's right," he said, smiling again. "I don't know you, do I? So who are you? Tell me—who am I helping?"

"Well, I really should introduce myself to you. After all, we've been through so much together already," I said, dragging out the words as dramatically as I could. "I'm Ora Pearl McGill— everyone calls me Pearl—from Grandview. If I can manage to stand the air around here and it doesn't kill me dead, I'll be starting a new job on Monday. I'll be here as long as it takes to earn enough money to get to college. From there, only the Fates know what will follow. That's me in a nutshell. And you? What's your story, Mr. Dime-Thrower?"

He laughed out loud. "My name is James. James Baker. I grew up in and now work here in this precious air of Muscatine. That's me in a—what did you call it?—a nutshell?" He paused and handed me his handkerchief, motioning for me to wipe something from my left cheek.

"It's soot. From the train. Actually, it looks good on you."

"I must look a sight," I said, wiping my cheek.

"Just the hazards of train travel," he said, leaning back and studying me from head to foot. "Yes, you'll pass muster now. You look fine. As a matter of fact, if you don't mind me saying so, I think you're a beautiful young woman. I'm sure that sounds like I'm being fresh, but I don't mean to be. I just say what's on my mind. Some would call that a character flaw, but it's one I'm stuck with. I've been this way all my life, and I doubt I'll be changing any time soon."

"I have the feeling you're typically *very* fresh," I replied, smiling, "but since it looks like you're now my Muscatine Sir Galahad—at least for the moment—I'll let it pass. Thank you for the compliment."

In all the commotion I hadn't paid much attention to him before, but now, as we sat there, I noticed he really was quite striking. He was tall, at least six feet. His hair, parted down the middle, was medium chestnut and wavy. It was his face, however, that struck me the most. It was angular, strong, yet he could in an instant produce a smile that offered sincerity and warmth. His eyes were light green and gentle. Yes, he was striking—and downright handsome.

James motioned over to the luggage carts and said, "Looks like the crowd's finally thinning. Let me help you get your bags. We need to get you home. You're probably all tuckered out."

"I am at that," I replied. "I just want to get to my new home, sit down, take off my shoes, and read a newspaper. I don't think that's asking too much, do you?"

"No, it isn't," he said, taking my arm and walking me to the carts. "As a matter of fact, that sounds darn good to me. I'm tired, too. It's been a long day."

He pulled a medium-sized suitcase from the end of the first cart, placed it at his feet, and then asked me to point out mine. I had just one, about the same size as his, and it was near the end of the second cart.

"You're traveling light," he said. "Just one case?"

"The job came up pretty fast, so I just brought the bare necessities. My mom is sending more of my clothes soon. If I don't get my purse back, I'll need them quicker than ever."

James suddenly seemed very preoccupied. When we reached the end of the platform he turned to me and said, "I'm going to loan you a few dollars. Here—take this—and don't argue with me. You can pay me back later. Until we get your purse back, you're going to need it."

He handed me a five-dollar bill. "I can't take this," I protested. "I don't know you well enough to…"

He cut me off. "This isn't a gift. I expect you to pay it back. In the meantime, use it to get home and for anything else you might need today."

Then, handing me a card, he continued, "Here's where you can find me if you need anything else. Now, one more thing. Where should I bring the purse after I find it? And I *will* find it."

I liked his confidence, his bravado. He was more than a little full of himself, but my father had an expression for people like this: "They're not braggin' if they can back it up." I suddenly had the feeling James could back up anything he put his mind to.

At that moment I realized something else. I couldn't provide him with my new address because it was on the back of a postcard in my purse! However, as quickly as the panic set in, it evaporated as I remembered the rooms were above a jewelry store. I relayed this information to him, and he said he'd be able to find me. Of that, I had no doubt.

Then, turning to me one last time, James said, softly, "I'd give anything if I could walk you home, but I have to meet some people, and it can't wait. I'm really sorry about that. Get a taxi and ask the driver to help you find the jewelry store. If memory serves, there are only two of them downtown. He'll help you find the right one. I have to go now. I hope you understand."

I was sad he had to leave so suddenly, but he had already done so much for me. "I understand," I said, reaching out to shake his hand. "Thank you for everything."

We stood staring at each other for what seemed an eternity. My hand was still in his, and I didn't want to let go. Finally, he gently squeezed my hand, backed away, tipped his hat, and said, "Take care of yourself, Miss McGill. Be safe. I'll be in touch soon."

I nodded, but didn't say anything. I just waved as he turned and walked away. I watched after him until he disappeared into a crowd forming at the other end of the platform.

Suddenly finding myself alone, I decided to go about the business of getting to my new home. The five-dollar bill was in the small pocket on the front of my dress. I *could* take a taxi, but I might need the money before all was said and done. "After all," I thought to myself, "how difficult could it be to find the jewelry store?"

I started to walk there instead.

….. ….. ….. …..

CHAPTER 2

My decision not to take the taxi and walk to my new home was not the smartest decision I've ever made.

Two blocks from the station I realized I had made a mistake. A big mistake.

In my haste to leave the station, I had not asked for directions to the main downtown district, so it didn't take me long to be utterly and completely lost and disoriented. To compound matters, as soon as I headed to my left down Front Street, assuming this was the correct direction, I simply could not believe my eyes. There before me, as if a curtain had suddenly been pulled aside, was the greatest commotion I'd seen since my stroll down the midway at the state fair.

Vendors were everywhere, hawking everything from fish to alcohol—smack in the middle of the street in the path of all walking by. Off to the side, groups of men in worn and dirty work coveralls were assembled every twenty or thirty feet. Most clutched buckets of beer as they laughed and teased those walking by them. Some of the groups, however, used language that put my tirade at the depot to shame. When that happened, the other groups of men nearest to them would howl their approval, much to the horror of the targets of these blue words.

I tried to stay out of their range by keeping toward the center of the street and behind vendor carts, but when a boiled peanut seller right in front of me suddenly and without warning skidded to a halt to make a sale, I crashed right into the back of the cart, causing a mound of peanuts to rain to the ground. The seller wasn't happy and glared angrily at me. A group of particularly vocal men lounging next to the street lamp across from me saw this, and the smallest member of the group shouted my direction, "It's Calamity Jane! Look out!" Several others laughed and pointed, but I didn't give them the satisfaction of a response. That would have just set them off again, so I quickly stepped to the side and kept moving down the street, which had become even more crowded.

As I continued along, I passed two barbershop quartets, one on each side of the street, obviously challenging each other to singing contests. They weren't half bad. I went by a pair of jugglers, one juggling burning sticks and the other trying to keep baseballs in the air. Near to them a woman sat at a small table with a sign that read, "Your Fortune and Future—I'm <u>Never</u> Wrong!—5 Cents." Several yards down from the fortuneteller, I came to an older gentleman selling live chickens. As I went past, he waved a small axe and shouted he'd dress one of his best while I waited, but all I was interested in was getting far away from him because he appeared to be enjoying the axe-waving just a little too much.

I had never been to a carnival, but this seemed like every picture I had ever seen of one come to life right before my eyes. I was, at the same time, fascinated and a little shocked and frightened. This was Muscatine, one of the best and most important towns in the whole state. At present, it also seemed more like a nest of drunks, bums, and barkers. On top of everything else around me, I noticed large piles—each at least ten feet high—of opened clam shells every fifty feet or so. These piles created something of an artificial fence and boundary between the groups assembled along the street. It also didn't take long for me to figure out these piles were producing the lion's share of the stench in the air. My nose was suffering more than ever, but at least the mystery was now solved.

"What in the world have I gotten myself into?" I shouted out loud.

No one even noticed.

I was about to stop someone and ask for directions where Front Street intersected the streetcar tracks when I suddenly saw him—the shoeshine boy! Our eyes met at the same time, and he ran off into the crowd. I started to chase him, but a wild elbow from my left suddenly caught me squarely in the stomach, and I stopped short, bending over and gasping for breath. The person belonging to the elbow didn't even look my direction as he continued making his way along. I gave up all thought of a pursuit of the shoeshine boy and concentrated on catching my breath, which was a significant task given the quality of the air I was inhaling and the fact I was standing just a few yards from one of the larger piles of clam shells.

When I finally gained my composure, I spotted three young women in their mid-twenties standing across the street in front of a dry goods store. I wasn't about to walk up to one of the rowdy groups of men, so I decided to ask the women for help locating my new address. As I moved closer to them, using my suitcase now as a battering ram to keep from being knocked into again, I noticed they were all dressed the same: faded and tattered men's overalls, hair tucked up under red and white polka dot handkerchiefs tied high on their heads, and ankle-high brown leather boots.

"Excuse me," I said, inching closer to them. "I'm lost. Terribly lost. I was wondering if you could…."

The oldest of the group cut me off, eyeing me from head to foot, "Just who invited you to this party? Who do you think you are, Dearie?"

"I'm sorry to interrupt you," I said. "It's just that I'm lost and can't find this address."

I reached down to open my purse and again remembered it was gone—and so was the postcard with the address. All I could remember was it was definitely on Second Street, and the rooms were above a jewelry store.

"Well, what are you waiting for, Dearie? Ain't got all day, you know. Can't you see how busy we are?"

The other two girls laughed loudly and swung their weight back and forth against the horse-hitching rail at the front of the store. At first glance, their faces appeared round, soft. However, as I moved closer to them, I noticed they sported about twice as much lipstick as they should have, and their cheeks were positively caked with a cheap, blood-red rouge. The contrast of the cosmetics and the work attire seemed absolutely in keeping with the rest of my new surroundings, so I didn't even blanch, didn't even break a smile. Instead, I repeated, slowly this time, "Look— I'm sorry I'm bothering you, but I'm new here and just want to get home."

Then, with as pathetic a face as I could draw up, I added, "I just want to get out of here, okay? Which way do I go to Second Street?"

The oldest turned deadly serious and pointed toward the Mississippi River Bridge looming just ahead of us. "You go right down there under this side of the bridge and enter the camp that's there. There's a road just inside the camp that loops back up right to the street you're looking for. The road behind us is all dug up because the streetcar line is being rebuilt all the way up Musser Hill, so you can't go the short way. That's tough, but that's the way it is. Go down to the camp, and anyone there can tell you how to get on the road you need. You won't get lost again. They'll be glad to help you."

"Thanks," I said, sighing heavily. "That's all I wanted to know. I'm sorry to have bothered you."

I turned to leave, stopped again, and added, my curiosity getting the best of me, "Just one more thing if you don't mind. Just what in the world is going on around here? It can't always be like this, can it?"

All three laughed heartily again. This time the youngest of the three spoke up, first coughing loudly to clear her throat. "Why, don't you really know? It's after 4:00 on Saturday afternoon. That's quittin'-time for the week. Nothing to do now but raisin' Cain until work time Monday. This is *our* time now. Ain't gonna think about work. Ain't gonna think about nothin' but this!"

She waved her right arm toward the now even larger and denser gathering of people inching up and down the street behind me. She looked like she wanted me to say something in response, but I didn't.

The long Mississippi River Bridge loomed eerily ahead and seemed to be very much out of proportion with the surroundings. Fascinated by its size, I kept my eyes focused on the bridge as I moved slowly and deliberately through the mass of humanity squeezing in on me. Its massive steel and concrete foundation was taller than any building I had ever seen. At the same time, automobiles and horse-drawn carts on its upper surface seemed as small as ants as they crept back and forth from one side of the river to the other. Looking at the bridge, I suddenly felt small—and very much alone.

It took several minutes to get down to the base of the bridge and the opening of what the girl had called the "camp." In sharp contrast to the bustle of the streets I had just left behind, the camp was nearly quiet as a new cemetery, which I took as a great relief. Large tents so close together they were nearly touching each other lined both sides of the worn dirt path through the center of the main area under the bridge's bed and ran all the way down to the river's edge. There were a few people walking up and down this path, and most of them seemed to be hauling heavy wooden buckets from a small dock down by the water up to their tents. From where I was standing, I couldn't tell if they were hauling water or something else.

An older woman smoking a corncob pipe was seated on a small stool next to one of the tents, so I decided to ask her to point me in the right direction. However, before I got three steps toward her, I felt a dull thud against the back of my head, followed by dust particles swirling around my face. Two more similar impacts quickly followed, one against the back of my neck and the other on the small of my back. I wasn't hurt, and at first I wasn't frightened.

It stunned me more than anything else. When I turned around to see what was happening, a tomato hit me squarely on my left shoulder, its juice running all down that side of my dress. My first thought was to run, but my feet wouldn't move.

Then I heard someone call out, "It's a Cutter. Get her!"

In an instant I dropped my suitcase and started to run the opposite direction. Tent flaps slapped open, and angry eyes peered out as I ran past them and back up the path. Just when I thought I was close to my freedom, a long pole came flying out of a tent and landed at my feet. I jumped and tried to dodge it, but my right shoe flew off, causing me to lose my balance. Down I went. Face first. Hard. I rolled over, looked up, and saw the Iowa end of the Mississippi River Bridge become darker, smaller, and farther away. And still farther and farther away…until it was gone…

....

When I came to, I was lying on a blanket at the river's edge. My upper body was dry, but my feet and ankles were dangling in the cool water as small waves lapped against them. My shoes were dry and by my side, and my suitcase was nearby. I sat up with a start and pulled my legs out of the water, but a gentle hand immediately urged me back down on the blanket.

"Don't be afraid," a man's voice said, calmly, reassuringly, each word spoken slowly and deliberately. "Just be still."

I turned and looked behind me, but the sun blocked my vision. As I raised a hand to mute the sunlight, I could see his outline against the hazy late afternoon sky. He quickly turned away from me so that all I could see was back of his head. When my focus returned, I could see his hair was long, raven-black, and nearly halfway down his back. His back and shoulders were thick, muscular.

Suddenly panicking, I bolted up, let out a short gasp, and asked, "Where am I? What happened? What…."

He interrupted me, "You'll be fine. You're safe now. I'll get you out of here." He paused, then added, "Keep your legs in the water. It'll cool you down, make you feel better."

"But, what happened?" I asked again, feeling anger and fear welling up inside of me. "Tell me now!"

"They thought you were a Cutter—a botton maker—and were trespassing. Maybe you are. Maybe you aren't. They were going to teach you a lesson. I stopped them. You're here. You're safe."

As he turned slowly toward me, I could see his face for the first time. He had a scraggly, full beard that covered most of his features except for his eyes. His eyes were light blue and quite striking in contrast to his black hair. But I couldn't see much else through the glare of the sun.

"I'll take you home," he said, softly. "We better get moving. Get up."

"Wait a minute," I said, reaching over to grab his arm. "I'm not leaving until I find out what happened."

"Would you like to ask them?" he replied, pointing to a small group of women staring angrily at us from the nearest tent.

"I understand your point," I said, bolting up to join him. "Let's go, and maybe you'll allow me a question or two after we're out of here."

"I doubt it," he responded, dryly.

After picking up my suitcase, he motioned for me to follow him along the river's edge and away from the camp.

"Watch where you walk," he said without turning back to face me. "Water's deep here. If you fall in, I'm not pulling you out."

I started to tell him what I thought of his rudeness, but stopped short when I caught one last glance at the women standing back at the tent. Several were making hand gestures, and their meanings were clear. *Very* clear.

I followed him without saying another word.

And as I did, one thought kept surfacing over and over again in my brain: "What have I gotten myself into?"

....

CHAPTER 3

I COULDN'T MAKE UP MY mind which was worse—the oppressive July heat or the stench of the Muscatine air.

The previous night had been one of the longest and roughest of my life. Because of the searing heat inside the room, I kept opening the windows to create any type of breeze that might offer relief. However, opening the windows let in the Muscatine air, which would come wafting through the screens like a stealthful predator, one my senses could not escape. I'd get back up to close the windows, and the cycle would repeat. This went on all night, so I finally just gave up about five o'clock and crawled out of bed, filled a pitcher with cool water, and slipped into the bathtub so I could sponge myself to try to escape the heat.

A robe belonging to one of my new roommates was hanging on the back of the bathroom door, so I helped myself to it and headed out to the kitchen for a bite to eat. I hadn't had a morsel since arriving in town the previous afternoon, and I was positively starved. However, after lighting a lamp, I checked all the cabinets, and there wasn't a scrap of food to be found anywhere. I suddenly remembered my mother wrapping a small, round block of cheese and some crackers in a kitchen towel and placing them in my suitcase right before I left Grandview. I practically ran to the suitcase and retrieved it. I then poured myself a glass of water, sliced enough cheese to make some cracker and cheese sandwiches, and settled on the divan next to the front window. From this vantage point, while I munched my breakfast, I could see a fair amount of traffic still moving up and down the street, even at this early hour.

The highlight of this activity came when I saw a fight break out right across the street. I couldn't tell what started it, but two very large men suddenly engaged in a knockdown, drag-out, round of fisticuffs. The donnybrook didn't last long as they both seemed to tire quickly. Finally, one waved weakly to the other, who seemed to take that as a sign of truce, and offered his foe a drink from a bottle he had in his pocket. The other man took a long draw on the bottle, handed it back, and both were soon arm-in-arm as they made their way down the street. However, after about twenty steps or so, they stopped short and suddenly started swinging at each other again.

My thoughts then, snapping back to the present, changed from "What have I gotten myself into?" to "What could possibly happen next!" Apparently, my life in Muscatine was going to be anything but dull....

While I watched the conflict continue across the street, I was still having something of a fight of my own, a fight that had raged through my mind all night long. My thoughts were jumbled and crashing together as I tried to make sense of the events of the previous afternoon. I could understand my purse being stolen. I had no one to blame but myself for that. My parents had warned me over and over again of the importance of holding fast to my personal belongings while travelling. I hadn't done that, and the result was exactly what they had said it would be. As much as I hated to admit it, they were right. Dead right.

It wasn't the events surrounding the purse that dominated my thoughts. What I couldn't get out of my head were the events at the camp down by the bridge. All I could remember was a small woman smoking a pipe next to a tent and some objects hitting me on the head and back. I remembered falling to the ground, but after that, I had no memory of anything until I woke up on a blanket next to the river.

The man sitting next to me when I came to had obviously come to my rescue, but I just couldn't figure out why a rescue had even been necessary. Had I trespassed in some way by stepping into the camp? It hadn't appeared that way, but I might have. Or, had I interrupted some activity involving the individuals carrying buckets up from the river? Had I been mistaken for someone else? After all, someone there had called me a *Cutter* right before I had been pelted.

My head throbbed as I tried to put together any reasonable answer to those questions, and this throbbing was growing worse by the minute. To compound matters, I had been able to gather very little information from the man who had walked me home.

We had walked along the river's edge a pretty fair distance until we came to a set of concrete steps that led back up the hill toward town. Without making a sound, he had motioned me to follow him up those steps. When I asked where we were going, he grunted, turned, stared at me a few seconds, pointed up the hill, and used his other hand to motion for me to follow him, and quickly.

At that point I'd had it. I was scared, and I was tired. Dog tired. I was also completely fed up with his rudeness and his commanding attitude. I had planted my feet heavily on the platform below the first step, slammed down my suitcase, and barked at him, "This is it! I'm not going anywhere until you answer some questions, the first of which is 'Where are you taking me?'"

He reached down, picked up my suitcase and tucked it under his arm, roughly took my hand, and started pulling me up the steps. I stumbled and nearly fell, but he held tightly to me and allowed me to keep my balance until I could right myself. He then stopped for a moment, pointed again back to the camp, and waved for me to follow close behind him as he quickly ascended the steps. I could see this was a standoff I wasn't going to win—and the fires of the camp still glowed menacingly behind us—so I picked up my pace and kept up with him as best I could.

At the top of the steps he turned to me and shrugged his shoulders, as if asking me where I wanted to be taken. I quickly explained I didn't know the exact address, that all I knew was it was above one of the two jewelry stores downtown on Second

Street. Without a word he pointed to our left, and we were off again.

Then, after just a few steps and so suddenly it made my breath catch, he stopped, turned, and said, sternly, "My name is Gaston."

That was all he said. He clutched my hand again, and we continued toward the main downtown area.

When we finally came to Second Street, we entered the same type of crowd I had seen earlier in the afternoon. Vendors and barkers were still everywhere. So were the small groups of men and women clustered next to the high piles of shells. The experience of moving through the crowd this time was, however, dramatically different.

Instead of just inching along while being surrounded by a mass of humanity, we moved quickly down a wide path as the crowd constantly and deliberately opened up before us. It seemed as soon as those around us discovered Gaston's presence, all immediately started stepping back. Many lowered their eyes and turned away, as if not wanting to be seen. Nothing was said, either by Gaston or those in the crowd. As a matter of fact, each section of the street we passed grew strangely quiet. I couldn't tell if this was happening out of respect—or fear. We owned the street, and no one dared to get in our way.

No one wanted to make eye contact with me either. "Guilt by association" passed more than once through my thoughts. Gaston still had a firm grip on my hand, so it must have looked to anyone as if I had somehow either wronged him or belonged to him. At that point, I didn't care what they thought. I just wanted to get home as fast as possible.

When we reached the intersection of Second and Cedar Street, Gaston pointed to Parmalie Jewelry, which was right on the southwest corner. From where we stood, it was obvious there were no rooms above the store, and my heart sank.

"It isn't this one. Can't be," I said, dejectedly. "Do you know where the other jewelry store is located?"

I then noticed, off to my left, standing next to her mother, a young girl pointing farther down the street. The young girl started calling out to me, "Newton's Jewelry is right down...." Her mother quickly covered her daughter's mouth and jerked her roughly back up on the sidewalk. Gaston saw this and glared at the mother, which caused her to turn and bolt back into the crowd behind her. Without a word to me, he motioned for us to continue. As we did, our path down the street became wider and wider as Gaston was recognized. And, as before, no one said a single word as we went by.

Three blocks later we came to Chestnut Street. There, on the corner at the northwest side of the street, was Newton's Jewelry. The side of the building running up Chestnut Street had a set of long, wooden steps that led to a balcony at the second floor. On the sill next to the door there, I could see the outline of two large flowerpots. Mattie had said in her note that a key would be waiting for me under a pot.

Turning to Gaston, I said, "I'm sure this is it."

Pulling my hand from his, I ran across the street and up the steps as fast as I could. There, under the first pot, was the key. I triumphantly held it up and waved it toward Gaston, who had moved into the shadows next to the building.

"Just a minute," I called down. "I'll be right back."

I placed the key in the lock, twisted it, and the door popped open. There was still enough light outside that I could see through the kitchen area and into a sitting room. I walked slowly inside and looked around. I spotted an envelope with Mattie's name on it lying on the small round table in the corner. I knew then I was finally home. I exhaled heavily and shook my head in relief.

Gaston still had my suitcase, so I headed back out and down the steps. When I got to the street, there was my suitcase next to the streetlamp.

Gaston was gone.

I looked around and called out his name, but nothing. When I asked an older gentleman standing off to the side if he had seen in which direction Gaston had gone, he quickly turned and walked away from me.

There didn't seem anything else to do, so I picked up my suitcase and climbed up the steps again. I turned one last time to scan the streets below, but there was no sign of him. At this point, I was unsure whether to feel sad or relieved. A sudden shiver shot down my back. Finally, I shrugged my shoulders—and went back inside.

For the rest of the evening I unpacked what little I had brought with me and did my best to relax and unwind. A copy of *The Lamplighter* was on the table in the kitchen area, and I tried my best to read into it. However, at the end of nearly every page I stopped, got up, and looked out the front window at the crowd below. The revelers were still going strong. I had never lived anywhere like this before, and I was fascinated by the commotion.

Finally I picked up the book, read a few pages, and drifted off to sleep. I woke up briefly just after midnight, when from then on the heat and the smell alternated waking me up nearly every hour for the rest of the night. It wasn't just unsettling. I was spent, emotionally and physically.

Muscatine had won round one. I had to concede that. However, the dawning of the new day had to be better.

It just had to be.

....

CHAPTER 4

I WAS JOLTED BACK TO the present by a sharp and insistent knocking at the door. I pulled the robe tightly around me and walked over to investigate. Sliding the curtains cautiously to the side, I quickly peeked out. A voice called through the glass, "Well, are you going to open up or make me stand here for the rest of the morning?"

There was no mistaking the voice: a touch of raspiness, a tinge of tugboat foghorn, and a smidge of the bark of an army general.

It was Mattie.

I opened the door to let her in, but she just stood there, hands on hips, smirking at me.

"How do you like my robe?" she asked, sarcastically. "Fit okay? Looks like you did go ahead and make yourself at home."

"Oh, I'm sorry," I said, quickly. "You're right—I should have asked first...."

Mattie smiled and cut me off. "Just wanted to see if I'd get a rise out of you. My place is yours and I could use the company. Viola drives me crazy. She's got the mind of a Colorado mockingbird—but never mind that. You'll see what I mean soon enough."

She paused, then added, "So, how you been, Pearl?"

Without waiting for a response, she handed me her small suitcase, picked up a paper bag and balanced it gingerly against her chest, and marched past me into the kitchen. She set the bag on the table and immediately started emptying its contents.

"Take a look at this," she said, excitedly. "Ever seen such beautiful fruit before? This, my dear, is our breakfast this morning."

She pulled out bananas, apples, oranges, and finally grapes, lining them up across the table.

"And this, too," she added, producing a small loaf of bread from inside the sack.

"Why, where'd you get the money for all this?" I asked, incredulously. "I've seen fruit prices this summer. My family couldn't afford any we didn't grow. You have a money tree out back or something?"

Without responding to or looking at me, she turned to the sideboard and picked up a knife, which she used skillfully to slice the fruit. I didn't know what else to say at this point, so I just watched in awe at the graceful movement of her hands.

"Nothing to it, really," she said matter of factly, placing a banana peeled and sliced lengthwise along the outer rim of a plate. "Just like opening shells and slicing out the meat at work, only easier."

"Just like what at work?" I asked.

"You'll find out soon enough. Which reminds me—I'll have to establish the 'finger pool' as soon as we get there tomorrow. By the look of those long digits of yours, there's a good chance you'll eventually lose one. Shoot—I'm guessing I won't be able to get more than short odds on you."

"Mattie, I haven't understood a word you've said since you got here. What are you jabbering about?"

"Nothing, Dear. Just forget it. I'm just being rude, which I am most of the time. Get used to it."

"There," she said, triumphantly, as she placed the last of the orange slices in the middle of the plate. "Help yourself while I unpack. I'll be back in two shakes of a lamb's tail, and we can eat and do some catching up. Sound good?"

"Sounds wonderful. If you'll show me where the coffee is, I'll get a pot going, too."

"Coffee?" she said, laughing. "The money tree doesn't grow *that* tall. Take a couple more of those oranges and squeeze us some orange juice. That's as exotic as we're going to get around here unless one of us gets a rich boyfriend or robs a bank."

I looked again at the fruit and bread and started to ask how she had afforded it when Mattie anticipated my question and cut me off.

"I stole it," she said, boldly. "And I don't want any lectures. With the slave wages we get around here, if you don't develop sticky fingers, a body would just about starve."

She saw my shocked expression and quickly exclaimed, "Oh, get over it. Tell me you've never swiped anything before. And besides, it really isn't stealing when you get right down to it. I look at it this way. The workers in this town get paid just enough to stay alive, just enough to get the work done for the fat owners. They're stealing from us and everybody knows it. We just can't do anything about it. Not yet anyway. They own everything in this town in one way or another. They even get a cut of the profits had by the poor street vendors who peddle this fruit."

She paused, walked over, placed a hand on my shoulder, looked me squarely in the eyes and said, "The owners don't pay us what they should. They control the prices of everything we buy around this rat hole of a town. Because they've got us over a barrel, they keep the money that's rightfully ours. That is, they keep it unless we find ways to get it back, and one of those ways is to help ourselves, when we can, to their other sources of profit, which includes some of the money made by the street vendors. So, by helping myself to the fruit and bread, I'm actually taking a piece of what is rightfully mine. See?"

I didn't see. Her logic escaped me, but it was clear that she felt she was very much in the right. I thought about arguing with her, but I was so hungry I decided to let it go—for the time being at least.

"We'll have to visit more about your *theories* one of these days. But, right now, I'll make the orange juice," I said, opening cabinet doors and looking for glasses.

Mattie again anticipated my question. "You'll find the glasses in the cupboard next to the sink. Oh—and by the way—I stole the glasses, too. From the diner around the corner."

She then picked up her suitcase and headed for the bedroom. I stopped looking for the glasses and looked around the kitchen, wondering to myself, "What in this kitchen *isn't* stolen?"

After inspecting everything from utensils to towels, I came up with my answer: "Not much!"

....

Mattie unpacked her suitcase quick enough, but then she spent a good half hour in the bathroom freshening up. When she finally returned to the kitchen table, some of the fruit, no doubt because of the July heat, had already started to turn brown around the edges.

"And another thing," she said while sitting down, as if she were already in the middle of a conversation, "you better learn to eat fast. Like a field hand. See how fast those apples are darkening? Food doesn't last long around here. And I'm not just talking about it spoiling. If you bring food in here, it typically won't be around long enough to go bad. That's because of Viola. You've never seen anything like her in all your life. Trust me on that. She eats like a jackal. Eats everything that even remotely smells like food. And what kills me is she never gains an ounce. Has the waist of a wasp. Me? I look at a glass of water and gain two pounds. Isn't fair. Just isn't."

I was holding a slice of banana a few inches from my mouth. When Mattie finally slowed down, I popped it in. "Mattie," I said through the banana, "when we were kids together, you never let me get a word in edgewise. I think...."

Mattie interrupted me and said, quietly, "I know I talk too much. I'm sorry. It's just that I get nervous, and my lips start flapping. I don't do it on purpose."

Here she paused, looked softly at me, and continued, "Look—do me a favor. In the future when I do this, just tell me to shut up. Okay? I won't take offense. And that reminds me—I want to tell you about the company so that *you* won't do anything stupid tomorrow. Well, at least nothing so stupid it'll follow you around from then on. I think you should...."

Smiling, I reached over, took her hand, and calmly said, "Mattie—shut up. Just shut up."

First she looked shocked, then smiled back. "Well, I guess I really did ask for it, didn't I?"

"Yes, you did," I said, patting the back of her hand. "And I'm no shrinking violet, so I'm not going to be shy about shutting you up. So, take no offense when I do."

We both reached for the grapes at the same time, our hands colliding roughly.

"It looks like you've got a pretty fair boarding house reach," I teased.

Mattie started to say something but stammered and stopped herself. We both laughed.

"I've got an idea," I said, finally. "Let's just not say anything for a few minutes. Let's just enjoy this, this...."

I was struggling for a word, a phrase. Mattie finished my sentence with, "Let's just call this 'fruits of the industry,' shall we? We'll debate other descriptions later."

I didn't reply. I knew that would only set her off again. So, I just nodded and picked up a slice of apple.

We looked at each other and giggled like schoolgirls.

My initial thoughts about her had been right. Living with Mattie was going to be anything but dull.

....

We spent the rest of the morning rearranging the furniture so I'd have a space of my own. Mattie and Viola shared the bed I had slept in the previous night, so a suitable pallet of some kind needed to be found for me. The previous tenant had left behind what at first glance appeared to be a beautiful divan. However, the pattern of flowers on its material hid some of the most vicious springs ever felt in a piece of furniture. Mattie had nicknamed the divan the "Venus Fly Trap"—and with good reason. She said more than one gentleman caller left with a hole in his trousers after flopping down on it. But, as uncomfortable as the divan might be, it was still the best alternative to the floor we could find. Therefore, of necessity, it was to be my new bed.

I also needed to find storage for the few clothes I had brought with me. I had hoped to find built-in closets like those I had recently read about in a magazine. No such luck here. Mattie suggested I hang my clothes in the kitchen pantry since the likelihood of it being full of food seemed remote at best.

"I just hope we don't have some man over who opens the pantry and finds your bloomers hanging in there," Mattie teased.

I didn't find that funny.

The last thing we needed to decide was how much my portion of the rent would be. Mattie wasn't bashful at all in bringing up this conversation. She started us off by saying, "You're not going to live here for free, you know. No bum bench here."

"I know," I said. "I fully expect to pay my own way. I just appreciate you taking me in. This is awfully kind of you."

"Kind nothing," she replied. "This is simple survival, my old friend. Rent for this palace is twenty-four dollars a month, which is robbery. The owners even get a share of the rent we pay. Can you believe it? If I could figure out a way to get back at them for this, I would. I'd steal some of the furniture and sell it if I thought I could get away with it, but none of it is worth a plugged nickel. So, for the time being, we're stuck. Viola and I have been splitting the cost, but it's killing us, puttin' us in a hole that keeps getting deeper and deeper."

She paused, then added, "Now that you're here, a three-way split will keep us from going completely under. I recall you were always the one with a head for numbers, so you've probably by now got it ciphered that you'll owe two dollars a week to the rent kitty."

"Two dollars," I said, shocked. "I didn't know it would be that much. I don't even know if I'll be able to afford that yet."

"You will—but just barely. Just by the skin of your teeth. I don't know exactly what you'll be doing at the company, but you'll likely start around six or seven dollars a week. That doesn't sound like much, and it isn't. You take two out of that and you've got about four dollars for food, clothes, and everything else, including your savings, if you're lucky enough to end up with any."

Two whole dollars per week for my part of the rent. For weeks I had been calculating how long it would take me to save enough money to go for my college studies. If Mattie were even half correct, those calculations would have to be thrown out the window. It would take much, much longer than I had guessed.

Mattie saw me blankly staring off into the distance, came over, and hugged me, which really surprised me. She wasn't, by my memory, a particularly kind or understanding person. Could she have changed?

"Don't worry about it," she said, brushing my hair away from my forehead. "We'll all probably be killed by some machine or chemical at work before we have a chance to save enough to do anything with it anyway. So no use worrying your pretty little noggin' about it."

She was *still* the same old Mattie.

"I'm going to become a teacher," I blurted out in response. "Nothing is going to keep me from that. I'm going to save every penny I can as fast as I can. I'll be out of here before next year. You'll see."

"And I hope you're right," Mattie said, walking over to look out the window. Then, pointing below, she added, "That's probably about the same thing all these fools have been saying for years. I don't know. Maybe you really will make it. I hope you do. I just have the feeling that's not in the cards for me."

This time it was my turn to speak up. "Mattie, I know you. When we were kids, you were headstrong and proud. There wasn't anything you couldn't do once you put your mind to it. It doesn't look to me like you've really changed any. If you say you can do something, I would never bet against you."

She looked back at me and smiled. I continued, "And besides, I'm here now. You may not remember it, but I can be just as stubborn as you. So get ready for it. I'm going to have my savings, and you're going to have yours. Then we're both getting out of here. I'll help see to that."

It was a lot of bragging on my part, but all the while I was saying it, I kept remembering my father's words: "It ain't braggin' if you can back it up."

I knew I could back it up. I just *knew* it.

....

With our home chores completed, Mattie suggested we get a Sunday paper and lounge around and read through the afternoon. Mattie walked over by the door and said, while opening it and quickly stepping outside, "Back soon!"

She returned in about five minutes with the paper. She had not taken her purse with her and I was going to ask how she paid for it, but I thought better of it.

I was afraid she'd start in on some story about how the owners got a share of the paper sales as well.

Mattie settled into an overstuffed chair next to the door, and I sat on the divan, just catching the tip of one of the springs on my lower thigh. I winced, and Mattie giggled.

"Thanks," I said, dryly. "Your sympathy overwhelms me."

"You are going to be more fun than Viola," she said. "I'm glad you're here."

While Mattie chose a section of the newspaper for me, I asked, "Now that you've brought her up, where is Viola? Is she coming back today?"

"Oh, she'll be here by and by. She's like a fed cat; she always returns."

It was really none of my business, but to make conversation I asked Mattie where she thought Viola was off to.

"I have absolutely no idea," Mattie replied, flipping open the front page. "She didn't say where she was going, and I didn't ask. But knowing her, I'd bet some man is involved somewhere, somehow. She does love her men."

"Mattie!" I scolded her. "What a terrible thing to say about someone. You should be ashamed."

"No," she replied. "I shouldn't be ashamed. It's Viola who should be ashamed, and that's all I'm going to say about that right now."

"Good," I said. "If you can't say something good about someone...."

"I know," Mattie interrupted, "if you can't say something good, then at least say something shocking. That's what people really want to hear, isn't it?"

"Not me," I said. "I'm just starting to get worried about her—and I don't even know her yet. And what about her job? What if she doesn't get back in time for work tomorrow?"

"It won't matter. You see, Viola isn't as lucky as some people. Unlike you, she doesn't have relatives to get her a job. She's a...."

That was over the line, and I wasn't going to sit there and take it. I put down my paper and said, "Just you wait a minute...."

Mattie waved a hand in front of me and said, calmly, while motioning me to sit back, "Now don't get your dander up. I meant no harm. Just stating a fact—that's all. No need to get riled. It's just my way of telling you not everyone around here walks into a job. Viola has been looking for something permanent a long time, and all she can find is what they call 'short work.' You're going to discover, and soon enough, a lot of people get badly injured in this business and can't come to work. Others get sick. When somebody doesn't show up, their jobs have to be taken care of or the process, the whole system, at a factory could grind to a halt. So, 'short workers' are brought in, usually for just a day or two, until the regulars come back to work or the bosses decide what else they want to do. A lot of people, like Viola, do this short work to get by."

Mattie paused, scanned through a few pages of the paper, and continued without looking my direction. "Every morning early—and I mean *early*—Viola and the others go down to a little shack by the train station. By sunup, a man called Muscatine Shorty, or just Shorts, has a list of the day's fill-in work, and he assigns the jobs as he sees fit. I wish I could say something good about him, but I don't think anyone can. He's been known to require special favors of people, especially women, before he'll give them a job—if you know what I mean."

I could guess exactly what she meant, so I didn't ask for any details. Mattie went on, "Anyway, Viola's been a short worker for a long time. She always manages somehow to pay her part of the rent, so I've learned not to worry about her. She works when she needs to—and she plays when she needs to. That's Viola."

She paused and looked down at the newspaper on her lap. "I thought we were going to sit here and read quietly. What about that, Miss Chatterbox?"

"Fine with me," I said, folding my section of the paper. "Pick a lock."

"Pick a what?" she asked.

"Never mind. Just read your paper." I held the paper higher to hide my smile.

She rolled up a section and threw it at me, hitting me in the head. "Okay," she said. "Not another word."

Somehow, I didn't believe her.

Mattie and I spent the rest of the morning and early afternoon reading the paper and swapping news about our families. When the conversation finally started drying up—or, rather, when Mattie got tired of talking about those subjects—she suddenly shifted to a diatribe against the button industry in general and the owners of the companies in specific. Something in one of the articles in the paper had set her off, and it soon became clear she wasn't going to shut up until she had her full say on the matter.

According to Mattie, button workers were among the most abused workers in the entire nation. She talked at length about the terrible injuries, often resulting in death, that happened regularly in the button factories. She talked about the lack of medical care for injured workers. She talked about company supervisors who were doing everything they could to keep wages as low as possible, including doctoring weighing and measuring scales and purposely miscounting items produced. Mattie even described workers just "disappearing" after standing up and demanding better working conditions. When I asked what she meant by that, she didn't pause to answer. She just kept rolling, spitting out one example after another of ways in which, according to her, the safety and well being of the workers were stomped upon by those in power in the companies. She even recounted the story of a nine-year-old boy who was recently killed in a button company in Washington, Iowa, when some crates of finished buttons fell on him. To my relief, Mattie finally said it wasn't as bad as all that at the Blanton factory, but she cautioned me there were still some supervisors who were very close to having a set of devil horns under the hair on their heads.

My uncle had warned me that I'd be hearing a lot of these stories once I got to Muscatine and that I should just take them with a grain of salt. He said some injuries were just going to happen when machines were involved, but most of these happened because of careless workers. These injuries were not, he emphasized, the fault of the companies. Those who complained the loudest, "bad apples," were usually people who were already unhappy with their stations in life and wouldn't be happy no matter what was done for them. My uncle said, and I tended to agree with him, that individuals had the power through their own hard work and initiative to make something of themselves, and these same people should not let the negative people of the world hold them back. When I interrupted Mattie and tried to share my uncle's views with her, she stopped me with a terse, "Well, your uncle's an idiot if he believes that."

There was no use arguing a point with Mattie once she got rolling. I just groaned and asked for another section of the paper.

....

It was about quarter after three when we heard creaking on the steps outside, followed by a loud knock at the door. Mattie jumped up and said, "Probably Viola. She never remembers her key or the one under the pot."

Mattie flung open the door and said, without looking outside, "Forget your key again, did you? You know, you're about as dumb as the sweat on a water bag."

"I beg your pardon," the familiar masculine voice said through the screen door. "Is this where Miss McGill lives?"

Mattie didn't apologize. Instead, she looked up and shot back, "And just who wants to know, Bub?"

"Mattie!" I shouted as I jumped up from the divan and rushed to the door. "I'll take care of this."

I tried to slide gracefully between Mattie and the door, but when she refused to budge, I resorted to a quick elbow.

"Hello, James," I said, through the screen. "I'm pleased to see you again… and so soon. What brings you this way?"

Before he could answer, Mattie called out, "Oh, for goodness sakes. Go ahead and invite him in. Isn't going to hurt having a man seen coming in here. Our reputations are already ruined."

I was too stunned to say anything. James just smiled, pulled open the screen door, and walked past me into the sitting room. As he did, I noticed it there in his left hand.

"My purse!" I shouted. "Wherever did you find it?"

"I made a few inquiries," he said, shrugging his shoulders. "That's all. I told you I'd get it back."

He handed it to me, and I quickly opened it to check its contents. Everything was there, from my money to my jewelry.

"I don't know how to thank you," I said, walking toward him.

"What's the matter with you?" Mattie scolded. "Go ahead and give the man a hug. A big one. And you should probably kiss him right on the lips, too!"

James laughed and said while pointing to Mattie, "I like her. Who is she?"

She didn't give me time to answer. "I'm Mattie Flynn, and if she won't give you a hug, I just might. You don't look half bad. As a matter of fact...."

Mattie's words trailed off while I must have been turning several shades of red. Her eyes suddenly got very wide, and her mouth fell open. I had seen this expression of hers before when she and I were little, and I knew this was not a good sign.

"I know you," Mattie said, crossing her arms. "I saw your picture in the paper about a week ago. You were in a photo with that socialite, Elizabeth Martin. You're getting engaged or something, right?"

James didn't respond. Instead, he frowned, turned to me, and said, "I was really worried about you last night. You don't know what a guilty conscience I had about leaving you alone at the station. Please tell me you had no trouble getting here."

I was still trying to get past the "You're getting engaged or something..." part of Mattie's comment and really didn't catch all of his words.

"I'm sorry," I said, looking up. "What did you say?"

"I asked if you made it home safely last night. No trouble, right?"

"Well, to be perfectly honest, I decided to save my money—your money—by walking home. Some girls I ran into on the street told me to take a shortcut down under the bridge and...."

"Oh no!" Mattie and James shouted at the same time. Then Mattie added, "Please tell me you didn't fall for *that* old gag. Girl, you better shake the straw out of your country hair right now or you'll never make it here in the big city. You're going to need a keeper!"

James laughed loudly and quickly added, "Oh, don't be so hard on her. The same thing happened to one of our best salesmen about a month ago when he came here to check out our new line of products. He ended up with nothing but a towel wrapped around himself when they finally set him free. I trust your experience wasn't that horrible."

His smile was warm, comforting, but it didn't last long. He quickly pulled his watch from his pocket and clicked it open. After studying it a few seconds, he turned to me and added, "I see you're now safe, and that's what's most important to me. I don't mind telling you I'd love details about your visit to the camp, but I'm running late again as usual. I guess I'll just have to be patient for now, but I do want to hear about it one of these days. I'm very sorry, but I've got to get going."

"Wait just a minute," Mattie said. "Maybe you don't want to hear about it, but I do—and every small detail. Pearl, what did they do to you?"

James suddenly turned serious and said to Mattie, "We can just be happy, for now, knowing she's safe. She's been through enough already."

Mattie glared at him, but, much to my surprise, kept her mouth shut.

The tension in the air started to thicken. I quickly said, "I'm okay. I survived and had a pretty fair adventure to boot. One day I just might decide to share it with you."

Then, turning to James, I said, "Please allow me to walk you out. Thank you so much for everything you've done for me. You've been very kind, and I'll never forget it."

We stepped out onto the landing and closed the door behind us. Once outside, I said as quickly as I could, "I want to apologize for Mattie. And you have to believe me when I say it really wasn't my idea to live here. Our mothers set this up to save us money. Truthfully. So please don't hold it against me. I'm only going to live here until…."

James interrupted me and said, gently, "You don't need to explain."

He studied me up and down and laughed heartily before continuing, "Let me see if I've got this right. You've been here for, what, less than twenty-four hours? And already you've been robbed, lost, and fallen for the oldest gag in town. Mattie was right. You *just may* need a keeper."

Then, studying his watch again, he added, "I'm sorry, but I really do have to go."

"I hope we'll meet again, Sir Galahad. Only I hope it will be different circumstances next time." Pointing to the door, I added, "And in a different location. I think that would be nice, too."

"We'll meet again," he replied, tipping his hat. "And soon."

"Thank you for bringing back my purse. Thank you for everything."

With that, he smiled, turned quickly, and headed down the steps. I watched him walk down the street until he disappeared around the corner.

It was then I saw just the head of a man peering at me from behind a streetlamp pole about halfway down the block. When our eyes met, he turned and started walking quickly into the alley behind him.

It was Gaston.

I started to wave, but he was already gone.

....

Mattie pounced the second I came back inside. "Okay, country girl," she said, folding her arms and tapping her right foot quickly and heavily on the floor, "how on this earth do you know James Baker? He's from one of the wealthiest and most powerful families in this whole area. They own one of the button factories and half the town to boot! I want details, and I want them now."

After how rude she'd just been, I couldn't resist playing with her. "Oh, he's just one of the many gentleman callers I'll be having over. I'll try to keep them down to one or two a day, except on holidays of course."

"No, no, no!" Mattie responded. "You're not going to clam up on me. Spit it out. I mean it. Now!"

Sitting back down and grabbing another section of the paper, I replied, without looking back at Mattie, "He's just a dear friend. That's all. And we country girls don't like to kiss and tell. So that's all you're going to get right now, like it or not."

Mattie took off a shoe and flung it weakly against the divan. "I'm not giving up," she said. "Today is still young. I'll bet money you crack before I do."

I didn't reply, which *really* made her mad. I heard her exhale loudly. I raised the paper and laughed softly. Her other shoe then landed with a thud against the wall behind me.

The rest of the day passed quietly, except for the times when Mattie would suddenly start pestering me again about James. I held out, however, and didn't break down. Teasing her was simply too much fun, and she deserved every minute of it.

At the same time, I started worrying again about Viola. Even after what Mattie had said earlier, and maybe *because* of what she had said earlier, I just couldn't get her out of my mind. When we had our light supper—fruit and bread again—I asked if we really shouldn't be worried, and Mattie replied, "If you're going to worry, worry about her soul."

I was afraid to ask for clarification, so I didn't.

Just before bedtime Mattie went into the bedroom and returned a few minutes later with coveralls and a headscarf very similar to those worn by the girls who had directed me to the camp under the bridge.

"You can borrow these until you get your feet on the ground, and then I want them back. This is the standard attire for women working at the company. Keep them in good shape because they're the only others I've got."

"Thanks," I said, surprised by her generosity. "I'll take care of them. I promise."

Then, sitting next to me on the divan, Mattie said, matter of factly, "That is, you can borrow them if you tell me about James. That's the condition."

She had been like a caged tiger all afternoon, so I knew I had played her long enough. "Well, if that's the way it is, I guess I don't have much choice, do I?" I said, frowning.

"Then spill the beans," she said, inching closer. "Let's have it."

If I had a dime for every time she rolled her eyes and said "Stupid, stupid, stupid!" as I told her about James, getting lost, and the bridge events, I could have bypassed working, repacked right away, and immediately left for my schooling. However, I took no offense at her admonishments. This was just Mattie being Mattie, and I knew I'd have to get used to it.

At the same time, I did not say anything about Gaston. Something inside me told me to keep that to myself.

We visited long into the night.

....

CHAPTER 5

THE DIVAN AND I WERE not going to be good friends.

The wayward springs woke me three times during the night, and each time I had a difficult time getting back to sleep. As much as anything, it was probably my anxiety over starting a new job that kept me awake. On top of all this, the acrid Muscatine air didn't help. I tossed and turned while trying to avoid another poke of the springs until I saw Mattie lighting a lamp in her room.

Before long she called out, "Out of bed, Sleepy Head! Time to get ready for work!"

After poking her head out of her room and making sure I was awake, she added, "I get the bathroom first. While I'm getting ready, you slice up some more fruit and get some bread ready to toast. We're going to have my famous toasted fruit sandwiches for breakfast this morning. You're in for a treat."

Without waiting for me to reply, she slipped into the bathroom and quickly closed the door.

"More fruit," I mumbled to myself. "I hope she can filch something better than that today."

....

Mattie was preparing those famous fruit sandwiches when I came out of the bathroom. The second she looked up at me, she let out a long, low whistle.

"Would you look at you!" she said, fighting back laughter. Shaking her head, she added, "Nobody will ever guess this is your first day."

"What?" I asked. "What is it?"

She could hold back the laughter no longer. When she regained a passing semblance of composure, she said, "Well, let's see. I'm some taller than you, but the coveralls fit fine enough. And the scarf is doing its job. You won't get your hair caught in any machine with it up that tight. But let me ask you a question or two. Where in heaven's name did you get those shoes? And earrings? Really? And what about that necklace—and that brooch?"

"What?" I repeated again. "I just want to look good my first day. That's all. Is there something wrong?"

"Well, for one thing, those look like church shoes to me, and after a few minutes of walking through the muck on the floor at the company, you'd never be able to wear them again. You'd have to throw them away. And get rid of all that jewelry. The company has a strict policy: absolutely no jewelry is allowed, not even wedding rings. You get that shiny stuff caught on a machine and it'll yank off a good chunk of some part of your body."

Then, turning more gentle, she said, "Country girl, get back in that bathroom and take off everything that even has a remote chance of catching itself on a machine. While you do that, I'll dig around and find some shoes you can borrow. I think Viola has an extra pair that'll do. I'll go fetch them."

"I'm sorry," I said, embarrassed by my naiveté. "I appreciate your help. I'll get the hang of it."

"You better," Mattie said, smartly. "I need your rent."

....

The Blanton Button Company, known locally as BBC, was about ten blocks from our rooms. A streetcar stop was less than a block away, but Mattie said we needed to walk.

First, she said we needed to save our money, that the fare could better be used for food. After three meals in a row of stolen fruit, I tended to agree with her.

Second, she said if we didn't get this daily exercise we'd end up getting fatter than hogs because the work at the company required standing or sitting for long hours at a single station. She said all I'd need to do was look around at the other women in the company to know what she was talking about.

Finally, Mattie said a nice, brisk walk past the vendors set up on the sides of the crowded streets would afford ample opportunity to get our lunches and suppers. I already knew she didn't mean *pay* for the food.

Even though I couldn't condone her helping herself to the food, her other reasons seemed sound.

We walked the ten blocks.

As we walked, I started thinking about just how much I really did know about the button industry. I may not have known what to wear to work, but I knew chapter and verse of its history. My family had seen to that, especially my uncle.

....

Uncle Sam Henry was peacock-proud of his place in the pearl button industry and never missed an opportunity to share with others something of its history, especially because his stories typically involved one of his dearest friends, John Frederick Boepple, the most famous man of all in the industry. As a child, I heard Uncle Sam Henry's stories so often at family gatherings I could practically recite them word for word. His favorite story, and my favorite to listen to on lazy Sunday afternoons, told of the beginnings of the button industry in Muscatine.

Mr. Boepple, a master button maker as a young man in Germany, had come to this country back in 1887. Button manufacturing in Germany had all but ceased because of the rising cost of shells, making it unprofitable to continue making the buttons there. Mr. Boepple had heard stories of a place in America where the mussel shells needed to make pearl buttons were more plentiful than any other place in the world and, better yet, were still free for the taking. So, even though he didn't speak a word of English, Mr. Boepple packed a few belongings, came to America, and immediately started searching for these shell beds of legend.

After studying maps of the Mississippi River, he made his way by train, horse, and eventually, when his money ran out, on foot to Muscatine because that section of the Mississippi River is one of only a few places along its entire length where the current runs east and west. Mr. Boepple knew the sudden bend in the river and shift in the current from north-south to east-west would form a natural trap where the shells could build up into massive beds. One day soon after his arrival to Muscatine, he was wading in the river just east of the town limits and stepped on a mussel shell, cutting his foot. When he reached down in the river to investigate, he discovered the shell beds he'd been searching for. They were real after all, and they were right beneath him. That one chance footstep was all it took to make history.

After securing the finances needed to put together a factory, Mr. Boepple started in Muscatine what would become the largest button manufacturing center not just in this country, but in the entire world. In just a few short years, so many buttons were being produced that Muscatine became known as the "Pearl Button Capital of the World" and "The Pearl City."

Mr. Boepple had started the industry and had given new life to Muscatine and dozens of other small towns in the region, and my uncle was proud of the part he was playing in this. My whole family had pitched in as well; my father and brothers had all, at one time or another, worked in the industry as blank cutters, polishers, and even as clammers. Even my mother had sewn buttons onto display and sales cards at night to earn a few extra dollars for us. And now, I would be adding to the family legacy by working at BBC. In turn, I hoped and prayed the industry would help me fulfill my dreams.

About halfway to the factory, Mattie turned to me and, without breaking stride, said, "Now don't take this the wrong way. I'm not trying to boss you around, but I want you to know some things before we get there."

She paused, took several more steps, and continued, "There are rules at the factory. I don't want you to embarrass me."

"Go ahead. I'd be grateful," I said, thinking about how I had initially dressed for work.

"Rule number one is simple. Unless you're given permission, don't touch anything that doesn't belong to you. Other than the big equipment, most things, from the drill bits that cut the shells to the sewing needles used to put the buttons on cards, are owned by the workers themselves. The owners *should* provide those things, but they don't. This is just one more way they take advantage of everyone, cut down on their costs, and increase their profits. So, if you touch something and break it, you could be destroying somebody's way of making a living. Some workers might just kill you for doing something like that. In short, keep your hands to yourself."

Without giving me time to say anything, she continued, "Rule number two: Keep your mouth shut and mind your own business. You're going to hear and see things that will shock you. Be seen and not heard—and never talk to the supervisors unless you absolutely have to."

"Give me more details," I cut in. "What do you mean?"

Turning very serious, Mattie said, sharply, "Pearl, I don't know you well enough yet to say anything more about this. You just keep your mouth shut while we're at work, and if you want to ask me questions, save them for when we get home. Understand?"

Although I really didn't, I nodded. That seemed to satisfy her, so she continued.

"Rule number three: Always look busy, even when you're not. Not all of them, but many of the supervisors would just as soon fire you as look at you. All they need is an excuse, and idle hands is one they jump on. I shouldn't be telling you this, but some of the supervisors fire people on purpose to open up jobs. Then they take money from those looking for work and put them in those spots. Basically, they sell jobs, and they're good at it. It's a racket, plain and simple. I don't think most of the owners know about this, but I doubt many would do anything about it even if they did. Make it look like you're busy at all times. You better—or you'll be out on the street, and I'll be out a share of the rent."

"Why doesn't somebody turn those supervisors in? That just isn't right." I said, huffing for breath as the incline of the street suddenly increased.

"Shake the straw out of your hair, Country Girl," Mattie replied, shaking her head. She continued, her voice rising, "Rule number four: Don't get hurt! If you get injured and miss work, this is what will happen. The company won't pay your medical bills; you'll have to cover that yourself, and you won't be able to afford it. Then, if you miss work, you won't get paid, and somebody else will be in your place when you try to come back. That's just the way it is. If you do get hurt, try to hide it if you can. Those supervisors might see you slow down and fire you for what they say will be for your own sake, which is just a lot of hooey. They will want you gone, so they can sell your job to someone else. So, if you get hurt, let me know, and I'll tell you what to do. Got it?"

"Yes, but that sounds so horrible. So inhumane. So...."

"So wrong?" Mattie shot back. "Again, shake out the straw. And another thing. Remember that finger pool I mentioned before? We always make bets, make a pool, every time a new worker comes on board. We bet on how long it will take for that person to lose a finger. Actually, it doesn't have to be a finger, although a lot of people do end up with less than ten. Any good injury with plenty of blood qualifies. The one closest to the date of the injury gets the whole pot of money. Hey, I have an idea. I'll pick a date a few weeks from now, and if you can keep from getting hurt until then, you can fake an injury or just get slightly hurt on my date, and we'll split the pot. That would pay for some decent suppers for a change. You up for that?"

I just glared at her and kept walking.

She then added, "Finally, rule number five—and most important of all— never, *ever*, talk about what we do in our factory with anyone who works in another factory. It's okay to socialize with those who work elsewhere, but the socializing is where it has to stop. The big bosses all think they have secret ways of running their businesses that make their products special. The truth is they're all pretty much the same from what I hear, but this is a little game played by the owners that we have to go along with. And there really might be some secret parts of the process in a factory that we don't know about or understand. Who knows? All I know is that there are plenty of stories of people who were fired for this—and even some stories of people who just up and disappeared and were never heard from again. The owners are dead-serious about keeping their little trade secrets to themselves."

Mattie added, "There are other rules as well, but you'll learn them soon on your own. This should be enough to keep you from getting fired or killed until you can settle in. If you have any questions, save them for when we get home at night. That's all for now."

"It's plenty," I said. "I'll do my best. I will. I need this job and would hate it if I did something dumb to cause me to lose it."

"You're welcome," she said, flatly. "But I didn't tell you all this just for you. I did it for me, too. Don't you go embarrassing me or getting me fired. Like you, I *need* this job."

The early morning sun was already heating up the day, and we were both wiping away perspiration as we made a sudden turn down an alley immediately to our left. "Shortcut," Mattie said, motioning me ahead.

About three-quarters of the way down the alley, she pointed to our right, and the Blanton Button Company came into view. I could barely believe my eyes. The brick and mortar building was three stories tall and nearly a block long. The side facing us—the side running parallel with the street—had large, rectangular windows tilted open and evenly spaced nearly its whole width. Large smokestacks stood front and rear of the building, and it appeared smaller ones formed something of a circle near the center of the roof. Steam was already billowing skyward from all of them.

I let out a low whistle, stopped firmly in my tracks, and exclaimed, "Sweet Savior! Would you look at that!"

Mattie grabbed my hand and pulled me forward with her. "Come on. Keep going, Country Girl. You haven't seen anything yet."

Too stunned to respond, I quietly followed her. We headed up a long sidewalk at the front of the building. Mattie was still holding my hand and yanked us to a stop just before we climbed the steps to the main entrance. There, she turned to me again and said, emphasizing each word, "Ye all who enter here, give up all hope."

Though that was a pretty rough version of Dante's sign at the gates of Hell, I got her point. As we entered the building, I knew my life would never be the same again.

....

CHAPTER 6

As SOON AS WE WERE inside the building, Mattie walked me to the main office and said, "This is where the boss holds court, and this is as far as I go. You're on your own now. Watch yourself. Tonight, when the whistle blows, meet me out front and we'll walk home together."

I leaned over to hug her, but she drew back quickly. "See you after work," she said, stepping even farther back. With that, she turned and headed down the hall.

I wondered if not showing emotion at work was rule number six. It was either that or Mattie just being Mattie. I decided to tuck it away and ask her on the way home.

As I walked into the office, a rather rotund secretary with black pincnez glasses looked up and asked, "May I help you?"

"I'm Pearl McGill," I replied. "I was told to report to work today."

"Oh yes, Miss McGill," she said, smiling broadly. "Nice to meet you. My name is Miss Fitch."

We shook hands, and her grip was impressive.

"Mr. Blanton is expecting you. Please take a seat over there. He'll be back here shortly and will meet with you just as soon as he can."

Just as I sat down, what sounded like a church bell suddenly started ringing, and it seemed to be coming from within the building. I looked at the clock over Miss Fitch's desk, and the time was 6:45 A.M.—fifteen minutes before the official workday began.

Miss Fitch struggled up and out of her chair and walked slowly from behind her desk. Stopping next to me she said, gently, "It just dawned on me that you might as well come with me. Mr. Blanton's going to address the employees. Does it every Monday morning before all get to work."

Seeing my confusion, she led me out into the hallway and down to a large open area on the main floor. I kept my mouth closed and followed her. There, in the back of this area, seated in long rows, were dozens of what were obviously, because of their manner of dress, employees of the company. None were talking. The room was absolutely quiet.

A tall, thin-faced, balding man I judged to be in his early fifties walked toward us from the opposite end of the hall. When he reached the open area, he stepped onto a small stage in front of one of the open windows and faced everyone. After looking slowly back and forth at the group assembled before him, he began, "Good morning, everyone. It's a glorious day."

While all in the room nodded politely toward him, Miss Fitch leaned close to my ear and whispered, "That's Mr. Blanton."

I nodded that I understood.

I looked back at Mr. Blanton and took note of how he was dressed. I had made quite a clothing blunder myself earlier, but his attire, by contrast, seemed downright foolish if nothing else. Even at this early hour of the morning, the temperature was already into the eighties, but he was dressed in a formal black suit and vest. He had to be roasting. Yet, he looked as comfortable as a cat on a feather bed.

He went on, his voice strong, forceful, "Just a few words today before we get to our stations. I want all of you to know production was up half a percent last week. That doesn't sound like much, but it's steady progress and for that I'm proud of all of you. I'm especially pleased with the work of those in the packing department. It doesn't make any difference how many buttons we make, if they aren't packed up and shipped out, they don't mean anything. By my count, we shipped out more product last week than we have in any one week in the past two years."

Here, everyone applauded, politely, but still no one said a word. He quickly added, "Our distributors in St. Louis have told us the last batch of Pinkies we sent out are selling like hotcakes in all the retail stores there. That color and luster is what every woman wants to use for the coming fall season. So, we should give credit where credit is due. We have our friend Gunboat Gaston to thank for this; the Pinkies were made from the shells he brings us."

Mr. Blanton gave an exaggerated grin, exhaled loudly, and shook his head as the others around the room smiled and nodded to each other—but still didn't utter a sound. As Gaston's name was mentioned, in my surprise, I let out an unconscious "Uh?" I composed myself, but my thoughts started racing a mile a minute. Was Gunboat Gaston *my* Gaston? If so, then why had he been called *Gunboat* Gaston? And what special shells did he have that others didn't? And why did all the others smile when his name was mentioned? Mattie had told me to keep my mouth shut in the factory, so I would do that. But, at the very first chance I was going to ask her all about this before my curiosity killed every cat in town.

Mr. Blanton then said, "I don't know if we can match that color exactly again, but if any of you working in the Sulfuric area can figure out a mixture that will duplicate the samples I'm going to send up, there'll be a handsome bonus for you."

He looked up as if expecting applause again, but when none came, he continued. "Finally, and I can't emphasize this enough, the cleanup crews need to be better. I expect these floors to be as clean and as free from shell dust as possible, and that's just not being done now. Get it done right."

He paused again for a moment and looked at his watch. "Everyone to your stations. Let's make some buttons."

The assembled group waited for him to step down from the stage and walk toward the office. Then, as a group, they stood and quickly made their way in all directions. I had never seen any group anywhere stay so silent for so long. It may have been out of respect for Mr. Blanton, or fear, a combination of both, or something yet to be known by me.

Miss Fitch took my hand and led me back to the office. I sat in a chair across from her desk while she stuck her head inside an inner office door and announced me. Then, turning to me, she said, "Mr. Blanton does that every Monday morning. It's good for the workers. And, if the truth be known, It's good for him, too."

Before she could say more, Mr. Blanton came out of his office and stood before me.

"Pearl McGill," he said, some astonishment in his voice. "My you've grown. Come on into my office and we'll visit some."

"Sir?" I asked.

"Why, you don't recognize me, do you?" he smiled. "I'm Richard Blanton. Back when you were a little girl, I used to come to your uncle's home all the time to pitch horseshoes. You used to sit on my lap and eat your ice cream because I always brought chocolate drops to put in it. Remember that?"

Suddenly, I remembered. My brothers, sisters, and I always called him "Mr. Chocolate" when he came to visit. I don't think any of us ever knew his real name.

"I sure do," I practically shouted, my eyes widening. "You're Mr. ...."

"I know," he said, grimacing. "You kids called me Mr. Chocolate. You didn't think I knew that, did you?"

We both laughed and sat back, studying each other. He broke the silence.

"Those were fun days. I loved your family. We were all poor as church mice back then, but we had each other, and that was enough to make us at least feel rich. I've got money now and, well, look at all of this."

He swung his arm wide and motioned to the office and beyond. "But I'd trade it all for just one more of those simple Sundays we all spent together. It's a different world now."

"And how about you?" he added. "Just look at you—a grown woman, and a pretty one at that. You've got your mother's features, that's for sure."

"Thank you. That's very kind," I replied, feeling my face redden. "Oh, my mother sends her best to you, and my father, too."

He nodded and we sat quietly before looking at each other and laughing again. "You're right, sir," I said, finally. "Those were special days. I'll always treasure them."

"Me, too," he said, softly. "Always."

He stood up, moved to the door, and closed it, firmly. Turning and facing me, I saw that his expression had changed completely. The softness in his eye from just moments before was gone. He seemed almost sad.

"Did your uncle talk to you about the job you're to have here?" he asked quietly while staring at his office door.

"No, Sir," I said, starting to feel more than a little unsettled by how quickly his demeanor had changed. "He just said I was to do exactly what you told me to do, that what I was going to be doing was important to you—and to him. I said that was good enough for me. So, I'll do anything I can to help you, Sir."

"He didn't say anything other than that?" he asked. "Nothing else?"

"No, Sir. He said you'd be talking to me about my duties."

"I wish he had explained at least some of this," he said, now pacing back and forth slowly in front of me. "This isn't going to be easy to explain."

He paused for a minute, pulled his desk chair next to where I was seated, and began, "Pearl, what we're asking you to do.... No, what *I'm* going to ask you to do is a lot to ask of someone so young. Frankly, it will also have its element of danger, and I'm going to be honest and tell you that right up front."

Here he got up and walked to the door to make sure it was shut tightly. He sat back down, scooted his chair even closer to me—so close that our knees were nearly touching—and continued, his voice much softer this time. "I've got a problem. We all do, including your uncle. The workers...." Here his voice trailed off and he looked at the door. "The workers, our employees, are about to drive us right under the ground. They're demanding higher wages and changes in the factories that we just aren't able to provide without going belly-up. To put it bluntly, what they are asking for would put us out of business."

Here he paused and appeared to be waiting for my response. "I know," I said, finally, matching the soft tone of his voice. "My uncle has told me all about this. He said the industry will dry up and die if the workers have their way."

"Good. I'm glad you understand that," he said, relief filling his voice. "We have to do something before it's too late. Your uncle and I think it might already be too late, but we've decided we're not going to go down without a fight. We've worked too hard and too long to get where we are to let a bunch of rabble tear it all down."

"Uncle Sam Henry calls them 'lazy, shiftless, good-for-nothings'—and a few other choice words as well," I added.

For the first time since he started talking about this, he cracked a slight smile. "Well, he and I definitely agree on that. And I've used a few other *choice* words myself."

His smile faded. "I'm just going to give it to you in plain language. Here's what we—I mean *I*—want you to do. We're going to let it get out that you're here as a special favor to your uncle, who happens to be a dear friend of mine. That is the truth, but, at the same time, it will also protect you and give you credibility and respect while you are here. We're also going to make sure everyone knows your uncle is in the button blank-cutting business, and he wants to expand his operation to become a finishing plant that will do everything in the button making process, like this one. We'll tell everyone you are here to learn how the business is run and how all the stations work together. At first, they'll think this is very unusual because owners never talk about their businesses with other owners. But since your uncle and I are such close friends, we're going to say we'll be going into business together, partners of a sort, when he gets his own factory ready. Your uncle likely didn't tell you that, but that is also true. That will make everything seem logical. To give you more protection, we're going to have it slip out that your uncle is going to need to hire workers for his new factory once it's ready—and that those who help you most while you are here will get first chance at those jobs, which will carry higher wages because his plant is far out in Grandview. That ought to get their attention—and ought to make you one incredibly popular girl."

I listened closely to him and understood what he said, but I still didn't understand exactly what he was expecting me to do. My confused look must have been obvious because he added, "Now to the heart of the matter. Pearl, you really are going to learn a great deal about the business. I'm going to have you work a week or two or three in every station in the factory, so you can watch and learn what is done there. Where it's practical, I'm also going to ask those at some of the stations to teach you how to do what they do, so you can learn something of their skills. Basically, you'll be like an apprentice for many tasks. We'll tell them that eventually you're going to help train workers in your uncle's new factory, so you, naturally, need to gain as much of this knowledge as you possibly can."

He suddenly stood up, walked to his desk, opened a drawer, and pulled out a ledger. He gently flipped it over to me, and I caught it on my lap.

"While you are observing and working at each station, I want you to get to know the workers there as much and as good as you can. I want you to find out their sympathies, whether they are loyal to the company—or if they're in that group of trash making noise about building up a workers' union. Take notes. Keep names. I want to know about everybody working in this factory. I want to know everything going on. If we can stop these people here, then we've got a chance to stop them everywhere else as well. They're like rats—and they multiply like wildfire. If we can douse the flames now, we just might be able to save the forest. We need your help to do this."

His message was clear. I exhaled loudly. So did he.

I didn't know how to say it delicately. "You want me to spy.

That's it, right?" I said.

"Let's not call it that," he said, curtly. "Some people think a spy gains information to hurt other people. That's not what this is all about, and if you think that, I'd rather you go back home right now and forget all about this—forget our whole conversation. No, I don't need a spy. Just the opposite. I need someone to help me save this factory, to save jobs for thousands of workers who depend upon this industry to provide food, clothing, and shelter for their families. If the scum in this industry have their way and get a union, just think what would happen to most of these workers when they lose their livlihood. I can't let that happen. I'm *not* going to let that happen. What I need to know now is whether you're willing to help me. Whether you'll help me save these jobs for the good people around here. If you are, we'll begin right away. If you feel you can't do this, I'd rather you go back home now. So, young lady, what will it be?"

Then, sitting back on the edge of his desk, he added, "This, no doubt, will be one of the biggest decisions of your life thus far. Be sure you think this through before giving me your answer."

I got up from my chair, walked past him and stood by his window, looking out at the well-manicured grounds below. My mind was still racing. On the one hand, his explanation seemed sound enough, and I trusted my uncle's beliefs. I had heard and read enough about unions destroying businesses around the country to know thousands of people really could lose their jobs if what my uncle and Mr. Blanton believed came true.

At the same time, just the thought of being a *spy* made me feel queasy, even if it was for a good cause. Plus, I didn't know if I could be a spy. What did it really mean? Would I have to steal secrets? I was thoroughly conflicted. I'd have to learn to lie and be very, very good at it. And, it suddenly occurred to me, I wouldn't just be lying; I'd be *living* a lie, which would be just about as bad as it could get. Mattie's words before we entered the building, "Ye all who enter here..." came back to me with great clarity. If I became a spy, I'd be entering a gate of a very similar sort.

This was all happening so fast I just didn't know what to think or do. Apparently Mr. Blanton could see this plainly on my face because he stepped next to me, put his arm around my shoulder, and said, calmly, "Why don't you take the rest of the day to think about it. Above all, I do want you to be sure. Come back tomorrow morning and we'll talk again."

"You're being very kind, and I appreciate that," I said turning to face him. "I think I'd like to have the rest of the morning if that's okay with you. I'd like to walk around and think about it. Walking is what I do when I have something I need to get sorted out in my mind. If I can have the morning, I'm sure I can let you know by the end of the afternoon."

Mr. Blanton smiled and said, "That'll be fine. Just be careful where you walk around here. There's a lot of construction down by the river on this side of town, and it's pretty dangerous there. I'd recommend, even though it's uphill, you go out the front door and head up to the park. That's where I go when I need to get away from everything. Good place to do some thinking. At least it always has been for me."

I walked over to the door, turned around, and said, "Sir, I'll be back this afternoon. Thank you for giving me this time to think about everything. Thank you for the trust you've shown in me. Whatever I decide, nothing we've talked about will ever be heard by anyone else. That I promise you."

"I know that," he replied. "You didn't have to say it. I'm a pretty fair judge of character, and I'm not worried about you at all."

He opened the door for me, and I left, pausing just long enough to say goodbye to Miss Fitch.

When I reached the end of the front sidewalk, I took Mr. Blanton's advice and headed across the street and up the long hill in front of me. The walk was steeper than I preferred, but it felt good. The dull ache I soon felt in my calves took my mind off the swirling thoughts in my head.

....

I sat down on a long bench near a thick row of lilac bushes. From this perch, I looked out and saw miles of the Mississippi River stretched out below. I could see far off to the right where the river suddenly started shifting south. I imagined that was one of the places Mr. Boepple first found the deep clam beds. Back to the east, the town of Muscatine spread as far as the eye could see. There was the Mississippi River Bridge and, underneath it, whisps of smoke drifting upward from fires at the clamming camp. I spotted the train depot and laughed as I thought of my introduction to the town. To my left, to the north, were more homes than I'd ever thought possible in any one town. If even half of what I'd heard in the past couple of days was true, then most of the people who lived in these homes were there because of the button industry.

I still didn't know how I felt about everything my uncle and Mr. Blanton believed, but I suddenly and with great clarity knew, by looking at all the sights below me, that the right thing to do would be to try to help the people who depended upon the industry for their livelihood. That much, at least, made sense. That much, at least, I could justify.

Even if it meant being a spy.

I had heard my uncle say that in order to help the people in the factories, the industry would have to remain strong. He believed the two were tied together and could not be separated; the health of one determined the health of the other. I thought about that over and over again for the better part of an hour. I didn't have everything sorted through, but I finally decided to give this my best try. If the information I gathered would help my uncle and Mr. Blanton, then they could help keep the industry healthy. That, in turn, could help the workers. In the end, then, everyone might prosper. My thoughts may have been more than a shade simplistic, but looking at the situation this way made sense to me. Having made up my mind so, I decided to walk down the hill and tell Mr. Blanton I had made my decision, that I'd be proud to help in any way I could.

When I reentered the main office, Miss Fitch smiled and said, "Go on in. He's expecting you."

I knocked gently, opened the door, and stepped in, quickly closing the door behind me. Mr. Blanton was standing by the window.

"I saw you coming back down the hill," he said. "Made up your mind so soon?"

"I need to be honest and tell you I'm not overjoyed about the spying," I replied. "I'm not going to kid myself; that's exactly what it is. But, I think I can live with that because if I have a chance to help everyone out, then I should do it. That just seems the right thing to do."

With our eyes locked, I said, boldly, "I'll do it. How do we begin?"

Mr. Blanton took me completely by surprise when he came over and hugged me, while saying, "You *are* doing the right thing. You'll see."

He then motioned for me to sit down and pulled his chair next to mine.

"Listen to me carefully. First of all, no one but the two of us, and your uncle, will know about this. No one. That is imperative. I won't even tell Miss Fitch, and she seems to know everything that goes on around here. Don't tell a soul, not even your closest friends. Your life may depend upon it."

Here he paused for emphasis, making sure I understood the seriousness. I nodded, and he continued.

"We'll meet once a week so you can give me a report. We'll meet after I have my Monday morning gathering with the employees. They'll just figure I'm meeting with you to give you additional information to pass along to your uncle. I want names, dates, and all the information you can get for me about this union talk and anything else you think might be important. They'd be stupid to do it, but I know there's also been some talk about a strike of some kind. See if you can find out about that, too. At the same time, guard that ledger with your life."

Mr. Blanton paused, took out his handkerchief, wiped his cheeks, and continued, this time seeming more relaxed. "You'll start tomorrow. I want you to go home now. I'll see to it word gets around today about what you'll be doing here, so you'll probably be quite popular when you get back here tomorrow morning. It won't be long before people will be asking you to recommend them for jobs at your uncle's new factory."

He then smiled and said, "I've saved the best for last—at least for you. So far we haven't talked about what you'll be getting out of this. Sam Henry told me you're here to earn the funds required to go get your teaching certificate. Going to school these days isn't cheap. It was a small fortune way back when I attended the University of Iowa, and now everything is even more expensive. I'm going to do what I can to help you along. You'll have a regular salary here, rather than being paid by piecework, which is pay earned by the quantity and quality of what one produces. You're going to earn eleven dollars per week, which is nearly double the normal starting wage. If our work together turns out to be successful and I find out what I'm looking for, there will be a thirty dollar bonus for you when you leave for school. That will be my personal contribution to your books and board. Does this arrangement sound acceptable to you?"

I nearly fell into shock. Eleven dollars per week! The time I'd have to be in Muscatine could be cut in half! And, on top of that, a *thirty dollar* bonus. That was more money than I'd ever seen in one place in my life.

Just as suddenly as my joy over the thought of that money entered my head, I had another thought. A very sobering thought.

Judas had been given *thirty* pieces of silver.

I wished he hadn't said anything about the money. At the same time, "Ye all who enter here..." once again popped into my thoughts. I couldn't shake it. Part of me was wavering badly, but another part of me—what my mother would probably call the Irish side of me—was telling me as long as one's heart is pure, the fight is always honorable. My heart wasn't one hundred percent pure on this issue, but it was as pure as it was going to get. That would have to be enough. I would take the rest on faith.

"It's acceptable," I said, standing and shaking his hand firmly. "And very generous."

"Good!" he said loudly—too loudly. We both winced and looked toward the door.

"Then I'll see you tomorrow morning. Take the rest of the day to gather yourself and get ready. As soon as you're here tomorrow, the first thing I want to do is give you a tour of the factory so you'll have an idea of everything we do here. This is a very different kind of operation than what your uncle has, so a lot of this will be brand new to you. The tour will also give me a chance to introduce you to those who don't get the word today. Then, after our walk-through, you'll begin your first job here. Your first station will be in packing and shipping. I'm going to have you start there and eventually work backward through all the stations. You'll have the advantage of seeing completed work before you learn how it is produced. This will allow you to see the whole picture before you start in with the brush, if you know what I mean."

"Enjoy the rest of the day," he added, stepping over to open the door.

"I will," I said. "I've got some walking—and thinking—to do."

He shook my hand firmly. We stood there and studied each other carefully, but neither of us spoke. I left without another word. Once in the outer office, I asked Miss Fitch if she would get word to Mattie that I'd meet her at home after work. She said that wouldn't be a problem, so I headed out the door.

....

CHAPTER 7

I WAS HAVING A TUG-OF-WAR with a spring in the divan when Mattie burst through the door.

"Why in the hell didn't you tell me what a big shot and how important you are?" she practically shouted as she threw down a small sack and plopped down next to me. "Everybody in the plant is buzzing about you. You're a celebrity, for heaven sakes! Here I've been calling you *Country Girl* ever since you got here, and it turns out I'm the one who doesn't know spit from Shinola. You've got some explaining to do."

She folded her arms and leaned back against a pillow. During my afternoon walk, thinking about what I was going to tell her, I'd decided to stay as close to the truth as I could, but I had no illusions. Some "stretchers" would be necessary. Facing Mattie, I chose my words carefully.

"My uncle didn't want there to be a lot of fuss when I got to the factory. For as long as I can remember, he's always been like a guardian angel for me. I didn't know what all I'd be doing until I met with Mr. Blanton today. All I really knew was my uncle had taken care of things for me. He's just like that."

That explanation wasn't nearly enough for Mattie, which she let me know by playfully kicking me on the shin with her heavy work shoe. "More!" she said, her eyes widening. "I want more!"

I thought about teasing her again, but I was starved and had my eyes focused on the sack she had dropped to the floor as she entered.

"That food?" I asked, pointing to the sack.

She nodded and scooted to the side to block my view of it.

"Well, I'm sure it's more of your ill-gotten gains, but here's a deal I'll propose. I'm hungry, so let's eat supper now. While we eat, I'll tell you as much as I can. Take it, or leave it."

"I'd rather hear everything now, but I'm not going to argue with you," she said, her voice clipped, almost stern. "It's a deal. Help me cut up the rest of our fruit. Then, get that sack and cut up what's in there so we can have sandwiches. You owe me a story, and it better be a good one."

"What's in there?" I asked, almost afraid of what I'd hear.

"Salami. I'm not wild about it, but it'll stick to our ribs. Bananas and Salami. Our stomachs are going to die if we don't get something better."

"Then why salami?"

Mattie screwed up her face and replied, "Because, Dearie, it was on a table right by the door in the shop."

"Oh," was all I could say. Her logic was, again, sound. At least for a petty crook.

I was no longer in a position to throw stones. So, I didn't say anything else. I cut the salami into thin slices and set them on a serving dish.

Bananas and salami it would be.

....

For the next hour I spun the best tale I could while we scarfed down the salami and bananas. It was an odd combination, but I was so hungry I'd have eaten just about anything pulled out of that sack.

While we ate, I told Mattie that my uncle, whom she had known when we were children, was going to be expanding his business and needed help to figure out everything from how a complete button factory, typically called a "finishing plant," needed to be organized to how the day-to-day operations were conducted. Mattie already knew my uncle produced only button blanks. I followed this up by doing my best job of predicting what his new factory would do for the little town of Grandview. I even suggested that Grandview might become a smaller version of Muscatine if everything went as planned. At this point, Mattie rolled her eyes and said, sarcastically, "That one-dog town? That'll be the day."

At least her attention was focused on our hometown and not on my real reason for being here, which was quite a relief for me. I knew, beyond a shadow of a doubt, that Mr. Blanton was right when he said absolutely no one else could know what I was doing. Mattie was right on top of that list, especially because past history indicated it didn't take much to turn her into "The Town Crier."

I could tell the wheels were spinning in Mattie's head because she was nervously picking at her hair and blinking her eyes rapidly. She finally picked up the serving plate and leaned forward to offer me more salami. As she did so, she practically blurted out, "I want to work for your uncle. I want you to put in a word for me. Please do it!"

She quickly turned away from me and avoided my eyes while folding her napkin in her lap. Mattie was never the sort to ask for favors of any kind, so this was unusual territory for her, and she didn't know quite how to act. As she continued waiting for my response and looking down at the table, I felt sorry for her. I knew her life had not been an easy one. Her mother was a kind and gentle sort, but my mother had told me Mattie's father frequently took to whiskey and a belt—and the belt was used on Mattie and her mother to the point that the local sheriff had to be called in to help keep the peace in their home. As I sat there and studied her face, I couldn't help but feel she might have been in Muscatine to escape the belt as much as anything else.

I reached over and gently put my hand on hers. As calmly and as softly as I could, I said, "I'd do that without having to be prompted. We go back a long way, Mattie."

Mattie just sat there, not saying a word. Her eyes were starting to tear up when she suddenly stood and walked toward the sink. Without turning around, she flipped a kitchen towel back toward me. I caught it and set it on the table. I expected her to follow that up by saying something, but she didn't. She continued to stand there, silently, her back to me. It didn't take a clairvoyant to tell she was on the tip of sharing something with me, but sudden and loud banging on the door startled both of us.

"What the...," Mattie shouted as we both turned to face the door.

"You want me to see who it is?" I asked, standing up.

"Well, the door isn't going to open by itself, is it?" Mattie barked.

From emotional to commanding in under a minute. That was Mattie. I walked over to the door and opened it.

A beautiful young woman with golden hair piled high on her head was standing before me on the landing.

"You're Pearl right?" she said.

"Yes," I replied. "And who are you?"

She didn't give her name. Instead, she asked, "So, what are you doing here in Muscatine?"

Before I could respond, Mattie shouted, "Oh, good grief! Viola, get your hiney inside. And close that door. You're letting in the heat and the bugs, and I don't want either of them. You can ask anything you want—but do it in here!"

I was surprised when Viola immediately hugged me and kissed me on the cheek. She glared at Mattie and said, "And nothing for you, you old crab."

"Old crab?" Mattie replied. "If I am, it's because some of us never let anybody else know where they're off to or what they're doing."

She paused for an instant, her face softening. "I was starting to get worried about you. But I can see now I shouldn't have been. That looks to me like a new pearl necklace I see around your neck. I'm betting that means you found another man, a rich one this time?"

The tone of Mattie's voice seemed to me to have as much a tinge of jealously as admonition. Viola seemed used to it because she didn't bat an eyelash. Instead, she completely ignored Mattie and turned back to me after sitting down in the kitchen chair closest to the door. It was obvious the words she directed to me were really intended for Mattie and that she was trying, not too subtly, to scold Mattie for her less than enthusiastic welcome.

"You didn't know the Knox brothers, did you?" Viola asked me, her voice now filled with emotion. "Claude and Odie? No, I guess you wouldn't. They lived up in Washington, Iowa in a beautiful little cabin overlooking the river. Up on Tower Street. You'd never in your life find two nicer brothers. Odie was always telling jokes, was always the life of a party. Claude was straight as rain, honest and true. And good looking. Both of them."

Mattie couldn't stand it any longer. She threw the other kitchen towel at Viola, just missing her head. "What's all this 'was' and 'were' manure? Where'd they go? Did they finally head down to Arkansas and leave us here? They promised to take us with them, those rats."

Mattie sat down at the table and squeezed her chair between mine and Viola's. I might as well have been invisible. Viola finally gave in and looked at Mattie, and Mattie smiled at her.

Viola didn't smile back.

Instead, she fell heavily back in her chair, placed her hands on her knees, and said, quietly, calmly, "They're dead, Mattie. Both of them."

Without looking at either of us, she picked up a slice of banana and started slowly nibbling on it.

"No!" Mattie screamed, standing up and kicking her chair so hard it slid and crashed into the sink.

Viola bolted up and hugged her tightly as both began sobbing.

Through her sobs, I could make out just enough of Mattie's words to know she had asked how it had happened. Viola's words were even harder to understand, but I was pretty sure I heard her say they had been in a terrible fight of some kind.

While Viola sobbed, she was breathing heavily and in short bursts. Mattie gently stroked her hair and continued to hold her tightly. Viola finally stepped back and pointed toward me while saying to Mattie, "There's something I have to tell you, but not in front of her."

Her tone didn't seem mean or cruel, so I took no offense. More than anything, she seemed in a state of shock.

Tears still choked her words, but Mattie looked at me and said, softly, "Would you mind? It'll only be for a little while."

I stood and said, "I am going to go for a walk before bed. I'll be back later."

On my way to the door I stopped and put my arms around both, giving them a quick squeeze. Then I stepped outside and made sure the door shut tightly behind me.

From this side of our second-story view, I could see a fair distance down Second Street, much farther than I could from the inside windows. Tonight there were no crowds, only an occasional wandering soul heading up and down the sidewalks banking both sides of the street. Off to my right, the Mississippi rolled gently along, the bright August stars reflected in its current. A light breeze was coming from the south, but it wasn't enough to wash away the terrible smell that hung heavily above the town. Added to it was a thick smoke smell, like large piles of brush were burning somewhere in the distance. The combination burned my eyes, and they began to water. Farther up the hill, behind our apartment, kerosene lamps were blinking softly in the windows of the homes on the streets running parallel to the river. If it weren't for the foul air, the early evening might have been described as beautiful. As it was, all I could do was hold my handkerchief tightly against my nose so as not to lose my salami and bananas. Muscatine was, if nothing else, a constant blend of the pretty and the putrid, and tonight the emphasis was on the latter side of the ledger.

I began to walk down Chestnut Street toward the river so I could see what types of shops were in that direction. Since I was still in my coveralls, I knew I'd blend in much better with the locals.

Whereas Second Street was lined with all type and manner of businesses butting against each other, shops on Chestnut were few and far between. I hadn't gone far when I realized this was because a honeycomb of alleys ran behind the stores facing Second Street—and they originated out on Chestnut. These alleys caused large gaps between buildings. There was a tailor shop, a bakery, and a small photography studio, but most of the other buildings this direction seemed to be serving as warehouses for furniture and building materials.

Just a few steps from Front Street, a man suddenly ran around the corner. As I tried to get out of the way, he grazed my arm with his own and continued on, gasping for air. He, too, wore work coveralls, and he had on a floppy hat pulled down nearly to his eyes. Twenty or thirty feet or so up the street, he stopped, turned around, and ran toward me again. His rush around the corner had been so sudden I hadn't had time to be frightened. Now, however, as he approached me again, I panicked and started running down the hill. I had only taken a few steps when I looked over my shoulder to see if he was still following, and as I did, I saw him stop at the alley there and stare right into my eyes.

Underneath those coveralls and hat was Gaston. Our eyes met for only an instant; then, he bolted down the alleyway. I started walking in that direction when, from behind me, I heard a large group of people shouting and yelling as they were drawing near to the corner of Front and Chestnut. I stopped directly in the front of the alley and waited to see what the commotion was about.

Not more than half a minute later, about a dozen men, some of them carrying clubs and one with a large hammer, rushed quickly my direction up the sidewalk. To put it mildly, they weren't happy. One called out, "We've got to find him!" Another shouted, "I'll skin his hide with this Arkansas Toothpick!" He brandished the largest knife I'd ever seen; it was a foot long and gleamed in the nearby lamplight. Still another called out, "I saw his coveralls. Damn unionist."

The obvious leader of the group, a burly man with a thick moustache curled up at the corners, saw me and huffed my direction. "Missy, you see anybody run this way? Anybody at all?"

"What'd he do?" I asked, as calmly as I could.

Someone behind him yelled, "He set the dock on fire! That's what he did. Whole loading area was ashes before we could do anything. Did you see him run by here?"

The leader stepped even closer to me, his breathing labored. "Well, did you?" he shouted right into my face, globs of his spit landing on the front of my coveralls.

It all happened so fast the words were out of my mouth before I had a chance to think. "I did see somebody, and he was running hard. He went down that alley across the street. I could see him go just about all the way down there, and it looked like he headed back down toward the river. He probably circled behind you."

"Why that dirty, lousy, piece of trash!" someone shouted from within the group. The leader looked closely into my eyes, exhaled heavily, and said, slowly and deliberately, "You better be telling me the truth. I'm going to remember your face."

Then, inching still closer until our faces were nearly touching, he added, "Did you recognize him? Did you know him? I see the way you're dressed. Was he one of yours?"

"I didn't get a good look at him. He had a hat pulled down over his face. He didn't look like any worker I've ever seen around here before. That much I can tell you. He looked like a... foreigner."

As the leader stared more intently at me, I started to get scared. My mouth was dry, and the last of my words to him were barely loud enough for him to hear.

"I'm going to remember your face," he repeated, this time drawing his index finger quickly across the front of his neck, indicating what could happen if I was lying to him.

He turned away, pointed to the alley across the way, and commanded, "Half of you go that way. The other half come with me—we'll head straight down to the river."

When the group didn't move, he added, clapping his hands sharply, "Come on! Let's go! I've got a five-dollar bill for the first man to grab him. Anybody want that?"

The mention of the money was all it took. The group split up and took off, whooping and hollering as they ran.

I stepped back and leaned against the building to keep from falling down.

As soon as they were out of sight, I turned and said with what little voice I had left, "They're gone."

Gaston stepped from behind a row of barrels along the wall. He removed his coveralls, revealing a regular pair of dungarees and a blue shirt. In one motion he removed his hat and shook his hair down. He rolled the hat up in the coveralls and threw the bundle over to me.

He then walked toward the edge of the alley, slowly and carefully peering out to look both directions. After studying my face briefly, and without so much as a "Thank you," he walked to the bakery, pulled down the fire escape ladder there, and started climbing. He pulled the bottom portion of the ladder up before continuing all the way to the upper landing. There, he jumped up, grabbed the edge of the roof, and pulled himself up and over. A few seconds later his head appeared again. It was starting to get very dark, but I could still see his face. His expression had changed, but I couldn't tell if I saw a smile or a frown.

Then he was gone.

I walked as quickly as I could back home.

....

"Where'd you get those?" Mattie asked as soon as I entered the door. "You rob and strip somebody?"

"Very funny," I said, gently placing the coveralls and hat on the table. "I found these down by Front Street. They're a little big, but I think we can take them in."

"You're learning," Mattie replied. "I'll make a crook out of you yet."

I wanted to tell Mattie what I had just seen, but I didn't have it straight in my own mind what had happened.

Mattie looked at me, and it suddenly dawned on me she must have been thinking I was still shaken from seeing her and Viola so emotionally torn up. She came over, led me by the hand over to the table, and motioned for me to sit down.

She turned serious again. "Viola went to bed, so let's keep it down. We've had a terrible shock, and she's taking it extra hard."

"Want to talk about it?" I asked, softly.

Mattie also sat down. She didn't say anything for a few minutes, and I didn't press the issue. Finally, she looked at me and said, as gently as I'd ever heard her speak, "Let's keep this between the two of us. Promise me you won't say a word to anyone."

I nodded. Mattie began, her voice full of sadness. "The Knox boys were the first really decent people we met in this stinkin' town. They were awful good to me and Viola when we first got here. I honestly don't think we could have made it without them. We met them at a huge town picnic at Weed Park. Odie took an immediate shine to Viola, and she immediately set her cap for him. Claude was good man. A little stiff and stodgy, but he still knew how to have fun when he let himself go. He and I became fast friends."

She paused and wiped her eyes. "Their father had been killed in a button plant back in '98—some kind of accident. Both the boys said his death was senseless, that it wouldn't have happened if anybody had given a hoot and a holler about safety of the workers there. Because of that—and you have to promise to keep this to yourself—they started getting involved with people who are interested in stopping accidents like this from happening again."

"You mean unionists?" I cut in a little too loudly. The minute it came out of my mouth, I knew it shouldn't have.

Mattie squirmed in her chair and pointed sternly at me and said, coldly, "Don't use that word in our home again. Just being suspected of being a part of something like that can lead to...."

Her voice trailed off. She started to get up from the table, but I grabbed her wrist and held firm. "I'm sorry," I said. "Sometime I talk when I should just keep my mouth shut. Please forgive me. Sit down and go on."

Mattie sat back down, heavily, and said, "I'm sorry, too. I'm upset. I'm upset because I'm tired of people close to me getting hurt or dying. I *hate* it when people die."

"Please, continue," I said. "Let me help if I can."

"I don't know what you could do to help," she said, looking over to the window. "I don't know what any of us can do."

We sat in silence until she finally decided to continue. "They just wanted to help keep people safe. For all their good efforts, they were paid with bullets. They were found face down in a shallow creek running off the river."

Here Mattie broke down, put her hands on her face, and sobbed. I went over and put my arms around her.

Neither one of us spoke the rest of the night.

....

CHAPTER 8

OUR SILENCE CONTINUED INTO THE next morning. As we dressed for work, we spoke only the occasional pleasantries required of three women sharing one bathroom.

It was during our toasted bread and banana breakfast sandwiches that Mattie finally spoke.

"My mamma always says mourning is just a way of remembering those we respected and loved. It hurts for a while, but eventually the memories will soothe. I'm going to remember the joy we had with Claude and Odie. At the same time, I'm going to remember something they believed in so that their dreams don't die."

She looked closely at me before continuing. "They meant well. They lived well. We won't forget them."

"Amen," Viola said, her eyes welling up again.

Then, as if a switch had been turned on, Mattie's voice grew stronger, bolder. "We've got work to do. We need payday or we'll be eating beans and hay before too long. And what about you, Viola? What are your plans?"

"I'm headed down to see Muscatine Shorty. There'll be work today. I just know it."

"There better be," Mattie said. "Your part of the rent is coming due, and we need you."

Turning to me, she said, "We better start now. Looks like a rain might be coming, and I don't want to be in wet clothes all day long."

We didn't speak much at first during our walk. Mattie was unusually quiet, and try as I might, I couldn't draw her into conversation.

I thought a couple of times about bringing up Gaston, but I still didn't know if I should. In the off chance I could pick up a little information about him, I decided to do a little fishing of my own. I told her that during my walk the night before I had heard some men talking about the dock burning and asked if that was serious. I didn't know if or exactly how Gaston might have been involved, but it couldn't hurt to gain whatever information I could.

I was shocked when Mattie started laughing so hard she had to stop walking.

"You're not pulling my leg, are you?" she finally asked.

"No. No. I'm not. What's so funny?"

"I'll tell you what's funny," she said, falling into even louder laughter. "Two of the loading docks down along the river got silted in so bad this summer they had to be closed. The dock you're talking about was the last one anywhere close that could be used to unload the shells we turn into buttons. Well, it was the last one except the dock over at the clamming camp. *That's* what's so funny. Can you see it now? The owners of the factories are now at the mercy of the clammers to get their materials delivered. Oh, this is going to be fun. Are you sure you heard them right? The dock really burned?"

"They said it was reduced to ashes."

"Then let the fun begin," Mattie practically howled. "Like the lamb lying with the wolf. Oh yes—this is going to be good."

The pieces of the puzzle seemed to be falling into place. If Gaston was part of the camp and if he had helped with the fire, it looked like monetary gain or some type of control might have been his motivation. But, then again, nothing I had seen to this point in Muscatine was exactly what it seemed to be. The town was like one big mirage.

Mattie interrupted my thoughts when she said, "And it serves the owners right. This is justice, plain and simple. Now maybe they'll be forced into listening to what the rest of us have to say. They have to. No shells, no buttons. Why didn't anyone think of this before. Burning that dock was a genius idea. Genius!"

Instead of laughing, this time she just smiled and shook her head over and over. My own thoughts turned back to Gaston. I wanted to know more about him, but if this situation was half as serious as Mattie described, I didn't want to say anything to connect him with this. After all, he had saved me from a fate I could only imagine at the clamming camp, and I owed him for that.

I kept my thoughts to myself as we quickened our pace. The wind was starting to pick up, and dark clouds were swirling toward us from the southwest. Because the wind had shifted, the air suddenly became heavy with the stench that had greeted me when I first arrived to town. Taking the first advice I had been given when I stepped off the train, I lowered my head and tried breathing through my hand. I may have looked like a hunchback, but at least I could breathe without gagging. Mattie looked over at me and said, "You're learning."

When we were finally just a couple of blocks from the factory, Mattie reminded me again of the rules of survival. This time she gave special emphasis to the importance of minding my own business and keeping my mouth shut. After what happened to the Knox brothers, this didn't surprise me one bit.

"I'll try," I said, "and I won't embarrass you at work."

Then, needling her to break the tension, I added, "Well, at least not on purpose."

It worked. Mattie gave me a squinty look and reached over and swatted me on the behind for good measure.

A light rain started falling just as the factory came into view. We quickened our pace and cut through a vacant lot across from the main entrance to save us from a good soaking. As we headed up the sidewalk to the front steps, I couldn't resist. Grabbing her arm to slow her down and get her attention, I pointed ahead of us and said, "Ye all who enter here, give up all hope."

Mattie flashed a devilish grin and responded, "You have no idea how true that is."

The way she said it stopped me in my tracks.

....

Miss Fitch appeared to be waiting for me when I entered the office.

"Good morning, Miss McGill," she said. "Nice to see you again. Go right on in. You're expected."

I tapped lightly on Mr. Blanton's door, and he responded, "Come!"

When I stepped inside and closed the door behind me, he greeted me warmly and asked, almost in a whisper, "And how is your resolve this morning?"

Resolve? I was still trying to believe what both my uncle and Mr. Blanton had said to me about what they saw as the problems in the industry. At the same time, Mattie, and even Gaston in an odd sort of way, had given me a lot to think about on the other side of that plate. Resolve? The only resolve I had at this point was a selfish, self-centered one. I wanted to earn money for school. I wanted my teaching career and all it would bring.

"My resolve is fine," I replied. "Just fine. I'm more than a little nervous about all of this, but I'll do my best not to let you down."

"Good!" he replied, slapping his hand on his desk. "Then let's get right to it."

He motioned for me to take a seat. "The first thing I want to do is give you an overview of what we do here—and what *you'll* be doing here. I want you to see every workstation we have, so we'll go on a tour of the building."

Mr. Blanton paused, his tone becoming much more serious, "There's also another, and more important, reason for the tour. As I mentioned yesterday, I want everyone to see you—and especially to see you with me. This will help cement why you are here. Word will spread like wildfire. Shoot—I bet everyone will be talking about us before we make it back here to the office."

He looked down. "I promised Sam Henry I'd look out for you. That I'd protect you. I aim to do that. Along those lines, I'm going to have you work *backward*."

"Backward?" I asked, confused.

"Well, at least in a manner of speaking. The very last work-station inside the building is the packing and shipping area. Actually, there is one more—the loading area. It's out back and I'll show it to you but won't have you do a stint there. It's important work, but it's still mostly grunt work and I'll spare you that. Packing and shipping is the best job in the business, and I reserve it for the most dedicated workers, those who have earned it. It's also the cleanest and safest section in the whole factory. You'll see why this is so once you visit with those who are there. I'm going to have you start with them and then work backward through all the different stations that come before it. This way you'll get the best overview of every step we go through. You'll see and be able to study the finished product before you learn how it was made. That should speed up your learning process quite a bit. I'll explain to everyone that this will help you better prepare for your work with your uncle and the factory he's going to build. They'll understand that. And, at the same time, it should be safer for you to learn what we do in this reverse order. Your uncle would never forgive me, and I'd never forgive myself, if you were injured here."

"I do appreciate all you are doing for me," I said, smiling up at him, noting his genuine concern. "I'll do my best for you."

"I know you will," he said, smiling back. "I have no doubts."

He took my hand and helped me to my feet. "Follow me," he said. "Let's begin our journey. You're going to *work backward*, but our tour will take us in the regular order. You'll see every step in what happens from the time shells get to us to when buttons get shipped out. If you don't see the natural order, then working in reverse wouldn't be as useful. So, let's begin."

As I followed him out of his office, the word flashed in my thoughts again: *resolve*.

Suddenly, my knees felt very weak.

....

I accompanied Mr. Blanton down the corridor on the main floor all the way to the back of the factory. The different workstations we passed were already buzzing with activity even though the official start of the workday was still a good ten minutes off. As we walked by each, nearly everyone paused at least momentarily to greet Mr. Blanton—and then stare pointedly at me. I started feeling as conspicuous as a pig in church. But that was exactly the point. Mr. Blanton wanted me to be noticed, and, from the looks I was getting, his plan was off to a fine start.

At the rear of the factory, huge doors were swung open to allow easy access to a loading dock attached to the building. Just inside these doors were steps going down on the left. To the right of the doors was an elevator attached to what looked like a pulley system to raise it up and down. One of the workers out on the dock called Mr. Blanton over to show him something on a clipboard, and I took the opportunity to step outside into the light rain to peer down a massive metal chute that was on a steep angle down to the floor below.

When Mr. Blanton finished his business, he returned. "Miss McGill, take a close look. This is where it all begins for us. Here at the dock we do three things, and these men here are my right arm when it comes to these."

Several of the men looked briefly at me and nodded respectfully before returning to their work. Most were cleaning the dock area and lining up shovels and rakes of various sizes and lengths.

Mr. Blanton looked on approvingly before saying, "We receive two types of loads here. First, this is where we unload the wagons full of shells that come five or six times a day."

He looked at his watch. "The first wagons should be here any minute now. When they get here, these raw shells get scooped into the chute over there for a ride to the first station down below. Secondly, two or three times a day we also take delivery of barrels of cut button blanks."

He smiled and added, "Of course, the very best of these come from a man by the name of Sam Henry McGill."

I felt a sudden blush and smiled as he continued, "These cut blanks are loaded right onto the elevator just inside and taken up to the sorting station. We'll see that later on our journey. We don't get as much profit from buttons made from the blanks we have brought in, but it takes so long for us to make our own that these outside blanks supplement what we can produce and help keep the factory moving smoothly. We don't use them all immediately; some are kept in the barrels and in reserve so we can use them in the winter. The clam harvesting season runs from about April to November, so if we didn't have the stored buttons, we'd be twirling our thumbs for about five months out of each year. So, by providing his blanks, your uncle does me a great service."

"I had no idea," I said, more proud of my uncle than ever. "This explains something I've always wondered about. My uncle keeps several warehouses full of shells close to his cutting building. He was storing for winter, wasn't he?"

"Now you're starting to get it," he said. "It's right out of *Aesop's Fables*. Remember the story of "The Ant and the Grasshopper"? Your uncle and I are both ants, always planning for the winter months."

Another worker handed him a clipboard, and as he studied it, he explained, "Miss McGill, the last step of the whole process takes place right here where we're standing. This is the Alpha and the Omega of the business. After the finished buttons have been readied for shipment, we bring them here to be loaded into wagons that will take them to the rail yard or a dock down at the river if they're going out by boat. Actually, you might find this interesting. I own just about all the wagons that come here. There are a few private individuals who have their own, but they're in the minority. By owning the wagons, I save time and money. We unload the shells, and then we refill the wagons with the boxes and crates of finished buttons. The wagons continue in this loop all the working day long."

He paused, and asked, "Any questions about this area? If you have questions, just pipe right up."

Motioning me to follow him down the steps just back inside the door, he stopped and pulled a small vial from his vest pocket, just as the porter had done at the station. He used his handkerchief to dab liquid from the vial to the area under and around his nose then he handed it to me and motioned for me to do the same. It took only a few seconds for me to understand why we had taken the time for this. While we headed down the steps, the stench became overpowering.

As soon as we stepped onto the lower level, I noticed several large fans built right into the walls. Their purpose was obvious—to draw as much of the smell as possible outside the building. They weren't doing a very good job of it, a fact brought home to me when my nostrils started burning and my eyes watered so badly I could barely see to move ahead. In marked contrast, Mr. Blanton seemed unfazed as he urged me along.

Immediately to our right, eight evenly-spaced women, all wearing tight-fitting coveralls, used small shovels to feed shells onto a conveyor. None of these women wore any kind of a mask as they worked. As I watched them, one thought kept surfacing: The air down here is so horrifying that their noses have to be dead as doornails.

The machines were loud, so Mr. Blanton had to shout in order for me to hear him. "This is the first stop for the shells—sorting and classifying. This may appear pretty simple, but it is one of the most important steps in the process. These ladies put the shells on rollers that run slightly out of parallel and get wider as they go along. This allows shells of different sizes to fall down into buckets along the way, depending on how big they are. The smaller shells fall first, and the big boys don't drop until just near the end. Sorting by size helps us quickly determine things like the size of buttons that can be made from the shells when they get upstairs. If you bend down, you'll be able to see the buckets underneath that catch them as they fall. When the buckets are full, those youngsters over there crawl underneath and drag them to the next station."

He pointed to a small group of ragamuffins, each somewhere around ten to twelve-years-old. Their clothes were torn and tattered, and most had cheeks that looked like they hadn't seen soap in weeks. They were also barefoot, which seemed a big risk around the sharp edges of the shells piled everywhere. I asked why they were dragging buckets and not at home helping with chores or in school, and Mr. Blanton just shrugged his shoulders. I didn't press the point, but I made a mental note to ask Mattie about it when I got home.

Mr. Blanton motioned for me to turn and follow him. On the other side of this lower level were huge tanks, some metal and some wood, full of brackish-looking water. I guessed each to be roughly fifteen feet in diameter and about three feet high. What struck me immediately was, from left to right, each had on its side, in bright yellow paint, the names of the days of the week. Right after we turned around, one of the bucket draggers struggled mightily to lift up his bucket and lower it gently into Tuesday. Mr. Blanton must have noticed my curiosity because he explained.

"These are Soaking Tanks. The sorted shells, still in their buckets, get placed in the water. If you look close, you'll see size markings on the rim of the tanks. If you are wondering about the days of the week, that's for practical reasons. We soak our shells a week before doing anything else to them. This makes them less brittle, much tougher, and stronger. This keeps them from breaking up when the blanks are cut out. The days of the week tell us when to take the soaked ones out and put the new ones in. Some of the sorters and about half of these kids come in near to four in the morning every day and pull out the correct buckets and haul them to the elevator, where they are taken up to the blank cutting stations. After the buckets are emptied, they are brought back down, and the process starts all over again. The Tuesday shells were already taken up this morning, so let's follow their path, shall we?"

I was hoping we'd take the elevator, but he motioned me

to follow him back up the steps. After reaching the main floor again, we climbed up two more flights. I was getting winded and understood right away why the elevator was used to bring the shells up. At the very top of the third floor and just off where the elevator stood, a row of button blank-cutting machines were in use. All of these workers were men. They all had on tight-fitting blue coveralls, but they wore no shirts underneath them. Whereas the lower level had the smell, the upper level had the heat, which was oppressive, even at this young hour of the day. Thus, Mr. Blanton explained, no shirts for the men.

I had been around button blank cutting-machines all my life because of visits to my uncle's business, but I had never seen anything of this magnitude. My uncle had two men who cut blanks; Mr. Blanton had sixteen, all working as fast as their fingers could move. Mechanisms down by their feet controlled all the cutting machines. Their feet turned their machines off and on, and their hands guided the shells under what was called a "drill chuck," a cylindrical tube with serrated teeth on the end that spun rapidly and cut through the shell, producing the blanks. The shells, in turn, started appearing like a piece of Swiss cheese as the blanks were cut out. Depending upon the size and contour of the shell—and the size of the drill chuck being used—as many as two dozen blanks could be cut from one shell. For safety reasons, some men held the shells with tongs. According to Mr. Blanton, the more skilled and daring of the lot would use just their fingers to hold the shells while they were drilled. This latter group could often be distinguished from the former because parts of fingers were missing, casualties of both mental and physical slips. For many, a lost digit was a badge of honor, a sign they were tough and possessed skills honed by sacrifice and practice. My uncle, not much impressed by missing body parts, always said shaking hands with one of these men was "like shaking hands with a rake." I always thought that was funny, but as I looked closely at the cutter closest to me and saw he was missing the entire length of the little finger on his left hand, no smile came to my lips.

Mr. Blanton interrupted my thoughts. "If you look over next to the wall to your right, you'll notice three machines that look different from all the rest. Those are my pride and joy, yet still something of an experiment. Take a close look. Those are run by electricity! We got those last spring when the electric wires were run over the hill and down here to the factory. The others are run by steam-driven pulleys and belts. But these three are really something. They cut just a little bit faster, which is nice, but their greatest attribute is they don't bog down as much, which means the cuts are cleaner. You're probably wondering why I don't have more of them. The answer to that one is simple. When the electricity goes out, which it does at some point nearly every day, those machines are dead and useless. That costs me money and plays havoc with the next steps in the process because the blanks aren't cut on time. And, to be perfectly honest with you, I'm still not completely convinced about this whole electricity thing. It may be just a passing fancy, and we'll all go back to using steam power for everything again. Time will tell, but I might as well give them a try and see what I can learn."

"Any questions here?" he finally asked. I had none and was mesmerized, completely in awe of the scale of the production process unfolding in front of me. In the time we had been standing next to this workstation, the men had produced dozens upon dozens of blanks of all sizes and varieties. By comparison, my uncle's shop was positively primitive.

"Let's step down this way now. Follow me," he said. "The next station is where all those blanks get sorted."

Large, white linen sheets hanging over what looked like a clothesline formed a light boundary between the blank cutters and the sorters. The sheets blew gently back and forth as ceiling fans twirled overhead. Every once in a while one of the third floor ragamuffins stood up and used a watering can to soak the top half of the sheets. Mr. Blanton anticipated my question and said, "It's cool water. The fan hits the wet sheets, and that helps keep this upper floor a little cooler. Plus, it keeps down the dust from the cutting machines. It's bad to breathe that dust."

When they weren't watering the sheets, the youngsters hauled buckets of blanks to the next station. These, like their counterparts at the lower level, should have been at home or in school. Their dirty faces and tattered clothes were their education for now, and my heart started aching for them. I reached over to pat one of the younger ones on the head, and he darted away from me as if he expected me to hit him. His wild eyes peered at me from behind a post, and I imagined he had likely experienced a swat once or twice in the past.

When we walked around the sheets and entered the Blank Sorting area, I saw Mattie. There were six women seated at long, rectangular tables. The movement of their fingers was positively cat-like as they moved blanks from a pile in front of them to various spots on the table. Mattie was so engaged in her work she didn't notice us enter the area.

Mr. Blanton spoke right up. They all looked at him for a second while their fingers kept moving. "Good morning, ladies. Nice to see all of you. I want to thank you for your hard work. Please keep it up. Without what you do, nothing else down the line can happen."

They looked at him—and then at me—for a second while their fingers kept to their work. Mattie did a double take when she saw me, but she didn't slow down her sorting. If anything, she picked up her pace. Mr. Blanton noticed this and said, "Nice work, Number Five. Keep it up!"

Mattie was in the second chair from the right, the chair with a large "5" painted on the back. I could see she smiled when she heard the compliment, but she didn't look up. I started to tell Mr. Blanton her name was Mattie, but I remembered her admonition that I not embarrass her.

Mr. Blanton turned his attention back to my lessons. "This is where the blanks are sorted by size—both diameter and thickness—and color. It's not an easy job because there are so many types of shells involved, and each type has its own individual characteristics that come to the fore in the blanks. Sam Henry has probably already told you this, but there are Heelsplitters, Pimplebacks, Pigtoes, Hickory Nut, Washboard, Elephant Ear, Money Face, Sheep's Nose, and just plain Muckets. Those are the most common around here, but there are even more than that. Overall there are about a hundred different varieties, and it is at this stage in the process that the differences really start to become important. That's why this sorting station exists. The blanks have to be sorted just right so those at the next stations can do their jobs properly. All this sorting has to be done quickly, as they are doing. These girls are good. Really good. I have no complaints about this station at all."

At this last compliment, I noticed smiles all around. Mr. Blanton then tugged on my arm and said, "Follow me to the other side of the room, over here."

As we walked, he leaned close to me and whispered, "Some companies have already replaced half their sorters with a conveyor system something like what you saw for the shells down below. I'll keep the human touch as long as I can, but costs keep going up, so I'll probably have to go that route eventually."

It was suddenly clear to me why Mattie was so worried about her position at the factory. Number Five would soon be expendable, a fact she very likely knew.

I couldn't believe what I saw next. Several young girls and boys were cranking handles that spun large metal drums around and around.

"Next, the sorted blanks are put into these drums, which are filled about a third of the way with water," Mr. Blanton began. "The drums are rotated like this, and the rough edges on the blanks get worn away as they bump into each other. It's crude, but it works. The blanks that are now being smoothed out won't go to the next station until tomorrow. The ones that were spun yesterday are already at the next station."

We walked to the far end of the floor. Again, wet sheets formed a barrier between the Blank Sorting area and the last workstation on this floor. Mr. Blanton motioned me to follow him around the sheets. On the other side, we entered what he called the Grinding Station. Once the blanks had tumbled and had become smooth around the edges, they were brought to the Grinding Station to have what was called the "bark" removed. When the blanks were first cut out, the outside layer of the shell stayed on the blank. This outer covering, this bark, had to be removed, and the best and most efficient way to do this was by grinding it off on special machines designed specifically for this purpose. After a good grinding, the blanks were placed in soaking tubs up along the front wall to soften them up in preparation for their next stop in the process.

As I followed Mr. Blanton out of the Grinding Station, he said, "We'll take the steps down a floor, where you'll see some really skilled work taking place. The blanks are now ready for finishing. In making a button, about four times as much work is done in preparation as in the finishing stations. This has to be done or the buttons won't stand up to regular use on shirts, dresses, shoes, or anything else. This factory takes a little longer than most others from start to finish, but I'm proud of the final product and those who work here are, too."

"My uncle always says you have the best buttons in the whole country, and I'm beginning to see why he feels that way," I said loudly, so as to be heard over the blank-cutting machines we were passing.

Mr. Blanton laughed and said, "You'll get used to the noise. Before long, you'll be able to speak in a normal voice and hear and be heard. It just takes time."

He led me quickly down the steps to the floor below, where a solid door sealed off this area of the factory. I hadn't noticed on the way up, but a guard with a revolver on his hip sat in a chair off to the side. Mr. Blanton explained that what I was about to see was a trade secret. All employees in this area had to take an oath and sign papers agreeing they wouldn't reveal this part of the process to anyone working in any other factory. Mattie had told me something of this, but I didn't understand the seriousness until my eyes found that revolver.

Mr. Blanton tugged at my elbow and stopped me before we entered the room. Looking very serious, he said, "I'm not going to make you sign and swear to secrecy, but whatever you see here must stay in here. Understand?"

"I do, Mr. Blanton," I replied. "You don't have to worry."

The guard opened the door for us, and we stepped in. A high-pitched hissing noise met us as we entered. On both sides of the center aisle, running three quarters or so the length of the floor, men operated devices that looked quite similar to the button blank-cutting machines I'd seen upstairs. The hissing noise was coming from these.

"On our left, those are the men working the Rounding and Scoring station. Their machines serve two functions. First, they smooth out on each blank any imperfections that might still be present. Second, they use their machines to make the depression in the face of what for the first time starts to look like a real button. The making of that depression is called 'scoring.' As soon as they accomplish that, the blanks are carried in small boxes across to our right, where you'll notice our Drilling station. Ever wonder who puts the holes in the buttons? Well, these men do. Go ahead. Take a closer look."

As I walked near one of the machines, I realized the hissing noise I had noticed earlier was coming from the fine drill bits making the holes. The pitch was so high my ears started to hurt, and I quickly backed away. The men operating this section wore no protection over their ears, and I didn't know how they could stand it.

Mr. Blanton motioned me aside and said, "Each company does this process slightly differently. Once you've been in this business a couple of years, you could have a pile of buttons in front of you representing all the companies in this area, and you'd be able to look at them and tell which company produced them. They're not exactly like snowflakes, but each does have unique

characteristics that separate them from the others. That makes a
world of difference to those who purchase them in stores. This is
why we guard the process as we do."

We left this area and continued walking down the aisle
toward the front of the building. Another closed door appeared
before us, but no guard was stationed there. This time the door
was there merely for a practical purpose: to separate the Polishing
station on the other side from the rest of the factory. Fans nearly
six feet in diameter were built into the walls on both sides of the
room. Through the whirling blades, I could see Muscatine to the
left and the Mississippi River to the right. The fans sucked out as
much of the fumes as they could from the acid bath now given
to the buttons. Mr. Blanton explained that this acid bath brought
out their natural color and uncovered their beautiful, natural sheen. The fumes, however, were not easy on the eyes, and
despite the best effort of the fans, my eyes immediately teared up.
Mr. Blanton's did, too.

Dabbing at his eyes with his handkerchief, he said, "Those
churns against the front wall are full of sawdust. After the bath,
the buttons are placed in there and jostled around so that the
acid is removed. This sawdust bath is actually the last step in the
manufacturing process. From here, all we have left is Sorting and
Grouping, Carding and Boxing, and Shipping. Those stations are
back down on the main floor. Let's head there, and our tour will
be complete."

We climbed back down the steps to the main floor and the
last of the stations. We had passed them before on our way to
the loading area, but I hadn't noticed them at the time because
all were behind doors on the right side of the main hallway.
Again, the doors served a practical purpose; once the buttons
were finished, it was important to move them to areas free from
dust and dirt so they could be made ready for shipment. All the
doors on that side of the hall led to a large open area that housed
three separate workstations. The first, and the one closest to Mr.
Blanton's office, was the Sorting and Grouping station. Here, four

women sorted the finished and polished buttons by color, luster, and grade. Once sorted, the buttons were moved to the station on the left, Carding and Boxing. Next, the buttons were sewn onto decorative cards that contained the button size, description, and company name. Six women performed this task. As soon as the buttons were sewn to the cards, they were placed in boxes for the last stop in the process: Shipping. Those at the Shipping station prepared and placed shipping labels on the boxes. When a group of boxes was ready, an elderly woman at the end of the table rang a small bell, which summoned still more ragamuffins, who moved the boxes out of the room and either to the dock out back or to a storage area on the other side of the building.

"See, nothing to it," Mr. Blanton grinned smartly and said as we left the Shipping station. "Miss McGill, the next time you button anything, you'll think of all the hands that touch a button as it makes its journey to your clothing."

His voice was filled with the pride of a new father, and the buttons, to him, were like his children. I had often heard the old expression "So proud buttons would pop," but it wasn't until this moment I understood it. If Mr. Blanton had been any more proud of his company, every button on his clothing would have flown skyward. His joy was so genuine and heartfelt that I wondered if I'd ever feel anything even akin to that. I sure hoped so.

"Well, I've got to go to work—and so do you. You're going to start right here. I'll have Marg McHugh, the older woman over there at the end of the table, show you how to make the shipping labels. That will be your first job."

Leaning close, he said, softly and genuinely, "Make us proud, Pearl. Me, Sam Henry, and especially yourself. I want you to feel proud of your time here."

Then he called over Mrs. McHugh, introduced us, and asked her to show me the ropes. As soon as he was sure she understood his orders, he turned, waved, and left the room, looking at his watch again.

"Sit right here, Miss McGill," Mrs. McHugh said, pulling up

a chair for me. "You're going to learn to do labels the right way."

Her voice was warm, friendly. I knew instantly I was going to like Mrs. McHugh. The big question rolling over and over in my mind was how many would like me if they really knew why I was here.

....

CHAPTER 9

THE NEXT TWO WEEKS FLEW by. On the home front, we settled into a routine, although I can't say it was a positive one. Every night Mattie continued to bring something she had "found" on her way home. I still wasn't happy about her actions, but I had thus far experienced just two paydays and, after paying my share of the rent and purchasing work clothes and shoes, I didn't have much money left to throw into the food coffers. Viola was working nearly every day, but short work didn't pay as much as a regular job, so she, too, was hard pressed when it came to adding variety to our meals. Most nights we ended up eating what Mattie called a "Slumgully Stew," which was a fitting name for "Just throw everything in a pot and see what comes of it." I couldn't say our suppers were tasty, but they were definitely filling, which was most important at this point.

Little free time came with the long hours we worked. Most nights after supper I'd take a walk to the Musser Public Library to get some time alone to think and relax. I occasionally checked out a book, but I was usually so tired when I got back home, I fell asleep before I could get very far through its pages.

Viola also liked to read, but the newspaper, the *Muscatine Journal*, was as far as she would venture. She favored stories about disasters. When she found what she considered a "good one," something like an earthquake or the sinking of a ship, she'd call us to attention and read the whole article aloud, punctuating accounts of injuries and deaths by shifting the tone of her voice to loud and solemn. She was so overly dramatic that Mattie and I had to cover our mouths to keep from laughing, which would have upset Viola something terrible. After reading us one of her "disasters," she'd look to us for approval, and we'd both just nod as she would then quickly flip the pages looking for still more death and destruction.

Viola also had an annoying habit of shouting out her home-made expressions of excitement and awe as she read the accounts. Most of these had to be homemade expressions because I had never heard any of them before, and my family had a pretty colorful range of vocabulary. The only one I faintly recognized was the declaration, "Well, I swan!" when she read something that shocked or surprised her. The other expressions, however, were completely foreign to me. Each evening I started playing a game in which I tried to figure out just what emotion Viola was expressing when one of these gems flowed from her mouth. She had quite a repertoire: "Roll up the paper and spank the mule"; "Never kiss a gift horse on the nose"; Two crows are worth three hens"; "Never jump and spit at the same time"; "Well, whistle Dixie and shoot the monkey"; and, "A watched clock never boils." Some of them seemed to make a sort of sense by the tone and inflection she used when uttering them. However, the last one, "A watched clock never boils," was one she used at varying times to indicate several emotions, and I could never quite figure out what she meant by it. I asked her about it one night, and she lowered her newspaper and gave me a look that said, "Boy, are you dumb!"

Mattie, by contrast, would usually flip casually through the paper to look for news related to the button industry or sales at local stores. It never took her more than two or three minutes to glance through the paper from start to finish. As it was when she was a child, she just could not sit still. I knew this was just part of her personality, but she was up and down like a child's yo-yo so many times a night she made me positively jumpy. In an attempt to occupy her time and at least to keep her hands busy, she brought home buttons from the factory to sew onto store cards, the small, colorful, often illustrated cardboard cards sold in stores all over the country. The current rate of pay for this work, known as "carding," was one penny per four completed cards, so it certainly wasn't the money that motivated her. She just couldn't stand to have idle hands, which started grating on me while I tried to concentrate on reading or my writing.

Every night right before going to bed I'd write a quick note on a penny postcard to send to my mother or pull out the ledger given to me by Mr. Blanton to make a few notes or entries. So Mattie and Viola wouldn't get suspicious, I told them I was jotting down information about the factory and the button-making process to share with my uncle in order to help with the creation of his new business. To make sure they were thrown off the trail, I'd often stop my writing and ask both of them simple questions about the manufacturing process. As they responded, I'd make it appear I was summarizing their explanations in the margin of the ledger, which always made them very happy. I hated deceiving them in this way, but if they had known my real purpose in keeping the ledger, the cat would have been out of the bag—and I would be out on the street.

My workdays started feeling terribly long, but I couldn't complain much because our tasks in the shipping department were relatively easy and not too physically demanding. The only real challenge for me was keeping the pace fast enough so the mailing labels could be prepared and attached as quickly as the boxes and cartons of buttons were made ready to be moved out to the loading area. The worst mistake of all in this station, one I almost made my second day there, was to place the wrong label on a box that was ready to be shipped. I was told if that happened and it was found out, everyone in the workstation would lose an hour of pay for the day, which would be disastrous given how little everyone was already taking home in the pay envelope. While it hadn't happened at Blanton since the last supervisor left, it was fairly common at other factories for supervisors to mix up labels during their checks of the stations so mistakes would be made and pay would be docked. This would, of course, save the company money, and some of the owners supposedly paid the unscrupulous supervisors a bonus each time this happened. It was shocking to me that any supervisor would stoop so low as to do this, but, then again, I was learning quickly not to be too shocked by anything that happened in the factory.

The three women with whom I worked closest in the shipping department were an interesting lot. The most experienced and the oldest was Mrs. McHugh, who was seventy if she was a day. Her fingers were gnarled and crooked, but she had learned to compensate for her lack of dexterity by growing her fingernails quite long, which made it easy for her to scoop up the address labels and attach them to the boxes. She never said much while we worked, but during breaks she'd chatter like a magpie about her grandchildren, all of whom she clearly adored. She took me under her wing and kindly and patiently taught me the proper way to attach the shipping labels to the different types of boxes. As easy as that task first sounded, I quickly learned several variables were involved in determining where the labels should go on the large variety of boxes constantly placed in front of us all day long. We had to be quick in our work, and we had to work as a team. Each day I tried to improve and did the very best I could, but I still knew Mrs. McHugh was frustrated with my lack of speed. To her credit, and much to my relief, she chose to provide me with steady encouragement rather than criticism.

The other two women in our station were responsible for adding the names and addresses to the labels before we could affix them to the boxes. Ocie Lee Morgan did this by hand. The labels she created were uncommonly beautiful because of her rich, flowing handwriting. She was a tall and attractive woman with dark, deeply-set brown eyes. Her husband had been killed a few years before in some type of logging accident. Ocie Lee had two young children, both girls, she was doing her best to support by way of the money she earned at the factory. She was very good at her work, but it was clear to all that while her body was with us, her mind was always with her children. In the very few times there would be a lull in our station, I'd catch her looking at a picture of her girls she kept in the top pocket of her coveralls.

The other label maker, Rebecca Littleton, I originally guessed to be about sixty. She was a small woman with a very pronounced Dowager's Hump on her back, the result of years of bending over to do a multitude of jobs in the factory. It was now impossible for her to stand up completely straight without being overcome by excruciating back pain. She used a typewriter to create her labels, and she was very fast. The rhythmic click-clack of her typewriter keys was a pleasant and welcome change from the constant high-pitched whirring noise we could hear coming from the machines in use on the floors above and below us. Rebecca lived alone in a rooming house on the western edge of town, and as far as anyone could tell, she seldom left her room there for any reason other than to come to work. In the middle of my first week I learned my estimate of her age was wrong. She wasn't close to sixty. She was forty-one years old. I was shocked. When I later told Mattie about this, she just shrugged her shoulders and said, "Every year working in the factory takes three years of toll on your body."

Mr. Blanton had told me he reserved jobs in the shipping department for the most loyal and deserving workers, but there was an underlying air of sadness about these women that I couldn't get over. It seemed to me their lives had become, in so many ways, their work in the factory, yet it was blatantly obvious they didn't find much pleasure in their work. Their work was simply a means to an end—a pay envelope every Saturday that allowed them a few precious moments away from the factory before they had to return once again. They were like moths to a flame, and all of them were being burned up. Their physical appearances and their solemn voices spoke volumes to this. "This," I said to myself over and over each day, "will never happen to me. I won't let it." Maybe they had said something very similar when they were younger, but I was resolute in my vow. This would not be my fate.

....

During our infrequent breaks in the workday, I'd sit quietly in locations where I could overhear the conversations around me. I'd usually sit with my eyes closed to make it appear I was napping. My ruse must have worked because people didn't lower their voices much after spotting me. During these breaks I heard of people who were stealing from the company, especially those who snuck both blanks and finished buttons out at night. Some workers would purposely damage a piece of equipment to get that part of the production shut down long enough for a nice break—but not long enough that their pay would be docked. Still other conversations revealed bits and pieces of information about the emerging Button Workers' Protective Union, which in conversation was usually shortened to just the "BWPU." I paid particular attention to those and took as many names as I could because I knew Mr. Blanton would be interested.

I was becoming a fair spy, but as each day went by my heart was less and less into it. The people who were stealing and damaging equipment were wrong to be doing that. Dead wrong. However, at the same time, the workers I was getting to know well were not the lazy, shiftless, good-for-nothings described by my uncle and Mr. Blanton. Quite to the contrary, they seemed to be good, God-fearing people just trying to eke out a living in what I could already tell were less than healthy working conditions. On top of that, they were being cheated, plain and simple. They were being cheated so that they'd earn just enough money to survive but not enough to be able to leave the factory for greener pastures. While I could never condone stealing and vandalism, I soon understood why many instances of these took place.

I didn't know how much of this Mr. Blanton knew about. In the short time I was there, I learned from Ocie Lee Morgan a few of what she called the "typical cheats." One of these involved the supervisors requiring the workers who were normally paid "by the piece" to produce what was called a "long gross" instead of a regular gross count. A "long gross" was a regular gross, 144, plus a dozen more of whatever was being produced in that particular station, to equal a grand total of 156. However, the workers were paid for just the initial 144. The supervisors said their "research" had demonstrated that about a dozen pieces out of every gross were defective or not up to the high quality required by the company. In reality, though, there were inspection stations all along the production process so that there was seldom anything wrong with the original gross produced. This long gross was just a way for the company to get free work from the employees.

Another popular method of taking advantage of the employees was to change the method by which they were paid. That is, on certain days, seeming to be at random, production for that day would be measured by weight, size, color—or some other characteristic chosen by the supervisor—instead of "by the piece," which was supposed to be the standard for measuring productivity. On the previous Thursday, for instance, it was suddenly announced that a formula for determining weight and volume of finished work would be used to determine how much workers would be paid for their efforts that day. This involved the blank cutting, polishing, and scoring stations. Since no time was taken to explain the specifics of this new method to the employees, they had to take the word of their individual supervisors at the end of the day when their production, and therefore their wages, was determined.

Those I worked with also told me about a dozen other ways their productivity around the factory had been suddenly and without explanation examined and valued. To me, the most disturbing of all involved "doctoring" the weighing scales used on days when productivity would be measured by weight. The workers were convinced that the springs in the scales had been lengthened by the supervisors so that everything would register a fraction of the actual weight. I asked how everyone could be so sure this was really happening and if they had any proof. As soon as I asked the question, Rebecca Littleton pointed to Olga Olsen, a robust woman stacking large boxes of buttons and a pull-cart, and asked me how much I thought she weighed. Judging from her size, I said I thought she might be in the range of two hundred pounds. Rebecca laughed before telling me that one day after work several of them had hung around to try out one of the scales up in the blank cutting station, and on that particular scale Olga weighed in at a svelte one hundred seventy five. It was then clear to all of them they were not just being taken advantage of: They were being swindled, and there was nothing they could do about it. These workplace injustices were brought up frequently when the need for the creation of a strong union was debated.

With each passing day, I began to realize these cheats were just the tip of the iceberg. There was another reason I was enjoying my role as a spy less and less. I couldn't side completely with the workers, but I also couldn't justify the behavior of those in charge of the factories. Plenty of fault could be pointed in both directions—toward both workers and owners—and it appeared to me some good, old-fashioned discussions between the two groups might put an end to the shenanigans being played out on both ends. However, from what I could gather from conversations I'd overheard among the workers, and from what Mr. Blanton had shared with me, the owners did not want to meet with their employees to address any issues. Hence, each passing day I overheard more and more debates in hushed tones about whether the emerging BWPU might be able to help get everyone together at least to talk. However, not all the workers felt a union was in their best interest. Many believed creating a union would somehow cost them their jobs or reduce the number of hours they could work each week. While listening to all this, I realized if I wasn't careful I'd end up right in the middle of everything—if I weren't already!

The workers had also heard rumors of "Pinks" being in town. I didn't know what that meant, so one evening after work I asked Mattie about it. After she gave her usual lecture about me needing to shake my country roots out of my hair, she told me Pinks was an abbreviation for the Pinkerton Detective Agency and its deputies. According to Mattie, the Pinks had been hired by the factory owners in Muscatine, as they had been in manufacturing communities all over the country, to help quell the establishment of unions. Mattie said she had it on good authority they were brutal thugs who stopped at nothing to get their message across. If people got involved in the creation of a union, they better be willing to withstand everything from threats to the safety of their families to beatings, and in some cases, worse. Because the Pinkerton men were officially licensed investigators and because most local police tended to look the other way, the Pinks could pretty much get away with anything. At least that's what the workers believed, and at this point, that was what mattered most. Just the knowledge that the Pinks were around placed a pall in our factory that could have been cut with a knife.

At the same time, the owners, as Mattie had predicted, were grieving the loss of the dock that had been burned. The dock in the clamming camp was the only practical alternative until a new one could be built. Rumor had it that those in the camp were asking an incredible fee for boats to load and unload there. The owners were over a barrel, so they had no choice but to give in to the clammers' demands.

Speculation was running wild regarding what had started the fire that destroyed the dock. Some suggested it was started by disgruntled workers, which would have been a logical assumption. Others thought it might have been the work of a small group of people trying to build the union, also a logical speculation. Still others, however, thought the fire might have been started by the Pinks to inflame the local atmosphere.

No one mentioned Gaston as a possibility, and I certainly wasn't about to. Gaston continued to enter my thoughts, especially after I spotted him one morning when he came to the loading dock to drop off a wagonload of his shells, which were highly prized by Mr. Blanton. Rebecca told me Gaston's visits always caused quite a stir, for two reasons. First, he was considered to be very dangerous and unpredictable, which caused everyone in the immediate area to be on guard. Mr. Blanton seemed to overlook this because he was most interested in the second reason Gaston's visits caused such a stir. Gaston's shells were the only ones that could be turned into what were called "pinkies," buttons with a unique bright and shiny pink luster. Stores could not stock enough of these on their shelves to keep up with customer demand. They commanded quite a premium—about ten times the cost of the average button—so they helped with profit margin. That was why Mr. Blanton was always so excited by Gaston's visits and why he tried to be so cordial toward him. Gaston's visit that morning coincided with one of our short morning breaks. I wasn't sure it was smart, but I decided to walk quickly out to the loading dock area just so he could see me. He did, and when he did, he did a double-take. He didn't smile. His face was expressionless. He stared blankly at me for a few seconds, then turned and walked to the other side of his wagon. My knees started shaking, so I headed back inside, tore into my work, and tried not to think of anything but the endless string of labels coming into my hands.

The past two weeks had gone quickly by, but with each passing day something other than a foul smell was starting to fill the Muscatine air: uncertainty. It was being felt by everyone. I was grateful when near the end of the second week Mattie and Viola invited me to come along with them to share in their upcoming Saturday night revelry. I couldn't wait. I needed that break.

....

CHAPTER 10

MATTIE AND VIOLA WERE TRUE to their word. When the 4:00 whistle blew on Saturday, Mattie and I hurried home to meet Viola and clean ourselves up before heading down to the growing commotion on Second Street. Viola was late meeting us, so Mattie paced back and forth in the living room until she showed up.

"You'll be late for your own funeral!" Mattie barked at her when Viola finally arrived.

Viola screwed up her face and replied, "I'll just be a minute, but what about you? You're really not going out with that grime on your face, are you?"

Mattie checked herself in the small mirror hanging in the kitchen and let out a high-pitched shriek. "Pearl, why didn't you tell me about this? I look like I've been hit with a hatchet!"

The truth was that Mattie got so crabby when she was in a hurry that I had learned to stay away from her and keep my mouth shut at those times.

After Viola had changed her shoes and Mattie was satisfied with her face, we headed down our steps into what we hoped would be enough diversion to allow us sweet escape from the drudgery of the work week. When we reached the corner of Chestnut and Second and saw the assembling crowd, Viola suddenly exclaimed, "Roosters on a raft!" That must have made sense somehow, but I just couldn't figure it out and didn't want to ask. So, I did the only thing I could think of. Shouting above the noise of the street, I repeated, "That's right—roosters on a raft!"

Mattie doubled over in laughter while Viola grabbed my hand and started pulling me down the street.

The carnival atmosphere I had seen on this street my first night in Muscatine was repeated every Saturday night for the benefit of those in the button factories, and for those in the lumber, garment, building, and river transportation industries, as well. What everyone had in common was a need to blow off steam and relax, even if just for a few hours, after the long grind of the work week.

Mattie and Viola favored getting a pail of beer and finding a good vantage point from which to watch the various vendors set up shop, but I never cared for spirits and didn't want to experience the morning-after effects that I'd seen more than a few revelers go through in the past. I enjoyed people-watching just about as much as anything, so I decided I'd still tag along with them.

We chose a spot across from a barber shop because, as Viola pointed out, "Men will want to get a shave before joining the fun, so the vendors will set up here to be the first to get at them when they leave the shop. Plus, we get first pick of those clean faces if we're so inclined."

Mattie and I scolded her for her brashness, but we did so with smiles on our lips because we couldn't fault her logic. This was a great spot for watching the vendors, but it was an even better location for inspecting the men. When the first two clean-shaven men came out of the shop and headed our direction, Viola shouted, "Roosters on a raft!"

This time I knew exactly what she meant. Mattie and I just shook our heads and laughed.

The range of vendors lining up on both sides of the street next to us was mesmerizing. Some of the vendors hawked food and drink, from sandwiches and fried frog legs to lemonade and pails of beer. I was too excited to eat anything, but my throat was dry, probably from the excitement, so I flagged down the first lemonade vendor to go by. Mattie and Viola got their beer, and we all sat on the curb and started enjoying the show—and especially the other vendors and their wares.

In some cases, the term *vendor* was used lightly. These men were definitely selling something, but it wasn't anything a person could eat or drink. Instead, they offered games of chance. Most of these had small wooden carts on wheels they could move up and down the streets, taking their games to where people were congregated, like at the barbershop.

One popular vendor offered a game of chance in which he quickly moved three facedown playing cards into different positions. One of these cards was the Queen of Hearts, and if a player could tell where the Queen was located after the cards had been moved, he won a quarter. If he lost, he'd lose his own quarter. It looked easy to me, but not many people managed to find the Queen. I started counting his winnings, and in five minutes that vendor made nearly as much money as I had in a whole week of work.

Viola told me about another game called "Button Tower." The object of this game was to stack rough button blanks of varying sizes as high as one could within a two-minute time limit. Four people played this game at once, each betting a dime. The contests lasted for exactly the two minutes, with the vendor watching the time carefully. The person with the tallest tower of buttons when time was called was given three dimes—and the vendor kept one. This was a great game for the vendor because he received a dime every time the game was played, regardless of who won.

As the evening wore on, a steady stream of these games continued in front of us. I finally got to see, in person, the "shell game" I had heard about from my father and uncle. The Muscatine version involved a man placing a small button under one of three clamshells and then moving them around in a very confusing pattern. As in the Queen of Hearts game, the players had to determine the final position of the targeted object, in this case the small button. Not many won this game, either.

There were also dice games, Bingo games, and even knife-throwing games, which Mattie said were always won by the men from the logging industry. I was having the time of my life watching them all. At the same time, there weren't many winners, so I didn't get the urge to join in.

The time flew by; I hadn't noticed it was starting to get dark. When Viola pointed out the emerging stars overhead and said, "Shotgun sky tonight," Mattie took a quick glance at her watch and exclaimed, "Oh, shoot! We've got to get down by the bridge. Get up! Get up! Get a move on."

I had no idea what Mattie was talking about, but Viola and I stood up, brushed off the back of our coveralls, and rushed to follow Mattie, who was already charging ahead through the crowded street. I followed Viola as closely as I could. She was obviously a seasoned veteran of dodging vendor carts and the catcalls of the men assembled in clusters along the sidewalks.

We managed to keep Mattie in our sight, but we couldn't catch up to her until we were past the depot and nearing the opening to the clamming camp. Memories of my last visit in this part of town caused me to grow more and more nervous with each step.

A large crowd of a hundred and fifty to two hundred people had gathered just under the end of the northern span of the bridge known to the locals as High Bridge, and very near to the entrance of the camp. A man standing precariously on top of a tall stepladder was addressing the crowd, but I couldn't make out his words. As we drew closer, a cheer erupted from those ahead of us as the man on the ladder raised his arms high into the air above his head.

"What's going on?" I asked Mattie as I looked around and saw people coming from all directions. Even those from the clamming camp had gathered and formed what looked like a skirmish line at the beginning of the road leading down into their area; most of them were armed with rakes and shovels.

Mattie was so focused on the man on the ladder she didn't respond, so I gently nudged the back of her leg and repeated my question. When she finally turned around, she said, "Pay attention. You might learn something. That's Howard Zey. He's a unionist. Half the town loves him, and the other half would like to see him lynched. You may find what he says interesting. Listen."

Just then an attractive and very tall and stocky man a few feet away turned our direction, saw Mattie, and came over to give her a hug. When she saw him, she reciprocated enthusiastically and added several kisses to his cheek.

"Finally!" the tall man said, first pointing to the man on the ladder and then raising his hands to the heavens.

"Amen!" Mattie responded, clapping her hands loudly and then hugging him again. "Have I missed much? What's he said?"

Viola, never one to be shy, rudely interrupted them by suddenly moving forward and positioning herself between them. She started introducing herself to the man when Mattie playfully shoved her to the side. In the same motion, Mattie urged me to come forward. She let out a loud sigh, and then introduced both of us.

"Girls, this is Stuart Alexander. He's known to his friends as Stoney. You can call him Mr. Alexander. He works for the Hawkeye Button Company. We used to run together. That is, we did before he got too big for his britches!"

"Very funny," he replied, facing us. "What she really means is she got tired of me hanging around and dumped me out with the trash. Isn't that right, Mattie?"

His tone was playful, but by the way he was looking at Mattie, it appeared he was still carrying a torch for her. Without looking at us, she said, "These miscreants are Viola and Pearl. Say hi to Stoney, girls."

Before we could, the crowd ahead let out another cheer. Mattie shushed all of us and motioned us to follow her farther into the group. When we were close enough that we could hear the speaker's words clearly, Mattie held out her arms and stopped us in our tracks. Her expression turned deadly serious as she turned and spoke.

"It'll probably be okay, but if anything happens, we'll split up and meet back home. Understand?"

I didn't understand. Not at all. Mattie whispered, "Howard Zey is a staunch unionist, and he's here to try to drum up some support. I didn't think you'd come if you knew."

Then, turning serious again, she said, "It might get a little hot around here later on, so we'll just stay for the main speech and then sneak out."

When a bright flash off to our left caught her attention, she added, "And one more thing. Turn your head as quickly as you can if you see any of those flashes. Those are cameras, and you don't want your face to show up in a picture of one of these gatherings. So, turn your head quickly after the flash so your face will blur in the picture. Got it?"

She turned away from me to concentrate on the speaker. Stoney on her left, and Viola on her right, moved toward her and locked arms with hers. I stayed behind them, unsure of what to do. One the one hand, I was upset with Mattie for not trusting me enough to tell me about the speaker. On the other, I was fascinated by the rumblings of the growing crowd around me. Mr. Blanton and my uncle would surely want to know about all this. Confused didn't begin to describe how I was feeling.

Suddenly the crowd turned very quiet. All eyes focused on the man atop the ladder. He paused for a minute, looked around at the crowd before him, and started speaking again.

"My friends," he began, "change is never easy. And the cost is often very high.

Now his voice became even more forceful. "But sometimes that cost must be paid, and this is one of those times!"

The crowd erupted in cheers. He allowed it for just a minute and then motioned everyone to settle down as he continued.

"How many people do you know who have sick children—children who need medical attention—but their parents can't afford it because they can't make a decent wage? How many of you have friends who have dust cough and lung complaints from working with shell dust swirling around them every single day in filthy and unsanitary factories? How many of you know men and women who go hungry at night so their children and other family members living with them can have just a few morsels of nourishment? How many of you!"

There were cheers from the crowd, followed by a chorus of "You tell it, Brother!" It was apparent many in the crowd had heard Mr. Howard Zey speak before.

Zey paused to wipe his forehead with a handkerchief, then continued loudly, in a commanding tone, "And look to my left —toward the camp. See our brothers and sisters over there. We have our differences, and nobody will deny that.

As he spoke, those lined up at the front edge of the camp inched closer together, forming an impressive wall of protection across the road at the entrance. They were sending a signal, and that signal appeared to say they didn't want any part of Mr. Zey. However, he seemed not to notice and continued.

"But even with all the differences that are there, we all still have one thing in common that no one can deny: We're all being taken advantage of, and it's time for us to put differences aside and, together, fight for what's rightfully ours!"

The wild applause and shouts that followed were deafening. Two flashes appeared, almost simultaneously, from my left, and, taking Mattie's advice, I quickly swung my head to the right and kept shaking it. I certainly didn't want my face showing up in the paper.

While the cheers continued, several men and women moved forward to the ladder and reached up to shake Zey's hand. He carefully walked down a couple of steps to be close enough to greet them. At one point, he seemed to lose his balance and almost fell off. A large man and a woman next to him grabbed the ladder and righted it before disaster struck. They were Mattie and Stoney! I hadn't noticed they had continued to inch forward through the crowd. When Zey regained his balance, he looked down and appeared to give Mattie a smile of recognition. Turning to Stoney, he did the same.

Zey climbed back to the top of the ladder. The crowd became silent, waiting for his next words.

"We've been cheated, and we've been crippled," he said, raising just his right hand into the air for all to see. Soft gasps spread through the crowd when we all saw he was missing his little finger and ring finger on that hand.

"And we've been starved. And we've been treated like animals. And we're not going to take it any more! It's time for you to join me—in the new Button Workers' Protective Union. It's time we had some rights, some dignity, some respect. That time is now!"

At first I thought more applause had erupted from the crowd, especially from my left. Then it seemed, from that same direction, as if members of the crowd were rushing toward Mr. Zey to congratulate him.

However, that wasn't at all what was happening.

In an instant, cheers were replaced by screams that spread quickly throughout the crowd. Fighting broke out from the left and spread like wildfire toward the center of the group. Mr. Zey's ladder was toppled, and he fell heavily to the ground, where I lost sight of him. Suddenly, arms all around me were swinging wildly, some of them in self-defense and others on the attack. Many fell to the ground and were trampled by others as people started running in all directions. A young man next to me fell at my feet, blood gushing from his nose. More flashes appeared from all directions, but I didn't have time to swing my head side to side. I was concentrating on keeping myself upright as sheer terror spread all around me.

Then, gunshots rang out. The crowd stopped moving and grew eerily quiet for just a second or two, acknowledging the shots, then the screams and fighting resumed at an even greater intensity. As one young man ran in front of me, he lowered his shoulder and tried to plow his way through. I tried to get out of his way, but it was too late. When he hit me, I lost my balance and went down. I wasn't hurt, but so many legs darted by me I was fearful of being trampled. I grabbed hold of a woman in front of me and pulled at her dress to steady and right myself.

I couldn't tell who was fighting whom. Everything was so confused, and one wild punch would inflict just as much injury as another. I spent the next minutes doing my best to keep my balance as I tried to back out of the crowd. When I was nearly out of the main disturbance, a hand from behind me placed a firm grip on my wrist and pulled me through two men who were punching each other and into a clearing. I turned to offer my thanks, and there he was.

Gaston.

"I owe you this," he said, urging me to follow him. "And I always repay a debt."

He took my hand, and I didn't hesitate as we ran toward the clamming camp. Those still standing vigil there with their rakes and shovels parted ranks just long enough for us to slip through. However, Gaston didn't slow down once we were past. We kept up a good pace until we were at the edge of the river. A boat was tied to the dock, and he motioned for me to climb in as he started untying its mooring ropes. When I stepped in, the boat wobbled. I lost my balance and fell forward, catching myself on a seat. I skinned my knee badly, but I was lucky. It could have been a lot worse. He saw this but didn't say anything. His concentration was still on a knot he was trying to undo.

He finally flung the rope back up on the dock and gently stepped aboard. With one sharp pull of a short rope, the engine at the back of the boat roared to life. In an instant, we were cutting across the current and heading out toward the middle of the river.

As I tried to catch my breath, I studied his face while he guided us farther and farther out into the current. He didn't appear frightened. As a matter of fact, the look on his face indicated disgust as much as anything. He constantly looked back and forth from the engine to the shore, as if trying to calculate distance and course. I hadn't noticed before, but his long hair was pulled back and tied together with a ribbon at the base of his neck. This allowed my first really clear view of his face. As I mentally erased the dirt and grime, his face was quite striking — even handsome. At the same time, it came to me he looked just like someone else I had met before. But whom? But where? An answer seemed right at the tip of my thoughts, but try as I might, nothing would come to me.

"Frightened?" he asked, quietly.

I nodded.

"Of me?" he continued.

This time I shook my head that I wasn't.

"Well, you should be," he said, flatly. "I'm Gunboat Gaston. I can only imagine what you've heard about me by now." He turned away to secure the boat's rudder with a looped rope. "That'll keep us out here in the current. We better stay here until that mess back on shore gets cleared out. If you truly aren't scared of me, then this won't be so bad. If you're lying and are, then I may just have to dump you into the river."

The boat bobbed up and down on small waves as our eyes met. Neither of us blinked for what seemed an eternity. Racing through my mind were all the stories I had heard about him. Nerves were still crashing inside me, and the first words out of me were completely inappropriate.

Pointing down the river I asked, "Did you burn that dock?"

His head snapped toward me as his eyes widened and his mouth dropped open. Then he smiled weakly and replied, "And what if I did?"

"I'm sorry. I shouldn't have asked that. That was uncalled for. Please forgive me. I should be thanking you for getting me away from that, that...."

I still didn't know what it was, what exactly had happened.

"I owed you," he said, bowing slightly toward me. "Because of that night. The night *somebody* burned the dock."

He smiled again, but I kept my mouth shut this time. If he'd been a part of that, and it now appeared from his expression he knew at least something of it, I wasn't going to go fishing for details. Instead, I looked back to the shore and saw fires growing where the fighting had broken out.

"What happened?" I finally asked. "What was that?"

"You don't know?" he asked, with more than a touch of incredulity in his voice.

When I said I really didn't, he continued. "We're going to see a lot more of this, but I doubt it will come to much good. I don't see how it can. The workers in the factories have been cheated and taken advantage of since the very beginning, and I don't see that changing any time soon, no matter what kind of union they try to build. It won't help. They can't get enough power."

In my earlier anxiety I hadn't taken notice of it, but it was at that moment, like a board hitting me across the head, I realized how he was talking to me. Gone were the short, clipped phrases and exclamations. Gone were the grunts and hand motions used to replace words. Instead, his speech was now articulate, polished. He was no longer the crude, uneducated hermit most believed him to be. I took a chance and asked about this sudden change.

"Since I've been in town, I have heard a lot about you. But now you're ruining the image. I don't think you're what people say you are."

He laughed and said, "I'm not completely sure that's a compliment, so I don't know what to say. I can only imagine what you've heard. No. Let me see if I can guess. Tell me if this is right."

Turning serious again, he began, "I bet you heard I was a killer with plenty of notches on my knives and guns and that I'd murder someone just for looking crooked in my direction. I'd also bet you were told I've been the cause of dozens of fires and robberies in factories and businesses all over town. Most say I grew up in the wild, raised by animals, and now live like one myself. And did you hear the one about how I cut out the hearts of two men who dared collect shells at my secret spot—and then ate their hearts in a special stew I prepared just for the occasion? Have I left much out?"

He didn't give me a chance to answer. Instead, he just shook his head before picking up a small bottle and tossing it to me. It was whiskey. I studied the bottle and then looked back at him.

"No, thank you," I said, leaning over to hand it back.

He laughed heartily and said, "I wondered if you'd take a swig."

Then, as his voice grew calm, even gentle, he added, "It's not for drinking. I can see blood spreading all around your knee. Roll up your coveralls and pour a little of this on the cut. It'll burn like fire and brimstone, but you better do it. The water's been bad around here for years because of the factories and all the people who dump their garbage into it. You're liable to get an infection, and it'd be a terrible shame if you lost that leg. Agree?"

I did agree. I quickly rolled up the stiff cloth and poured the whiskey all over the area where I had skinned myself. He was right about the pain, and I winced and sucked in my breath.

"That should do it," he said, reaching over to take the bottle. "Keep it clean for two or three more days and you should be fine. You'll be up and running from more union events before you know it."

"Thanks," I said, dryly. "I can't wait."

"Oh—and one more thing," I added. "You just about hit the nail on the head before. Yes, I've heard most of those stories about you, but what about the one where you blew up a boat and killed half a dozen men who snuck into your clamming area where you find your Pinkie shells? Don't leave that one out. It's a great story."

He laughed again, then replied, "Well, I hate to bring that one up because it's partly true. I actually did sink their boat, but none of them died. And it wasn't six. It was three of the nastiest scallywags you've ever seen, and they all did make it back to shore, even though they didn't deserve to."

Motioning me to turn around, he continued, "See that small canon attached to the rail behind you? I fire it off once in a while just to keep people away and keep the stories boiling back on shore. To make a long story short, I caught those river rats poaching in my section early one morning, so I fired a shot over their bow to scare them off. I must have had too much gunpowder packed in because a huge fireball also shot out, and it landed smack in the middle of their boat. It was instantly engulfed in flames, and they dove into the water and swam away like the devil himself was chasing them. I'm glad they didn't drown because, in a way, I owe them a favor. The story they later made up actually did me a lot of good. Nobody came near me for months. And that's how I got the name Gunboat Gaston. I like it. It suits me."

He peered at me and said, "But don't you go telling anyone what really happened. You have to promise me that—or you may not make it back to shore."

I nodded I would. Something in his voice, something in his eyes, made me believe him. I still was far from sure what he was exactly, but it was more and more clear to me that he wasn't the fiend the residents of Muscatine believed him to be. But what was he? One the one hand, there appeared to be a soft, gentle side to him that made me feel very much at ease. On the other, this was a man who looked like he could chew the heads off live chickens, and he really did fire his cannon at others. Who was this man? Where'd he come from? Why was he staying on the river?

We sat in silence, each looking back at the shore. The area where the commotion had taken place was now nearly empty, save for the fires blazing even higher. I could still see people standing at the opening of the clamming camp, but their ranks had shrunk significantly. When what sounded like three quick gunshots echoed across the river toward us, I looked over at Gaston.

Ignoring the gunshots, he said, matter of factly, "I know your uncle. How's old Sam Henry getting along these days?"

"What? How do you know...?" I asked, taken back completely by his words.

"Doesn't matter," he said. "What does matter is that if I know it, then it won't be long before the unionists know it. That means you're walking a really thin tightrope, and there isn't any safely net under you like at the circus. You better be careful or I'll likely find you floating down the river one day, and I would hate that."

I tried to explain to him that everyone already knew about my uncle, that they knew I was working at Blanton partly to help my uncle get a new business underway. I was an open secret, and safety wasn't a concern of mine. Not in the least.

He would have none of it.

"Keep telling yourself that," he said, sarcastically.

I tried again to explain, but he didn't seem to be listening to me at all and I'd had it. I knelt forward and said, "I'm sure this is great advice coming from a man with your reputation, but you'll have to forgive me if I don't take it. I don't believe a word you're saying. I'm perfectly safe. It's you who should be on the lookout. They're going to get you one of these days. And it isn't going to be pretty when they do. If you have any family left, I'm sure they'll be very proud of you then. Very proud."

At the mention of family, his demeanor changed in an instant. The playful smile on his face disappeared. He looked away from me and dropped his head. I had somehow crossed a line, and I immediately regretted it. No matter what he had said to me, I had no cause to dig into him. He had saved me from harm—again—and I should have just been grateful.

"I'm sorry," I said, softly. "I didn't mean to. I mean, I should have...I...."

I reached over to take his hand, but he stood up and pointed back to the shore.

"They're putting out the fires now. My guess would be there are also a few police hanging around in case anybody else shows up. This round is over, and I'd award it to the union busters. It was probably the Pinkerton men. That's their style—beat up a bunch of unarmed people who don't even know how to fight back. And the clammers sure weren't going to get involved. This isn't their fight, even though that speaker tried his best to make it theirs. That's a divide that will never be breached. Not in our lifetimes anyway."

He paused before continuing. "What you saw tonight was just the start. A bigger fight is coming. And the people who fight it, on all sides, are going to know how to fight. You can bet your bottom dollar on that. This was just a skirmish tonight. The war is coming."

Turning to face me, he added, "And what about you? Which side are you going to be on? Your uncle's? You'd like to be, but something tells me you aren't sure."

He was right, but it was beyond me how he knew. If my uncertainty was that clearly written across my face, then I was in trouble. I didn't answer his question. Instead, I tried putting the light back on him.

"And what about you?" I asked. "Which side are you on?"

"Not my fight," he replied without hesitation. He seemed to choose his words carefully. "I do have family here. Their sympathies are not my own. I want nothing to do with this—or them. I won't fight them. I'm going to stay out of this. If you are smart, you'll do the same."

"You're probably right," I said, studying his face. "What I need most right now is some time to think."

"Do it quick," he said, sharply. "You're an easy target because of your uncle."

"You're really not concerned about me, are you?" I asked, trying to break the tension that was building.

Mimicking me, he said. "Haven't made up my mind yet. What I need most right now is some time to think."

We laughed, but the lighter mood didn't last long. More gunshots rang out on shore.

"I'll get you home," he said, untying the rudder. "I'll land you on the other end of town, and you can walk home from that direction. You'll be safe if you come back down Third Street. Keep on the sidewalk and in the shadows. Now hang on. We'd better hurry."

When we reached the riverbank just west of downtown, he stopped the boat next to a small concrete landing. He threw a rope over a piling to keep the boat steady before helping me to my feet. Taking my hand, he led me out onto the landing. The boat had been pulled so close my feet didn't get wet.

"Listen to me carefully," he said, his face hidden in the shadows. "If you ever need me, go back to the camp and tell them you want to buy a scarlet pearl. Remember that—a scarlet pearl. They'll either bring you to me or send me the word."

Then, stepping out into the light, he added, "There's also something I want you to remember."

"Yes, I know," I said, cutting him off. "I'm an easy target. But don't you worry. I can take care of myself."

"That's not what I was going to say," he said, suddenly and sharply reaching out and drawing me to him. Before I could back away, he kissed me full on the lips, gently at first, then drawing me even closer.

It happened so quickly I was stunned and didn't even try breaking free. He finally stepped back and said, "Remember that."

That was all. He stepped back in the boat, gunned the motor, and was gone. I just stood there, motionless. I felt I should call out something to him, but nothing rose in my throat. I didn't move a muscle until I lost sight of his boat near the middle of the river. Then, still numb, I walked as quickly as I could toward Third Street.

As I made my way up the hill, I raised my hand and touched my lips. I then stopped, turned back, and looked out at the dark Mississippi.

....

I made it back safely and climbed up the long flight of creaky steps as quietly as I could to the dark apartment and went inside. I moved to the table next to the divan to light a lamp. Suddenly, to my right, something moved. My heart skipped a beat as I jumped back and gasped.

"That you, Viola?" a voice called out from the right end of the divan.

It took me a couple of seconds, but I finally realized the voice was Mattie's. "No—it's me, Pearl. What are you doing there in the dark? What's going on?"

"Pearl! I'm glad you're okay."

She got up, ran over to me, and hugged me tightly. Against my shoulder, I could tell her cheeks were wet.

"What is it?" I asked. "What's going on?"

"I was so worried," she said, choking back tears. "After all hell broke loose, I didn't see you anywhere, so I figured you got out. But Viola...."

Backing away from me, she added, "But I saw Viola being hauled off by what must have been Pinks. Stoney and I tried to catch up with them, but when the fighting spread, we couldn't get through the crowd fast enough. We finally had to give up, so I came home. There was nothing else to do. I've been worried sick ever since. You didn't see her later, did you?"

"No, I didn't," I said, handing her my handkerchief. "I made it down by the river. It was safe there. What should we do?"

"There's not much we can do but wait. That's what I've been doing. And praying. She better be okay. She better be."

"She's a tough girl," I said, trying to calm Mattie down. "Why, she's probably just hiding out until it's safe to come home."

Mattie uncharacteristically didn't respond with some smart comment. Instead, she hugged me again, tighter still, and asked me to sit with her.

We waited on the divan long into the night.

Viola never came home.

....

CHAPTER 11

MATTIE AND I WERE STILL sound asleep on the divan when someone pounded on the door just after seven. I rushed to the door and there was Stoney, out of breath.

"Let's go," he said, sternly. "Viola needs you. Now!"

"Slow down," I said, rubbing sleep from my eyes. "What are you talking about?"

"Where's Viola?" Mattie urged. "Is she all right?"

"No, she's not all right," Stoney shot back. "She's in Bellevue Hospital. Get up! We've got to get over there."

"What happened?" I asked. "How'd she end up there?"

"We're wasting time," Stoney practically shouted at both of us. "I'll tell you what I know while we're on the way."

Without another word, Mattie and I rushed at the same time to the bathroom. We shared the small space as best we could, each taking a quick turn in front of the mirror. I came out first, and when I did, Stoney asked, "You got another pair of coveralls? That one's got blood on your knee. You shouldn't wear that to the hospital in case the police are still there. Get my meaning?"

I did and immediately hurried to the bedroom to change. I didn't have other coveralls, so I quickly slipped on one of my church dresses.

Mattie and Stoney were waiting at the door for me when I returned. "Let's go!" Stoney urged, pushing us ahead of him and closing the door behind us.

When we were on Third Street and hurrying up the long, steep sidewalk toward Bellevue Hospital, Stoney finally spoke. "Near as I can gather, Viola was one of the first grabbed by the union-breakers. Not sure if it was the Pinks. Whoever grabbed her shoved her in a wagon and took her across High Bridge to the woods on the Illinois side. That makes it an Illinois problem, so the Muscatine cops probably won't lift a finger. They beat the tar out of her there. And not just Viola. They had three or four other women and at least two men. They wanted to know who in the factories were getting in with the new union—and who were just thinking about it—and I guess they tortured them to find out. Stopped short of killing them. Barely."

"How bad is she?" Mattie interrupted.

Stoney didn't stop to answer. Instead, he continued, breathing hard as we moved farther up the hill, "It looks like some talked. Not sure if Viola did. Because of those who did talk, a lot of people will be packing up and moving away today. That is, they will if they don't want to be beaten themselves or to have their families harmed."

"Why'd they take Viola?" I asked when he finally slowed to take a breath. "Why her?"

Mattie and Stoney looked at each other quickly. Mattie shook her head and then looked at me to see if I had noticed. I had, but I pretended I was looking the other way. "Well," Stoney added, "they must have thought she knew something about the union—or they mistook her for someone else. What matters now is that she's in a hospital bed and is asking for you two."

"How'd you find out she's there?" Mattie asked, also out of breath.

"One of the others they took was Steven Wiegand, one of my best friends. His cousin, Sissy, nurses there during the overnight. She came and got me this morning soon as she got off work. Wanted me to make sure nothing else happened to him. I rushed over as soon as I could and found out Viola was there, too. A doctor was looking at Steven, so I snuck in to see Viola when the nurses weren't looking. I got most of the story from her before she fell back asleep. I think they gave her something to knock her out. Face was a real mess and an arm was bandaged. Before she went out, she asked me to bring you. That's all I know."

We were all gasping for breath, but Mattie managed a, "Why those dirty..." before she motioned for all of us to stop for a minute.

"No use killing ourselves. Let's slow down and think about what we're going to do once we get there."

We started walking again, but slowly this time. There was still a long way to go, but Mattie was right. We needed to decide what we were going to do once at the hospital. If Viola was hurt that badly, chances were they wouldn't even let us in to see her since we weren't blood kin.

It wasn't more than a minute later that Mattie said, "I've got it. This'll work. Pearl, you're the only one of us who doesn't look like a button worker. Good thing you put on that dress. Tell them you're her sister. That should get you in. We'll try to sneak in behind you, if we can."

Between hard-fought breaths during the steepest part of the hike up Third Street, Mattie told me to make sure of three things. First, I needed to make up a story for the doctors and nurses to explain that Viola was accidentally mixed up in whatever had taken place—that she was just in the wrong place at the wrong time. Mattie said those who work in hospitals, like little pitchers, have big ears—and word would get out to the right people that Viola was not mixed up in union activity. Next, I was to find out how badly she was hurt. Mattie said Viola had an uncle in Washington, Iowa, who was a doctor, and we could send for him if she needed extra care. Finally, I was to ask Viola if she knew what had been said to those who took them. Specifically, she wanted me to find out names that had been given. Viola had been too groggy earlier to say anything to Stoney, so Mattie said I needed to ask right away. In the past couple of days I had come to understand much more about Mattie's sympathies toward the emerging union, so this final request didn't shock me. I nodded, and we quickened our pace.

Mattie had been right. When we arrived at the hospital, the nurse at the main desk did not want to let any of us in to see

Viola. I immediately informed her I was Viola's sister, and that did the trick; I was told I could visit with her for just a few minutes. Mattie and Stoney were told to stay in the waiting area off to the left.

The nurse led me to a small ward down the main hallway. There were a dozen beds or so in the room, and Viola was in the one farthest from the door. She was still sleeping when we walked up. The nurse said I could sit quietly in a chair next to the bed and hold her hand. She turned and left the room without checking on any of the other patients. Once she had gone, I leaned down and kissed Viola gently on the cheek. As I did, her eyes opened, startling me for an instant.

"Pearl?" she asked, blinking rapidly.

"Yes, I'm here," I said, sitting carefully on her bed. I squeezed her hand and didn't say anything for a minute. She had a large bandage wrapped around her forehead and a strip of gauze taped to her right cheek. Her right arm was also wrapped from her wrist to her shoulder. When she rolled toward me, I could see her right eye was swollen shut, and a large, dark circle was forming around it.

"How you feeling? Anything I can do?" I asked, quietly.

Viola smiled weakly and said, "I must look a sight. I feel like a sight. My jaw hurts so bad. And my eye...."

"You look fine," I said, brushing some hair away from the bandage at her forehead. "Why, in no time at all you'll be back at the old grind."

"You're a terrible liar," she replied.

After trying to raise up and look around, she added, "Where's Mattie?" She winced in pain, and I urged her back down.

"She's fine," I said. "She's out in the waiting area. They wouldn't let her in. By the way, I'm your sister in case the nurse comes back. That's the only way I could get in here."

"I'm proud to be your sister," she said, squeezing my hand.

Viola closed her eyes for a few seconds before continuing, "Tell Mattie something for me, okay?"

I leaned closer so she could whisper in my ear.

"Tell her the furniture store on Cedar Street needs to be closed. Then tell her there were no singers. No choir."

Viola was growing weaker. "I heard the doctor say I have a concussion of some kind. My brain's swelled up. This is the first time anyone has ever said anything about my brains. Pig in a poke, right?"

She tried to laugh, but closed her eyes tightly as the pain swept over her. I knew she needed rest. Leaning down once again to kiss her cheek, I said, "I'm going to take off now. Get some sleep. We'll be back tonight to check on you. In the meantime, you just rest as much as you can."

Viola closed her eyes and was asleep almost instantly. When I left the ward, Mattie and Stoney were talking with the nurse. As I approached them, Mattie was saying that Viola had just been coming home from choir practice when she heard all the commotion down by the bridge and had gone there to investigate. Wrong place, wrong time. Simple as that. When everyone turned and saw me, they asked at the same time how Viola was doing. After I reassured them she was resting again, the nurse started down another hallway, and Mattie and Stoney motioned me to follow them outside.

"Well?" Mattie asked as soon as we were down the front sidewalk.

"They did a good job on her," I said, shaking my head. "She's got a concussion and plenty of cuts and bruises. I thought it was bad when my brother fell out of the loft, but what happened to him couldn't hold a candle to what Viola went through. But I think she'll live, God willing."

Mattie grabbed my arm and said, "What'd she say? Anything about names?"

I pulled my arm away and said, as boldly as I could under the circumstances, "I'm not stupid, you know. I know what's going on here. I know what you wanted me to find out."

I was tired of being treated like a child—like I was just a

pawn to be used as she saw fit. But, more than anything, I was tired of all the whispers and cloaked gestures when I was around.

Mattie bit her lower lip and looked away from me.

"I think we need to talk, don't you?" I said, moving toward her.

Mattie turned to Stoney and said, "Go on. We'll talk later. I guess it's time Pearl and I had a few words together."

"If that's what you want," Stoney said, looking quickly back and forth between the two of us. "If you think it's best."

"I do," Mattie replied, curtly. "It's time."

With that, Stoney started walking away. He didn't say goodbye.

"Reservoir Park is just a couple blocks from here—and it's downhill—so let's go there. Might as well be comfortable while we do this," Mattie said, resignation in her voice.

"Fine with me," I said. "Lead the way."

I had a good notion of what I was about to hear; I also knew a door was going to open that I could never shut again.

....

"First, you've got to understand something," Mattie began, as we sat across from each other at a picnic table in the park. "Viola's father and older brother were both killed in an explosion in a button factory up in Washington. It didn't have to happen. After they died, the owners of the factory were so uncaring they wouldn't even let Viola's mother reclaim his tools. To the owners, he was just a piece of grit to be fed to the hogs."

When I didn't say anything, Mattie continued, "Then her little brother lost a hand in a sorting machine. Know what happened then? The owners gave him five dollars. They had a sliding scale, ranging from a dollar for a finger to ten dollars for an eye. They can put a price on anything, except safety and a fair wage."

She was getting wound up, her voice getting louder and louder. "I know your uncle, and he treats his people good. Real good. I know that. And Blanton isn't a bad man. Oh, I still think he looks the other way for too many of his supervisors, but his actions are those of a scared man who knows change is coming that he can't do a thing about. But your uncle and Blanton are the exceptions to the rule. You have no idea—absolutely no idea at all—what most of the factories in town are like. Do you want me to tell you? Do you?"

I finally spoke. "Go ahead. I'd like to hear what you have to say."

"Whether you believe what I'm going to say or not, it's all true. All the gospel truth." Here she stood up and walked back and forth in front of me as she spoke, her voice rising even higher. "There are about twenty-five hundred workers in button factories all across Muscatine. The average worker puts in sixty to seventy-two hours a week to earn five dollars a week if a woman, and seven or eight dollars a week if a man. Out of this pitiful wage, they have to buy their own work tools and other equipment, and those aren't cheap. After paying for rent and food, they might be able, if they're lucky, to keep starvation and disease just outside their door. And let's talk about disease just for a minute. Did you know over half of those in the factories have lung complaints, like Dust Lung, that will greatly shorten their lives? Everybody knows this, but no one does anything about it. And on top of this, there are more cases of pneumonia, typhus, and gangrene here than any other place in the Midwest."

She sat back down before adding, "You've seen the children working in our factory. In others, kids as young as six and seven work forty-hour weeks. Many of them are there to pay off debts owed by their parents to the owners. They can never pay these debts back completely, so this is nothing more than slavery. Nothing more. And let's talk more about safety and health. At Blanton we're lucky that we have sawdust spread out on the floors every morning before work to help keep down the shell dust. Most other factories don't do this. Did you know shell dust is the leading cause of blindness in the industry? There are so many eye patches in town we look like a bunch of runaway pirates. And remember how I joked about the finger jar at work? That's not a joke at all. Most places actually have one—and one for eyes as well. What do you think about that?"

I started to respond, but she didn't want me to. She kept rolling.

"Most factories don't even have basic safety precautions for the acid bath rooms. There have been countless, needless cases of facial burns and blindings because of the acid process—and they could have been prevented with just a few dollars' worth of safety equipment on hand."

She slowed down, and her voice became almost a whisper. "There are also hidden tragedies, those not known outside of our little world. No one is quite sure why it happens, but women who work in button factories have five times the number of miscarriages as other women in town. On the other side of that coin, men in the factories have more bladder diseases and cancers than any other group of workers in the nation. I can go on and on if you want me to. Are you starting to get the picture?"

This time, she really was waiting for a response, so I chose my words carefully. "Mattie, I have no reason to doubt what you've said. I believe you. But this isn't a simple problem. I know some changes would help—and are needed. I know that, but I also know, and deep down I think you do, too, there's only so much the owners can do and still stay in business. What would you have them do?"

"They can listen," Mattie said, bluntly. "That would be a start, and it would also be a first. All these workers want is a decent, honest living, which right now they can never have. I know what you're thinking. If it is so bad, then why don't they just move on and do something else? The answer to that is easy—and sad at the same time. Other industries right now aren't any better. There isn't a monopoly on abuses here. All have their own problems to solve, and the workers are the ones who will always suffer until change comes. This work is all they know how to do, all they want to do—and the owners know it and take advantage of it. They have us over a barrel."

Then, looking right at me, she added, "This is America. Do we have the right here to have a safe and healthy place to work at a fair wage—or do we continue to allow the owners to be the only people with decent lives? Right now, it's a one-way road, and we aren't even allowed to begin the journey. Is that just? You answer me that."

She put her head down on the picnic table and closed her eyes. It was clear she had spoken from her heart, that she believed everything she said to be absolutely true. I was about to speak when she suddenly raised up and added, "And how can I be so sure of this? I'll tell you. But before I say anything, you also better understand this, too. If you tell anyone about what I'm going to say, Viola could be killed—and maybe you and me, too, just by association. You think about that before you get any type of urge to open your mouth. I'm trusting you now—with our very lives."

Becoming quiet to the point of whispering, she leaned close to me and said, "Viola's a patsy. Do you know what that means?"

I nodded that I did—as I shivered and felt myself blush at the same time.

"That's why she does nothing but short work. The short work gets her into all the factories in town, and she can report on all of them to those who need to know. She's good at her job because she seems so dense, which she actually is at times. But, overall, she's one of the best. Ever wonder how she can pay her part of the rent with just once in a while short work? The union is actually paying her a good salary. That's how the rent money magically appears. She started doing this because of what happened to her family. Then, after she saw what was going on in the other factories, she's doing it for all of us. This might be why she was beaten. Could be. Or, she really could have just been in the wrong place at the wrong time. If the union busters know about her, then we've got to get her the heck out of here. And we might have to go, too. Do you understand any of this?"

I did, but I didn't know what to say. I had plenty of notions about Mattie's leanings, but the revelation about Viola caught me completely off guard. At the same time, the irony of the situation also hit me hard. Viola was gathering information for the union at the same time I was gathering information for the owners. And all under one roof. Nothing could have better shown the complete and utter lack of communication between the two parties. I wasn't completely sure I bought everything Mattie had shared with me, but I did believe, more than ever, both parties needed to listen to each other. If this didn't happen, a war was sure to follow and, as Gaston had suggested, it wouldn't be pretty.

"Well, speak to me," Mattie urged. "You've got to have something to say."

I chose my words carefully. "Mattie, if what you say is true, then I do understand why you and Viola feel the way you do. At the same time, my uncle has told me enough stories about terrible things workers have done that have damaged the industry. My best guess is the truth of the matter is probably somewhere in between. If that is the case, then I agree with you now is the time for something to be done. But I have a question for you. Is a union completely necessary? Isn't there another way to get everyone to the table to talk about the concerns of both sides?"

She stared off to her right, to the Mississippi River below, before continuing, "I wish I had an easy answer to your question. If there's any way other than building a strong union, then I don't know it—and nobody I know does either. Unions are built to represent those who can't represent themselves. So far, the owners haven't let anyone come to the table. Maybe—just maybe—if the Button Workers' Protective Union grows the way I think it can, the owners will be forced to listen. Oh, I know it's a two-way road. There are workers who aren't worth the gunpowder it would take to blow their heads off. Maybe the union would make it so the bad workers and bad owners would lose their voices. Maybe the good and the just would come, like fresh cream, to the top. Then again, maybe I'm dreaming. Maybe a union can't do what needs to be done. All I know is that right now it seems to be the only option we have, and I'm going to help with all I can offer. So, there it is. I'm a low-down, good-for-nothing, shiftless unionist. That's me."

I didn't say anything. Instead, I smiled again and squeezed her hands. There was so much I wanted to tell her, but I was hanging on a high fence. Yes, the truth was probably somewhere in the middle of what I had heard on both sides, but I wanted to make up my own mind.

Mattie seemed disappointed I didn't have much to say in response. I told her I'd honor our life-long friendship by keeping my mouth shut. I told her I'd think about everything she said. I also promised we'd talk again—and soon. In the meantime, I asked her to honor my desire to go off and think things through.

Before we left the park, the tension between us was still thick. I didn't want to talk anymore about the union, but I knew something needed to be said. Mattie had bared her soul to me, so I thought the least I could do in return was share a very private detail with her. My news wasn't in the same league as hers, but there are some bonds that women just understand, cherish, and use to build common ground.

"You'll never guess what I did last night," I said as we reached the street and started down the long hill.

I didn't wait for her to respond. I quickly blurted out, "I got kissed by Gunboat Gaston. Can you believe it?"

The questions came in waves all the way home, and they united us once again.

....

CHAPTER 12

THE REST OF THE DAY was a tug-of-war, with Mattie pressing me for information about Gaston, and me trying to drag out of her more information about the plight of the workers in the button factories. By late afternoon, a stalemate of sorts set in. I agreed to tell her just one more piece of information about Gaston, and she promised to tell me more about Viola's short work scheme. For my side of the bargain, I told her about Gaston saving me the first night I came to town. She followed by sharing how Viola knew more about the workings of the individual factories than anyone else in town because she had worked in every one of them—and in nearly every station in each. From those experiences, she had been able to provide the emerging union with vital information. Mattie still wanted to hear more about Gaston, and I was still very curious about how Viola's information would be used by the union, but we were both emotionally drained. There'd be other days, other discussions. So, finally, a truce ensued. Mattie prepared banana and celery sandwiches for us, and we sat at the table and ate them in silence.

When we had eaten and cleared the dishes, we spoke again, this time more seriously. According to Mattie, the information I had received from Viola was incredibly important and needed to be passed along as before nightfall. The "no singing" and "no choir" was clear enough, even to me. These meant none of those abducted and beaten had given up the names of individuals involved in or sympathetic to the union. Mattie said this was a great relief to her because several "sudden" disappearances had already taken place in their ranks.

The part of her message about the furniture store took longer for me to figure out. I passed my guess by Mattie, and she confirmed the furniture store was the secret meeting place of one branch of the union membership. Someone had given up this information, probably believing it would save his life, so it was no longer safe for anyone to be seen going in and out of that building in the evenings. Word had to be gotten out quickly to the members who would be going there for their usual Sunday night meeting.

It was growing late in the day, and Mattie said she needed to rush off to deliver a message to some friends. I knew what she meant. When I asked if I could tag along, she told me that wouldn't be such a grand idea. The union membership had a grapevine it used in spreading messages quickly, and, according to Mattie, it would be safer for me at this point not to know anything about other branches of that vine. This sounded logical to me, and I appreciated her candor.

We decided I could be most useful by going back to visit Viola to find out if she had remembered anything else. At the same time, I could check to see how she was getting along, just in case we did need to contact her uncle. I was glad to be going. No matter what she was in union circles, Viola was my friend.

As Mattie and I headed out the door, she turned to me and said, kindness filling her words, "Thanks, Pearl. Thanks for everything."

Tears welled up in her eyes. I didn't respond. I just patted her on the shoulder and headed down the steps.

....

As her "sister," I was permitted to sit with Viola for nearly two hours. She drifted in and out of sleep regularly that whole time. A nurse came in during one of Viola's naps and showed me how to apply a cool compress to her bandaged arm to help reduce the swelling. Doctors still weren't sure if the arm was broken or if the muscles had been damaged—or both. The nurse explained they wouldn't be sure until the swelling dropped enough for a thorough examination of the area. Viola said the compress made her arm feel like it was burning, so I waited until she dropped off to sleep before gently pressing it over the bandages. Several times while she slept blood trickled out of her nose and dripped down to her neck. When I was finally able to get another nurse to stop and visit with me, I asked about this and was told it was part of the concussion and not to worry about it—yet.

At times when Viola was awake, we spoke quietly again about what she could remember of the previous evening. The blow to her head had dulled most of her memory, but she could remember quite clearly the faces of those who had abducted her. They were dressed very well: tight suits, jackets, and vests. Each wore a black derby. She didn't see any badges, but she was becoming more certain these men were Pinkertons. There were other men with them as well, and Viola said she recognized one of them as being from Muscatine. She couldn't yet place him, but she was fairly certain he worked in one of the factories as a supervisor or a clerk. She said it would come to her eventually.

She sobbed quietly and her breathing came in short, jerky bursts when she described what she could recall. Those abducted with her were taken one at a time from the back of a large wagon and tied to trees in a thickly-wooded area down by the river-bank. The trees were close enough together that all could still see and hear what was happening to the others. One person would be asked a question, and if he or she did not provide an answer, a terrible beating would follow—and was witnessed by the others waiting for questions to be posed to them. Viola said the waiting was the hardest of all, knowing that the brutality was soon coming. To their credit, none of those questioned gave up any names, no matter what was done to them. Viola said one of the last to be questioned was a young woman who was clearly with child. The person who seemed in charge of the abductors stood before her with a piece of steel pipe about a yard long in his left hand. Viola said he very calmly told her that if she couldn't provide them with any type of useful information about the union, he was going beat the child out of her. At that point, all those tied to trees started screaming and begging the man not to harm the woman. When the woman didn't respond right away, he raised the pipe above his head and started counting backward from ten toward one. At five, the woman caved in. She said that while she was not affiliated with the union in any way, she had overheard some workers at the billiard parlor on Walnut Street talking about the furniture store that was being used for meetings. This seemed to satisfy the man with the pipe, so he cut her loose and told her to get back in the wagon.

Viola was the last to be questioned. They asked her everything from what she had heard about the union to whether she knew anyone directly involved. When she refused to give up names or other information, three men took turns hitting her with short pieces of what appeared to be canvas hose and round, tapered pieces of wood. At one point, the largest of the men got right in her face and screamed at her as he clubbed her on the head. She could remember nothing after that until waking up at the hospital. She didn't even know who had brought her to Bellevue.

Near the end of my visit and just before Viola drifted off to sleep again, I asked if there was anything I could do for her. She motioned for me to lean down close to her lips, and she whispered to me, "Tell Mattie this name: Robinson. She'll understand. That's all I remember."

Then Viola closed her eyes and she was asleep. On the way out, I stopped by the nurse's station and asked if anyone knew how long she was likely to be staying. The nurse said it would depend upon how quickly the swelling in her brain subsided, and no one could predict that at this point. I thanked her and left.

I bought a Sunday paper on the way home and tried to read it while waiting for Mattie to return. I hoped there would be a story about the previous night's events, but there wasn't a single word. Not one. Mattie had told me the owners controlled what went into the papers, but I hadn't believed her. As I flipped page after page and didn't find even a short blurb, I started to wonder if Mattie might be right. I finally settled for the comics and the light, local news. Several times I attempted to get through a long story about a man who had just set some record for swimming back and forth across the Mississippi, but my mind would wander each time I started, and I never did finish it. Matttie finally got back near dusk. She plopped down next to me on the divan, sprawed back, and threw her legs over mine.

"Did you get your... your work done?" I asked, pushing her legs off me.

"I did," she said. "And just in the nick of time. And how about you? How was your afternoon? How's Viola?"

"Still awfully banged up. Oh Mattie—the men who did this to her should be horsewhipped and then boiled in a clam vat. And even that is too good for them."

"Is she going to be all right?"

"Too soon to tell for sure," I said, "but they're hopeful. It's the concussion that has everyone most worried—and me, too."

I paused, then said, "There's not much we can do right now. Like I said before, we just need to pray."

"I'm doing that," Mattie replied. Turning even more serious, she asked, "Did she say anything else about what happened that I should know about?"

I repeated as best I could what Viola had told me about the beatings. Mattie put her face in her hands and cursed softly as I relayed the story. When I finished, Mattie looked up and asked, "She say anything else?"

"Yes, she said I should tell you the name Robinson. She didn't say anything about it. She just told me to give you the name. Does that mean anything to you?"

"It does," Mattie said weakly, her face growing pale. She stood up, grabbed her handbag, and headed toward the door.

"I've got one more thing to do tonight," she said. "Don't wait up for me—and don't worry. Get some sleep. I'll be back in time to work tomorrow morning."

"Where you going?" I asked. "Anything I can do? Want me to come along?"

"What I need to do right now, I need to do alone. I wish I could say more, but I better not. I'll just say I love you, Pearl— and I don't want anything to happen to you."

I walked over and hugged her tightly. "I won't ask anything else. I'll do as you say and trust you. You just promise to be careful. That much I am going to ask."

She nodded solelmly, turned, and stepped outside. I locked the door behind her and returned to my newspaper.

I tried to read the story about the swimmer at least a dozen more times before finally falling asleep.

....

CHAPTER 13

MATTIE SHOOK MY SHOULDERS, AND I snapped awake about five thirty.

"Rise and shine. Chickens are already up," she bellowed while marching into the bathroom.

I yawned, stretched out, and made my way slowly to the bathroom door. Knocking lightly upon it, I asked, "You okay? You get the rest of your work done last night?"

"Dig out a pan and see if you can fry us up some eggs," she replied. "I found some chickens on my way back last night, and their eggs just followed me home. Also found some good, fresh bread, too. Toast some. You'll find a jar of orange marmalade next to the sack."

"Where did you..." was all I could muster before heading for the kitchen. Eggs? Orange marmalade? We hadn't eaten this well in the whole time I'd been here. Compared to our usual breakfast fare, this was going to be a feast. I was so hungry I resisted the urge to go back and ask any more questions.

As quickly as I could, I scrambled six eggs and prepared the toast. Normally, I'd have gotten dressed before we sat down to the table, but not this morning. Our meals had been so light of late I was half afraid I'd come back from the bathroom and find all the platters clean.

When the food was ready and the table set, I called out, "Come get it while it's hot—and before I eat everything."

The last part of my announcement did the trick. Mattie bolted into the kitchen so fast she slid right into her chair. We both laughed.

"I'm not even going to ask how the eggs managed to follow you home," I said, handing her a piece of toasted bread. "Say, you didn't by chance have any of the chickens follow you home, did you? We haven't had any meat in over a week."

"Sorry," she said, while spreading the marmalade evenly across her toast. "Maybe next time. It was all I could do to get home with this."

"This is perfect," I said, taking my first bite of egg. "My stomach won't know what to think!"

"Remember that expression we had when we were kids?" Mattie asked. "How'd it go? 'Over the lips, through the gums, look out stomach, here it comes!'—or something like that. Remember that?"

"I certainly do, and that old expression was made for just this occasion. Look out stomach—here it comes!"

Mattie beamed as I started preparing my toast. This truly was the finest meal we'd had together. We ate in silence until our plates were nearly empty. Then, at the same time, we each took a small piece of toast and wiped up the rest of the egg and marmalade on our plates.

I started to thank her again, but she cut me off and said, "We don't have time for it now, but I did manage to come across something else."

Standing and walking over near the farthest kitchen cabinet, she opened its door to reveal a small tin of coffee.

"Are you're pulling my leg!" I screamed loud enough I was sure people on the street below could have heard. "Coffee!"

"As Viola would say, 'Put a rag in it!'" Mattie replied, laughing softly.

"I can't stand it anymore. Where'd you get all of this?" I asked, pointing from the table and then to the cabinet.

"Let's just say I found it and didn't want it to go to waste."

"In other words," I replied, "you don't want me to ask any questions, right? You just want me to shut up."

"Right," she answered back. "But I do want to say just one

more thing, and then you better get dressed. We've still got work, you know."

"Well, what is it?" I asked, drumming my fingers on the table.

"This was just a simple meal," she began. "Just some eggs and lathered toast. Not a big thing, right?" Before I could answer, she continued, "Then why is this the first time we've eaten together like this? I'm going to tell you why. It's because we don't make enough money to have even the simple, normal things. And why is that? It's because there are those who don't want us to have a stinkin' thing. Not even decent food or places to live. And why is that? Because if we're starved out, sick, or hurt, we won't have the energy to do anything about it. We'll just continue on, scratching and clawing for anything we can get. And who wants us to be this way? Three guesses, and the first two don't count. The owners—that's who! They'd just as soon see us die off one by one than do anything to let us improve our lives. I'm sorry Pearl, but this is the way it truly is, and the sooner you understand this...."

Her voice trailed off. She turned away from me and looked out the window, avoiding my eyes.

Finally, and without turning to face me, she added, "Eggs and toast. Funny how something as small as that can make life so beautiful in the early morning. No, *funny* isn't the right word. I think *pitiful* is more like it. Wouldn't you agree?"

Her last words were stern, cold. It was also clear she was then waiting for me to say something.

"You're right. It shouldn't be so hard to have a good, simple life. We all deserve that. Each and every one of us. I know that and I'll do what I can, Mattie. That much I promise you."

I then added, "I feel guilty asking because you provided all of this, but if you'll wash the dishes, I'll go get dressed. Would that be okay with you?"

Mattie didn't answer. She just stood there, looking out the window. As I reached the bathroom, I heard her say, softly, "Eggs and toast."

....

On our walk to work, Mattie explained to me what we'd likely find waiting for us.

"Every time there's a incident involving the industry, and especially if they suspect anything related to the union is involved, the owners crack down and try to drive more nails into the coffin. Expect today to be pretty grim."

"What do you mean?" I asked. "What will Mr. Blanton do?"

"Oh, he won't do much," Mattie replied. "He's not like most of the owners who go out of their way to keep everyone pinned down. He'll just likely remind us that if it weren't for the factory, we'd all be dead. Overly dramatic, yes—but also quite effective."

I'd soon enough find out what she meant. Quickly changing the subject, I told Mattie more about my visit with Viola. We both vowed to head to the hospital as soon as we could after work.

The rest of the way to the factory neither one of us uttered a word.

....

Mattie's words were prophetic.When everyone had assembled for Mr. Blanton's usual early Monday pep-talk, the room was absolutely silent. I couldn't detect a single motion in the room. Everyone seemed frozen, locked in place, almost afraid to move. All eyes were focused straight ahead as Mr. Blanton began speaking. Instead of his usual greeting, he jumped right into business.

"Last week production was just about even with what we did the week before. That's not bad. Not at all. But I know we can do better. I want you to really concentrate this week. I don't care if you're rounding, cutting, sorting, or packing, keep your mind on two things. First, I want you to keep in front of you pride in your work. We're a small company. We're not big like Hawkeye or Pioneer or McKee. We're a small, family-owned concern. We can't produce anywhere near the quantities they can. So, why are we still in business when we could have been swallowed up? Our pride in our workmanship—that's why. Our product, while smaller in quantity, is better in quality. That quality is what separates us from everyone else."

He paused, took a sip of water, and looked around the room. "This brings me to my second point. I said to you earlier we're a small, family-owned concern. I want you to think about what I mean by family for a minute. All of us here at Blanton are part of this. Think about it. What would happen to me, to you, if the factory closed? Our family would collapse. That's why I say keep pride firmly in your hearts this week, and help make our family stronger than ever. We can do it. I know we can. And we need it now more than ever. I think this morning we all know why."

At this point, his face nearly ashen, he stopped talking and just stood there, looking around the room. I also scanned the group, and most people lowered their eyes to the floor and remained absolutely still, appearing for all the world like scolded children. After a good two minutes—uncomfortable for everyone—he finally walked down from the platform and headed quickly straight for his office. He didn't even pause to order all to their stations, as was his custom. The group, as if stunned by his demeanor and uncertain of what they should do, finally started walking slowly and deliberately out of the room.

"I've never seen anything like that before," Mattie said quietly to me. "I guess he's more worried about what happened than I expected he'd be. Played to our emotions. That was smart. Really smart."

"But there wasn't anything in the papers," I said. "How does he know?"

"Of course there wasn't. But that doesn't mean the owners don't know about every single thing that happened. I bet Blanton and the others knew everything not more than thirty minutes afterward. They've got their stooges in the police and the papers. Yes, he's sweating this now. That's good. If he's this worried, that probably means the other owners are having fits."

There was no more time, so Mattie went to her station, and I started for the main office for my meeting with Mr. Blanton. Under the circumstances, I wasn't sure he still wanted to meet with me.

As soon as I entered the office, Miss Fitch motioned me to sit in a chair by the door. She wasn't her usual cheery self and didn't say a word. Somehow, she, too, must have known what had happened Saturday night.

I waited about five minutes before Mr. Blanton opened his door and roughly motioned me inside.

"It's good to see a friendly face," he said, exhaling deeply when I was seated. "You've heard what happened the other night, I suppose."

He was clearly agitated, his voice cracking as he spoke. He sat against the edge of his desk and started popping his knuckles, one after the other.

"What is it, Sir?" I asked, gently. "What's wrong?"

"Pearl, I've got a problem," he replied. "We've all got a problem. Maybe you haven't heard. If you haven't, then you need to know about it. It was exactly what your uncle and I predicted. Unionists! Meeting right out in the open here in Muscatine! We knew there were nests of them all over the place, but now they're starting to show their faces right out in public! What is this world coming to?"

I didn't want to let on I knew anything about it, so I tried to keep my face expressionless and waited for him to continue. I didn't have to wait long to hear his side of the story.

"Saturday night a large group of unionists met down by High Bridge. The leader was a known Socialist called Zey. Ever hear of him?"

Thankfully, he didn't wait for me to answer. He continued, "They blocked the bridge so no one could get across and started fires everywhere all along the river. Muscatine was under seige! With the heat and the wind this time of the year, the whole town could have been burned to the ground by a spark from any of

those fires. They would have liked that. Then, they started fighting everyone who came into the area. Women and children, too.
It was a terrible row. Dozens of our best citizens were injured by
those hooligans. Can you believe it? Unionists have no respect
for law and order. All they know is violence."

He walked around his desk and sat down, resting his face
in his hands. I stood, poured him a glass of water, and set it in
front of him. He had a large handkerchief in his vest pocket, so I
reached over, pulled it out, and soaked the end of it in the water
pitcher.

"Here," I said, handing him the handkerchief. "My grandmother always said there's nothing like cool water to soothe the
spirits. Hold this over your forehead and eyes. You'll feel better."

"Thanks," he said, pressing the damp cloth to his forehead.
"I'll try anything at this point."

While he steadied himself, I started thinking about his version of Saturday night. I didn't know where he had gotten his
news, but from what I had been able to see that night, nothing
was further from the truth. As a matter of fact, what he said was
exactly the opposite of what really took place! I wanted to tell
him, but in doing so I would have had to reveal that I was there.

His version also solidified something I'd been thinking about
for some time. To me, one of the biggest problems facing the
workers and the owners was the absence of simple, basic, honest
communication. If a man like Mr. Blanton could end up with
such a twisted version of the actual events, then I shuddered to
think what the other owners were thinking this morning. It was
more and more clear to me that sometime, somehow, both parties would have to talk to each other openly and honestly before
anything else could happen. At the same time, no one could be
naive enough to believe that truth alone would settle the range of
issues pressing on both sides, but without this common bond of
truth and communication, a next level could never be reached.

Mr. Blanton grimaced as he held his handkerchief on his
forehead. As I looked at him, I felt sorry for him. He wasn't one

of the bad owners Mattie always talked about. He was just one of the many souls in town groping in the dark for a solution to a problem that was already affecting many, a problem that could, potentially, destroy the whole industry.

"Mr. Blanton," I began, cautiously, "it isn't my place to say anything, so I'm going to ask you to forgive me in advance. I've listened to my uncle talk about this same problem for quite a long time now. The more I hear about it—that is, about what the workers seem to want—the more I believe a fight everyone seems to think is coming might be avoided. Maybe an outside voice would help."

He started to smile, which made me feel he wasn't giving me much credence. I couldn't blame him, but I hoped he'd at least hear me through.

I was relieved when he said, "Go on. I'm listening."

Again choosing my words carefully, I continued. "I'd like to ask you a question I don't know the answer to. I don't know anything about unions, but what would happen if everyone sat down and just listened to each other talk? From what I can gather from my uncle, he says the unionists don't have a clue what it takes to run the industry. As a matter of fact, he says they're a mostly a bunch of ninnies."

Mr. Blanton smiled again, this time more broadly, as I added, "Now please don't take any offense, but my uncle also said some of the owners aren't the best listeners in the world. To me—and I know I'm terribly inexperienced—it seems like if the owners of the factories would at least agree to listen to what the workers have to say, and if the workers would try to understand even a smidge of what it takes to run the industry, that might help everyone avoid a war. What do you think?"

Mr. Blanton laughed out loud.

As he did, my face burned red. I felt anger welling up in me, but I knew better than to let it out. I sat there and suffered him.

When he gained enough composure to speak, he began, "Pearl, you're one in a million. I wish I had a daughter like you.

You see nothing but the good in the world, a world that can be so ugly at times. I wish everybody could be like that."

Possibly sensing how uncomfortable I was, he poured a glass of water and handed it to me. "What you're suggesting, while I'll admit is good in theory, would be the beginning of the end. You don't know the unionists. Most of them are socialists. If they get a toe-hold, their influence will spread like a disease until the industry crumbles right before our eyes. They'll want everything without having to work to get it. No, if they get their way, we're all cooked, plain and simple."

"Look," he said, his voice utterly condescending, "you're a smart girl. I'm sure you're good at math, so I'll put this in terms I'm sure you'll be able to understand. In this industry, we live, or die, based upon a simple mathematical formula. It takes a certain amount of money to operate the factories and maintain them. On top of that, costs of raw materials keep going up. Every year they go up. And, on top of that, it takes a tremendous amount of money to prepare for the future, to purchase new equipment. Now, let's say we raise wages even a fraction of what the unionists are talking about. And then if we add in the 'worker benefits' they say everyone must have, then that reduces the amount of money we have to keep the factories open, maintain everything, plan for the future, and so on. If that money is reduced significantly, what would happen to the factories? We'd have to make serious cuts somewhere. We might have to reduce our hours of operation to keep up with maintenance issues, which would mean a reduction in product and profit—which would then mean we'd have to let workers go. If we did all that, we could find ourselves with plenty of factories and nothing going on inside them. We'd be finished."

He stood again and walked back and forth in front of his window, looking out at the town of Muscatine. "No," he said, emphatically, "talking to the unionists will only lead to disaster. I appreciate your candor. But you just don't understand the way it is. That isn't your fault. We're all taught by the Good Book that life is a precious gift, one that is to be earned by hard work and dedication. We all believe that. Well, all apparently except the unionists. Many of them don't even believe in God. No wonder they always seem to want something for nothing. That's the real problem. Until they understand that what they want has to be earned, no amount of talk is going to do anyone a bit of good."

It was clear his views were firm and his mind was made up. It was also clear that, like Mattie on her side of the fence, he believed everything he was saying was true. I couldn't imagine two better representatives of the opposing views could be found than Mattie and Mr. Blanton. They were fire and ice. At the same time, they were both what was wrong in the industry. Stubbornness. Plain, simple, unbending stubbornness. I could just picture the two of them sitting down to discuss their views. They would make the Civil War look civil. As I sat there, I kept going back to my earlier thoughts. Someone, sometime, was going to have to step forward. For now, sadly, I couldn't imagine which side that would be.

Mr. Blanton came over and put his arm around me. "There, there," he said, genuine concern in his voice. "What you said took a lot of guts to share. I'm proud of you. And Sam Henry would be, too. You just don't have the experience we have with this. I'm afraid we're going to have a fight. Hopefully, we'll get you enough money before that happens so that you can get to school and get that teaching certificate you want so badly. Trust me—you'll be lucky to be out of here."

He laughed. "In some ways—and on some days—I wish I could be going with you!"

He didn't mean it, but it was kind of him to say. His heart was here in the industry he had helped create. He was a man searching for answers, and they were not going to come easily.

Mr. Blanton sat back down as his face turned serious again. I knew what was coming next. I had hoped the events of the weekend would distract him enough that he would forget about it, but I was to have no such luck.

"So, what have you learned for me?" he asked, leaning his chair back against the wall.

After the events of the past several days, I wasn't sure I wanted anything more to do with my work as his patsy. My heart wasn't into it. I could see there was plenty of finger pointing that could be done on all sides. There were some workers who were taking every opportunity to steal from or hurt the factory, but now I was thinking maybe they felt they were right and just in what they were doing. Stealing was stealing any way it was sliced, but maybe it was like Mattie had said—that they were just taking what was rightfully theirs. And maybe they were trying to damage the factory in hopes that changes would have to be made to improve the safety and health issues that were everywhere. This was all swimming in my mind when Mr. Blanton asked me to share what I'd learned. I didn't want to lie to him. At the same time, it didn't feel right blowing the whistle on people I really didn't know well enough to judge. So, I did the only thing I could think of to do. I said just enough to satisfy him—but not enough to feel an overwhelming sense of guilt. In short, I filtered the information the same way the sorting machines separated the shells. I offered information I thought he already knew, so I wasn't worried that my words would cause anyone to lose a job.

I began, "Mr. Blanton, I was able to find out some things that really shocked me, and they may be quite upsetting to you. Most of this I found out from listening in on conversations during the breaks."

Here I paused, leaned forward, and said in almost a whisper, "I wasn't able to get specific names, but I learned that workers are somehow sneaking buttons home to sew to cards. I don't know how they get them, but many of these cards are from other factories. That means they are earning money by selling your buttons to other companies, who then sell them as their own. In other words, your buttons are being sold in stores on other companies' cards."

"I knew it!" he shouted, pounding his fist on his desk. "Dirty, lousy thieves. I had no proof, but I still knew it. I'll find a way to put a stop to that. You can bet on it. My buttons being sold by someone else—that won't happen any more!"

"Go on," he said, completely wound up. "What else?"

"I don't have all the details about this, but it looks like when supervisors switch from piece-work to weight scales to determine daily wages, the blank cutters slip heavy steel washers into the buckets to make it appear they've done more work than they really have."

"That'll stop," he said, his voice rising and his face even more agitated. "Try to let a man earn a decent wage, and what happens? I'll tell you what happens. Give an inch, and they want the whole nine yards."

I quickly interrupted. "Mr. Blanton, only a few workers here are doing these things. Most are completely loyal to you. So, please don't think this is something too many are involved in. It doesn't seem to be that many."

"But you didn't get any names? That right?"

"I'm sorry," I said. "I just picked this up from what I heard others saying. If you want, I'll see if I can find out who's involved."

I had no intention of following through with this, but I knew it was what he wanted to hear. "Please do," he said. "We've got to weed out these people. We've got enough trouble already without this going on right in front of our faces."

He added, "Any talk about people wanting to join up with the union? Did you hear anything—anything at all?"

The truth was I hadn't heard very much. Well, at least not at work, which is what he asked about. I told him, with a straight face, that I had not.

He looked at his watch. Our meeting was just about finished, so I spoke quickly. I tried telling myself it was only a white lie, but I knew, deep down, it wasn't. It was a true lie—and now also something I felt was a necessity, for my own sake. Mattie had been right that I needed to know more about what the workers in all the stations were going through. At the rate I was going, it would be months before I'd get through the factory. So, I needed to speed this up.

"Sir, I have a favor to ask of you. My uncle's new building is coming along much faster than anyone expected, which is good news. At the same time, I know I'm here in part to help him out, to learn as much as I can about the different stations. Do you think it might be possible for me to move from station to station a little more quickly than what we originally planned? I'll understand if we can't. I was just thinking that if I move along more quickly I'd still get a fine overview, only in less time. I'd appreciate it, and I know my uncle would too."

"Nothing's too good for Sam Henry," he said, already looking past me to Miss Fitch, who was now standing in the doorway. "Your appointment is here," Miss Fitch said to him, quietly.

"I'll be right out," he replied. Then, turning to me, he added, "We'll work that out. Don't you worry. I'm sorry, but I've another meeting now, so you'll have to excuse me. We'll meet again next week. And thank you," he said, smiling again, "for everything you're doing for me."

I left the office and walked as quickly as I could to my station. Today, continuing with my reverse-process learning, I was to learn the skill and art of packing the buttons into the shipping boxes, and I was already terribly late.

When I got to the station door, I paused before entering. My thoughts were more jumbled than ever but I came to a decision right on the spot: My days as a spy were over. I still wanted to learn all that I could about every station in the factory, but my motivation had now changed. I wanted to learn this information for myself. The reasons for this were still more than a tad foggy to me, but I knew I needed this knowledge. I had to have this knowledge. After my talks with Mattie and Mr. Blanton, I was sure of the winds of change. Which direction they blew and to what effect I had no clue, but I wanted to prepare myself for whatever was to come.

....

CHAPTER 14

THE NEXT WEEK FLEW BY, while the tension in the factory became as thick as the foul Muscatine air. News of Saturday night's violence spread quickly, and as it did, more and more workers who had been on the fence about whether to listen to the union seemed to be sliding further that direction. The conversations during breaks in the workday were now focused almost solely on how the people could attend meetings and become involved without suffering severe consequences. It was clear to me now the owners had been wrong to instigate the violence at the gathering by the bridge. They had unwittingly created a rallying point, one that seemed likely to haunt them for a long time to come.

This was magnified because Howard Zey had disappeared during the commotion, and no one had seen hide nor hair of him since. There were all sorts of theories, ranging from he simply feared for his life and lit out for points unknown to speculation he was quietly taken from town, murdered, and dumped somewhere along the river. The latter theory was discussed the most, and each time I heard a version of it, more and more speculation was provided—to the point it started sounding like fact. For all any of us knew, it could have been fact. That was enough to fan the flames of the union talk.

At the same time, a type of what could only be called a "game"—and a very dangerous one at that—started gaining momentum. Some workers started to hint they were affiliated somehow with the emerging union but always stopped short of coming out and directly saying so. They were like little children playing with fire, and if some weren't careful, I thought, they were going to be consumed by the flames. It became typical in the small groups that formed during breaks that someone would suddenly say something like, "Well, at the last meeting, we all decided..."—and then cut the sentence off, look around, and pretend as if he had forgotten where he was and shouldn't have said anything at all. Then the person would laugh and say, "Oops! Better watch what I say!"

Everyone around would join in the laughter and nod knowingly. The person who caused the greatest stir in this game was Obadiah Krukshank, a short, greasy looking man in the blank cutting station. One day during the lunch break, he said loud enough for everyone around him to hear, "I hear there's a meeting tonight on the bluff overlooking High Bridge. I think I'll...." He then smiled as he covered his mouth with his hand and pretended to look embarrassed. Just as those around him started laughing, a short woman from the polishing station drew everyone close, whispered, and everyone suddenly gasped and headed back to their stations. Later I found out that while Obadiah was just trying to be funny and didn't know it, there really was a meeting scheduled for that night in a store up on that same bluff. No one could say how many people heard Obadiah, so a message was sent to cancel the meeting in case the wrong ears had been listening.

I finally asked Mattie about this game, and she said she thought it was a clever idea, one that was spreading throughout all the factories in town. She said the owners were starting to come up with lists of those they suspected of being involved in union activity, and if everyone could be seen joking about this, then their lists would become useless because all names would be included.

"Tough to pick out one pig in a mudhole," she said, sounding very much like Viola. She had a point. The "game" being played would allow the real unionists to hide in plain sight. Mattie suggested the unionists might even have started the game to throw off suspicion from themselves. That sounded plausible. All I knew was I'd never be caught pretending to be part of the union. It wasn't my kind of game.

Mattie and I spent every night that week visiting Viola at the hospital. The doctor said she seemed to be generally improving, but her vision continued to be a concern. She was having frequent periods of blurred vision and dizziness. The doctor suspected these were related to the concussion, but he also said it would likely be a couple more weeks before anything would be known for sure. In the meantime, he wanted to keep her there for observation and treatment of her other injuries. Her arm, as it turned out, wasn't broken, but several of her ribs were, and it was still difficult for her to breathe without wincing. Her frequent nosebleeds continued, and these were now of great concern. We did our best each night to entertain her and take her mind off her pain. Mattie would bring the evening paper and read aloud to Viola, with great drama in her voice, the stories of the day's tragedies from around the country and world. Viola would much rather have read the stories to us, as she used to every night back at home, but with her vision as it was, she had no choice but to lie back and listen. We played card games like "Authors" and "Gin Rummy," but Mattie wasn't very discreet about her cheating, and on most nights Viola and I would grow disgusted with her and throw our cards up in the air out of frustration. More than once a nurse had to ask us to lower our voices so as not to bother the other patients.

Near the end of our nightly visits, Mattie would ask me to leave the room, so the two of them could have some private time together. I knew they were probably talking about news of the union, so I took no offense when I was asked to wait out in the lobby. Some nights after we got back home, she'd let me know a little of what they had talked about. Other nights, her lips remained tighter than a snare drum, which was quite an accomplishment for her. I never pressed her for details. I knew Mattie was waiting for me to settle on one or the other side of the fence, and until that time, both of us knew it would be best if we kept our talks about union issues to a minimum. One item she did share with me was that she had gone ahead and contacted Viola's uncle, so he knew of the situation. If need be, Mattie had said, Viola could be moved to his home for additional treatment. At the same time, it could be a place for her to hide out if that need arose.

The week at work provided plenty of food for thought for me. Mr. Blanton had sped up my "reverse order" work so much so that in a few days I had been able to see the workings of and participate in, at least in a small way, several other stations. Working backward from shipping and packing, I first experienced the smoothing and polishing stations. To put it mildly, I wasn't at all prepared for what I was to learn. Smoothing and polishing were among the most important steps along the process of creating a finished button, but they were also right up there with the most dangerous. It seemed incredibly and sadly ironic that those who made the buttons look so beautiful sacrificed their own appearance in order to do so.

In the process of smoothing and polishing, the buttons were placed into churns of sulfuric acid for exactly an hour. During that hour, the acid removed the top layers of dull finish on the buttons and started them on their way toward a beautiful sheen. Then, after the sulfuric acid had done its job, the buttons were transferred to still other drums containing hydrochloric acid. This second acid bath removed the rest of the impurities and finalized the process of bringing out both luster and color. Finally, the acids had to be removed from the buttons. This was accomplished through a process involving sawdust to soak up the dangerous liquid. After all traces of acid were removed, the buttons were ready to be moved to the packing station.

While the buttons at this point were quite beautiful to look at, the workers in this station were not. As cruel as that sounded the first time I shared the observation with Mattie, it was true—and horribly so.

Even though fans, both in the ceiling and in the side wall, provided some circulation, acid fumes clung to the heavy air in the room and, therefore, to the skin and lungs of the workers. Most workers appeared spotted, with large, irregularly shaped patches of different shades, from completely white all the way up to dark-brown, covering their arms and faces. These patches were particularly noticeable on the backs of their hands and just under their eyes. The backs of their hands, as a result of acid burns, were a ghostly white. The patches under their eyelids made their eyes appear darker and more intense. I noticed the men and women in this station didn't often look directly at each other. I couldn't tell if this was out of embarrassment related to their appearance or the fact that they seldom looked anywhere other than at what they were doing in that very instant because of the danger. Whatever it was, this station had an eerie and sad quality about it that I couldn't shake even after going home at night.

In addition to the outward signs, every person in this station had a low cough that sounded as if they were constantly clearing their throats. During breaks, nearly all would rush to a smoking area down the back stairwell and immediately light up pipes or self-rolled cigarettes. One day I asked why everyone smoked, and a veteran of the station, Helga Marsund, said it was well-known that tobacco smoke was healthy—and would coat the lungs and protect from the dreaded "acid cough" that had felled so many workers in the past. One afternoon during a break I was offered a cigarette, but I declined, reluctantly. That afternoon my breathing had seemed to be more difficult, so I was sorely tempted to give the tobacco a try. If I had been staying longer in that station, I definitely would have.

Others in the station talked of continual eye and ear infections and sore throats. They also had a yellowish border around their fingernails that wouldn't go away, even after vigorous scrubbing with the harshest of soaps. Most grew ill at least once a week with upset stomachs that made it difficult for them to hold down food. When these spells occurred, they enacted a plan to gain temporary relief that was so simple the supervisors never caught on. I certainly would not have understood what I was watching if Viola hadn't explained it to me one night at the hospital when I was talking with her about how sickly these poor people always seemed to be. In this same station, the drums of water and sawdust used to soak up the acids couldn't be reused and, therefore, had to be dumped regularly. Whenever anyone would feel a stomach spell coming on, he or she would be allowed by the others to jump in and take an extra turn carrying pails of the old water and sawdust down the back stairs to a small platform where they were placed in wagons tied up there. When the wagons were full of pails, those in the station took turns driving them to a section of woods down by the river where they could be dumped in the thick sand. Because nearly everyone in the station was dotted with the skin patches and looked so much alike, the supervisors never caught on that the person carrying the pails often switched places with the wagon driver, thus allowing the person nearly an extra hour of time out in the fresh air, time badly needed to regain at least a temporary semblance of health. I quickly grew truly sorry for those working in this station, but, a the same time, I discovered there was a long line of those waiting for a chance to work there because it carried an extra two dollars a week over most other stations in the factory. Was the extra two dollars worth it? Many thought so.

Then, toward the end of the week, again working backward, I moved to the facing and drilling stations. It was here I learned the value of what the workers called "vision and precision." That meant each worker needed to drill shapes and holes with remarkable precision at lightning pace. Speed was vitally important because these workers were paid by the piece. At the same time, they were penalized heavily for any buttons that split or cracked while they were working on them. It didn't seem fair to me, but every damaged button, regardless of how the damage occurred, resulted in a count of three buttons subtracted from the worker's daily final total. Quite often a button would become damaged not because of poor workmanship but because of a flaw in the button itself. That didn't matter. Every bad button came out of the worker's hide. And, with every bad button, the foulest words I'd ever heard before erupted from the mouths of those at the machines. At first I was shocked, but it didn't take long to tolerate those words under the circumstances. Just a few bad buttons a day could mean the difference between having an average day and a terrible day.

This station, too, had its own particular health and safety issues. I hadn't noticed it on my first walk-through with Mr. Blanton, but the floor in this area was covered with a half-inch layer of rough sawdust that the workers were careful not to disturb as they moved about. When the faces of the buttons were drilled down, small clouds of resulting shell dust would swirl like miniature tornadoes around the room. This got into the eyes and throats of the workers, making them blink almost constantly and fall into prolonged coughing fits. The shell dust eventually fell to the floor, where it was trapped in the sawdust. If it weren't for the protection provided by that sawdust, everyone in the station probably would have suffocated. I was at the station for just two days, but by the end of my time there, I had a cough that sounded like I had diptheria.

....

As the week passed, and through my work and observations at the different stations, I started understanding more about what those in sympathy with the union were striving for. Yet the working conditions at Blanton were heads and above better than at other factories. After what I had seen, if that were truly the case, then the other factories must have been on a par with Hades itself.

At the same time, I saw first-hand why the owners believed they needed to increase their profits. If they were going to use those profits to improve maintenance and purchase new equipment, both of which they believed would at the same time improve safety and health issues, then maybe the end did justify the means for them. On the other hand, if what Mattie said was true and the owners were going to do nothing more than line their own pockets with the money, that was a different kettle of fish entirely.

My experiences moved me beyond any question of who was wrong and who was right. What I could now see, more than ever, was that both parties were going to have to be willing to give some ground, or the walls would most certainly come crumbling down upon everyone.

It was time for workers and owners alike to sit together and at least listen to what the other had to say. That just made sense to me.

If it was true that pride came before a fall, both were looking right over the edge into the depths of a deep ravine. Would they both fall in—or would they sacrifice some pride in the name of self-preservation? Only time would tell.

〉〉〉〉〉 〉〉〉〉〉 〉〉〉〉〉 〉〉〉〉〉 〉〉〉〉〉

CHAPTER 15

AN UNEASY FEELING SWEPT OVER Mattie and me as the work week ended and Saturday night approached—but for very different reasons.

After what had happened the previous weekend, I was worried that more violence would erupt, and neither side seemed capable of withstanding much more of that. I suggested a visit to Viola at the hospital and then staying home to read the paper and relax. I didn't think it was wise to head down to Second Street in the current climate.

Mattie, on the other hand, said if the workers didn't partake of the reverie on the streets, that would signal to the owners the skirmish the week before had done its job and put their employees back in their places once again. According to Mattie, it was our duty to go out and have a good time. We owed it, she said, to every worker in Muscatine.

I didn't agree with her, but once Mattie got on her high horse about such things, she wasn't going to back down. I also didn't want her going out alone, so I reluctantly decided, against my better judgment, to tag along.

As soon as the whistle blew on Saturday, we met outside on the sidewalk and headed straight up the hill to see Viola. She appeared somewhat better and scolded us for wasting so much of our time coming to see her, especially on a Saturday night. Like Mattie, she wanted us to get downtown to enjoy the night. At the same time, she cautioned us to stay clear of any large crowds that formed. Viola was her own living cautionary tale, a fact not lost on us. As we stood there and looked at Viola while saying our goodbyes, I could tell Mattie and I were thinking the same thing:

There would be no crowds for us on this night.

When we left the hospital, Mattie turned to me and asked, "How about if we skip going home? It'll be faster if we just head back down toward the river and cross through Turner's Field to get to Second. I know we could use some freshening up, but I doubt this will be a night for romance."

"Thanks a million," I said, dryly. "I needed to hear that."

"Don't you worry about tonight. Everything will be fine. You'll see." Her voice was confident, but I had my doubts.

When we finally reached Second Street, the general atmosphere was what could have been described as friendly—but subdued. The vendors pushed their carts back and forth in front of us, but their barking was quieter than usual. The street was about half as crowded as it had been the previous Saturday night. The biggest difference, however, could be seen in the groups gathered along the sidewalks. All groups—from the barbershop quartets to the leering louts who seemed to live to embarrass women passing by—seemed half-heartedly going through the motions. At one point, when Mattie stepped into the street to get us a bag of peanuts from a vendor she knew, the right shoulder strap on her coverall snapped loose. This was seen by a group of loafers well into their pails of beer, yet they chose only to "Oooh" and "Ahhh"—and didn't even throw out crude catcalls. I was shocked by their restraint.

As soon as Mattie returned with the peanuts, I said, "This is spooky. Look over there at the vendor who does the shell game. Nobody's playing! Just what in the world is going on? This is like we've walked into a different world, like this is a Jules Verne story."

Mattie replied, "I told you it'd be different tonight, but this sure beats me. Looks to me like people are just plain scared."

From the river below, a low boat whistle echoed up the hill and down the street in front of us.

"Hear that?" Mattie asked. "The fact that we can hear it tells just how spooked this town is right now. On a normal Saturday night, I can't hear myself think here. Now we're all standing around and listening to boats going up and down the Mississippi."

She flagged down a lemonade cart and bought us two large bottles. Handing me one, she said, "Let's go back down by the bridge. I want to see something."

I didn't move. The bridge area seemed to me to be the one place we definitely needed to stay away from on this night. Another of my grandfather's old expressions came to me in that moment: "Why put your head in the lion's mouth if you don't have to?" As I looked at Mattie, I thought, "Why, indeed?"

Seeing my reluctance, she said, "Oh, don't worry. It's not what you think. I just want to check on something. If we see another big crowd down there, we'll turn around right away. I'm not stupid, you know."

"What do you want to check?" I asked, almost afraid of the answer.

"Never mind," she replied, grabbing my hand and pulling me behind her. "Just come along. It'll only take a couple of minutes."

We made our way through the streets with ease. There were still plenty of folks milling around, but all seemed strangely polite and respectful of others walking by. In an odd sort of way, this was unsettling to me. I never thought I'd miss the rowdy, raucous behavior, but I did—because of what it represented. And now, I was worried about what the lack of it represented. The life had been sucked out of the town.

We paused at the train depot just long enough for Mattie to clear her throat and say, "Stay close."

I started to ask what we were looking for when Mattie interrupted me and said, pulling me back toward the main entrance to the station, "Just as I thought. Take a look. Those are the Pinkerton men, all around the clearing."

"How can you tell?" I asked, ducking behind a luggage cart.

"See how they're dressed? Who else would be wearing a derby and a vest in this heat."

I inched forward to get a better view, but Mattie pulled me back. "Know why they wear that kind of hat?" she added, quietly. "So if gunfire breaks out they won't shoot each other."

She got on tiptoes and peeked over the end of the cart toward the river.

"That clinches it," she said, shaking her head. "The clammers are armed to the teeth and spread all along the opening to their camp. Look for yourself."

She was right. A picket line was still there, composed of grim-faced men and women wielding rakes, shovels, and picks. Two Pinkerton men were leaning against a tree not more than a hundred feet from the entrance staring intently at the clammers.

"I don't know how they do it," Mattie said, "but the clammers always know when trouble's brewing. They must have a sixth sense or something."

Suddenly, from behind us, a voice bellowed, "Can I help you, ladies?"

Mattie and I both jerked around at the same time. There before us stood a very tall man wearing a brown vest and matching derby.

My breath caught as he added, "I have to ask what you are doing here."

"And what business is it of yours?" Mattie shouted back at him. "You scared the you-know-what out of us. You should be ashamed of yourself—sneaking up on us like that."

He stepped back, tipped his hat lightly, and said, this time more evenly, "I'm terribly sorry I startled you. I apologize."

As he leisurely put his hands in his pockets, his left arm brushed his vest just enough to the side to reveal a shiny silver badge. If I had any doubts before, they were immediately erased. He was definitely what Mattie and Viola called a "Pink."

From all I had heard, I fully expected him to have everything but horns on his head. He didn't. As a matter of fact, he looked very much like a businessman one would see in one of the nicer stores uptown. His face was youthful, tanned. His eyes were a soft light blue. His shoes were also well-shined and buffed. He even wore a high school ring. Nothing about this man spelled the devil. The sharp contrast from what I was expecting was so pronounced I could barely believe what I was seeing.

Turning to me, he said, "I suggest you leave and head back toward town."

Nothing in his voice was ugly or commanding. His tone was that of someone genuinely concerned about our safety.

"And why would that be?" Mattie shot back, anger rising in her voice. "It's a free country, isn't it?"

He smiled, pulled his hands from his pockets, and crossed his arms. "Last time I checked," he said. "I just think it's best for you not to be around here tonight."

"And why is that?" Mattie shouted, inching closer to him. "Are you afraid? You afraid there's going to be more…trouble?"

The smile quickly left his face. He then looked back and forth from Mattie to me as he studied us closely.

"I see you're both wearing coveralls," he said, looking directly at Mattie. "You work in a factory around here?"

"And what if we do?" Mattie said, her voice rising again. "What business is it of yours?"

The two stared at each other, neither blinking.

As the tension mounted, I had to do something.

"We were just leaving," I said, taking hold of Mattie's arm. "Thank you for your concern. That was very kind of you."

Mattie looked at me as if I'd lost my mind. I didn't give her a chance to respond.

"We're late for our dinner," I said to Mattie, also making sure he heard me. "I'm actually quite hungry. We better run along."

Off to our right another man with vest and derby approached, this one much older. "What's the problem here?" he asked no one in particular.

"Nothing, sir," the younger man replied. "I was just giving

directions to these ladies. They're lost. They were looking for that restaurant where we ate the other night. The one with the great pie."

Then, turning to face us, he added, "It's right up that way, ladies. Just around the corner to your right once you come to Third Street. You can't miss it."

Just before turning to face the other man, he smiled again and winked at me. The older man pulled out his watch and said, "Time for you to take Charley's place up on the bridge. Say good-bye to your lady friends."

He tipped his hat once again, turned, and started walking away. Mattie was just about to say something to the older man when I jerked roughly on her arm and said, gruffly, "This way, Sis. Try to keep up with me this time."

As soon as we were out of earshot, I turned to Mattie and started scolding her. "What was that all about? You had no cause to speak to that man that way. I don't care who he is."

"But he's a Pinkerton!" Mattie shouted back at me. "A dirty, rotten Pink!"

I added, curtly, "I didn't see any pitchfork in his hands. What makes you so sure all of them are bad men? He seemed polite and kind to me. And don't you start with that 'Shake the straw out of your hair' bologna again. I'm tired of that."

"Why you poor little fool," Mattie said, her voice easing up. "You don't have a clue what these men have done before, do you? Are you really that naive? You gussy up to one handsome man wearing a badge, and all of a sudden all the rest of them are just like him, right?"

"I didn't say or mean that," I replied, as calmly as I could. "Who told you these men are as evil as you've been saying they are. Do you have any proof?"

"Proof?" Mattie said, laughing softly. "Everybody knows they are nothing more than hired guns. Thugs. Union breakers deluxe. Ask anybody. And what about Viola? It might have been them, you know."

"In other words," I said, "you've only heard these things from others, right? You don't have any direct proof, right?"

I shouldn't have been so rough on her, but I was tired of all the rumor and innuendo hovering over the town. I was tired—and hungry.

"Let's just go home," I finally said, "I'm sorry. I'm just tired, and I know you are, too. Can we just go, please?"

Mattie frowned and replied, "Ever since we were kids you always found a silver lining in everything, so I guess I can't be too mad at you. You're not going to change, and neither am I. Viola's always saying you can't paint over zebra stripes—or something like that."

I smiled weakly.

She should have stopped there, but she just had to get in the last word as we started back up to Second Street.

Pointing back behind us, she added, "When push comes to shove, the Pinks will fight to the last man for the owners. You'll see."

I was going to reserve judgment about the Pinkerton men. It was likely their reputation was augmented considerably by those in the union. It was becoming more and more clear to me both sides were very good at creating common enemies for people to rally behind. In conflicts like this, truth and fiction were often mighty hard to separate.

At the same time, I realized something else as I turned around and took one last look at those standing across the entrance to the clamming camp.

Muscatine was a powder keg, and it wasn't going to take much for anyone to light the fuse.

〉〉〉〉〉 〉〉〉〉〉 〉〉〉〉〉 〉〉〉〉〉 〉〉〉〉〉〉

CHAPTER 16

OUR EXPERIENCE WITH THE PINKERTON men upset Mattie to the point all she wanted to do was go home and settle in with the evening paper. If I went with her, I'd be stuck listening all night long to diatribes about how horrible the Pinks were and how much a strong union could do for the workers of Muscatine. Not in the mood for more of her lectures, I told her I thought I'd go back up to Second Street to do some more people-watching, and I'd get home early. She cautioned me again about the need to keep extra vigil—and to stay away from crowds—and we went our separate ways.

When I reached Second Street, the atmosphere wasn't nearly as restrained as it had been just a short while earlier. The sidewalks were finally starting to fill, and vendor carts were again spread out the length of the street. One of the barbershop quartets even offered up a song for those passing by, although their volume was decidedly lowered. For my people-watching, I decided a fine vantage point would be directly across from one of the more popular shell games, evidenced by a long line of what Mattie called "suckers" waiting for their chance to step to the table. The rapid movement of the shells and the steady and loud banter of the man switching them around fascinated me. The line of those waiting to play grew longer with every passing minute.

Those playing the game were an interesting mix. One woman who must have been seventy if a day closed her eyes the whole time the shells were moved around—and finally pointed to the shell on the far right. It was not the shell with the button, and the woman shrugged her shoulders and started to leave. The man running the game stopped her and asked why she kept her eyes closed. She replied, "I can't see good no more, so I thought I'd try to 'hear' where that dad-blasted button would end up." Upon hearing her response, the man running the game looked dumbstruck, while those waiting in line laughed heartily. The next person in line, a short man with a rich shock of red hair shooting all directions, rocked his head back and forth, trying to match the movements of the shell he believed to be hiding the button. When the shells stopped moving, he was absolutely convinced he knew the correct shell and, while rubbing his neck, let out a high-pitched "Yahoo!" His excitement didn't last long; he, too, chose the wrong shell.

My favorite player, a woman near thirty, stepped to the table after four or five others had tried their luck. She had on black coveralls, the uniform of women in the logging industry. What struck me most about her were her arms, which were thick and muscular. Her shirtsleeves were cut off at the shoulder, which allowed all around her a clear view of her ample physique. After watching the shells deftly swept around and around, she chose the one in the middle. When it was lifted and she saw the button wasn't there, she reached over, grabbed the man running the game by his arms, lifted him over a foot off the ground, and shook him violently back and forth. All of us watching were too stunned to move or do anything else. After a few seconds, she gently lowered him to the ground, brushed off the front of his vest, and said, "I oughta marry you. You'd always have money, and I see now I could sure whoop you if I needed to. Whadda ya say?"

The man, still stunned, quickly replied, "I'd say I better get out of here!" He started to bolt, but the woman grabbed the back of his trousers and held him firm as his feet ran in place. All around burst into laughter at the sight of this poor little man trying to make good his escape. The woman, laughing with the rest of us, finally shouted, "You can stop your tusslin' now. You're too scrawny for me. I think I'll throw you back."

Turning to face those behind her, she added, "He's all yours.

I've had enough of him."

As soon as she was out of earshot, the man finally spoke. "Somebody please step up and play—and help me take my mind off that ... that ...."

"Future wife of yours!" someone called out from the back of the line.

The laughter grew again as the poor man shook his head and called out, "Next! Who's next?"

I watched the game long enough to see someone won about every fifth game, and when this happened, the button seemed to alternate being under the outside shells. My family was definitely not a gambling lot, and it was drilled into me from a very young age that games of chance were to be avoided, but I suddenly felt an urge to try my luck with this game. A dime was a lot of money to risk, but I hadn't spent a red cent on anything but necessities since arriving in Muscatine. "One time won't hurt," I said to myself as I moved toward the rear of the line.

I positioned myself just to the side of the line so I could see whether those playing won or lost. After a man won—he chose the shell on the outside to the right—I counted those in front of me, and there were nine. I needed to be the tenth in line, so I told the man behind me he could go ahead—that I needed more time to get ready. The man gave me an odd look, but he did step in front. If all went according to plan, the button would be under the shell on the far right when it was my turn at the table.

I was anxiously waiting my turn and turning my dime over and over between my thumb and index finger when a hand tapped me on the shoulder and someone whispered, "Well, I thought you were smarter than that."

At first I thought it was just someone being fresh, but when I turned around, my breath caught. Gaston stood before me, arms folded, eyes squinted.

His hair was pulled back, a tattered straw hat hid most of his face, and he had on a loose-fitting pair of logging coveralls and knee-high boots.

"What are you...?" was all I could manage to say before he grabbed my arm and pulled me out of the line.

"Come with me," he said, gently. "Let's go where we can talk."

He led me onto a small porch at the front of a dry goods store across the street, where we sat on the railing, our backs facing the street. From this perch, those walking by couldn't see our faces.

"You should know better than that," he scolded me. "That game's fixed, and everybody knows it."

Then, a smile betraying him, he added, "Everyone but you and those geniuses in line with you."

"For your information," I replied, "I was going to win that game. Before you so unceremoniously and rudely pulled me away, I watched and learned. I know how that game can be won."

"I'm sure you do," he said, laughing loudly. "Sometime I want to see that. That'd be a sight for sure. But for now, I can show you a better time than standing there and trying to match wits with a man playing with shells. If you're up to it, I'd like to show you how people really have fun—and it won't cost you a dime. Interested?"

"What would we do?" I asked. "Where would we go?"

"You ask too many questions," he replied. "From what I've just seen, looks like you're a gambling woman, so I challenge you to take a gamble now. You've got to lose those coveralls, so go home and put on your simplest, plainest dress. And I mean plain. Pull your hair back and tie it. Put on some shoes you can walk in without falling down. Then, meet me at the entrance of the camp. Don't go in. Wait up by the road. I'll come get you when I see you. We'll meet in, say, about twenty minutes. That should be enough time for both of us. I've got to shed these clothes, too."

He placed his hand gently against my cheek and asked, "You willing to take a gamble?"

I had no idea what he had in mind, but I was intrigued. I should have said "no," but said "yes" almost instantly.

"I'll probably end up regretting this, but I'll do it," I said, moving off the railing. "I can be there in twenty minutes."

"Then one more thing," he said, moving toward me. "Let me see that dime you had in your hand."

I handed it to him, and he studied it a few seconds before placing it in his pocket.

"I'm keeping it," he said, smiling again. "To teach you a lesson."

"And what lesson would that be?" I asked, playfully trying to retrieve the dime.

"You'll see," he said, quickly stepping back from me. "You can tell me later—after tonight."

As he left the porch, he drew his hat tighter and lowered it so his face was hidden.

"Be on time," he said, not turning again to face me. Then he walked quickly away.

I was only a couple of blocks from home, but twenty minutes wasn't much time. I'd have to hurry. Thankfully, when I reached Chestnut, the crowd had thinned to just a few people sitting along the sidewalks, so I was able to make good time.

Mattie was reading at the kitchen table when I came in. I walked past her as quickly as I could, retrieved a dress from the pantry, and got into the bathroom before she even looked up. I dressed, tied back my hair, and was on my way back to the front door in what must have been record time. Mattie was still focused on the paper as I slipped by her.

"Be back in a while," I said. "Don't wait up."

"Where are you...?" was all Mattie could manage before I stepped out to the landing and closed the door behind me. I was already at the bottom of the steps when I saw her open the door. She yelled something, but I was already too far away to hear what it was.

I wasn't anxious to have a repeat of the earlier experience with the Pinkerton men, so I hurried directly down to and across Front Street and headed east across the open field there. I knew this would take me just below the entrance to the camp. Save for a pack of dogs that darted by, the field was deserted.

As I neared the camp, I came to a long row of trees, finally stopping where I could see several clammers still on guard at the entrance. I didn't want to walk out and stand directly in the open—for fear the Pinkertons would see me—so I hid myself the best I could behind a leafy branch and watched for Gaston to show himself.

A few long minutes later I saw him standing near the middle of the group. He was looking straight ahead as if he expected to see me by the road. I tried waving to get his attention, but the tree hid me too well. I finally decided to take a chance and ran across the field toward him. As I did, he spotted me and walked quickly out to meet me.

"You're right on time," he said. "I'm glad you came."

"I took the round-about way here. Those men up by the road are Pinkertons, and I don't know about you, but I've already had my fill of them. If you don't mind, let's not stand around here."

"My sentiments exactly," he replied. "Come with me. This way."

"To the camp?" I asked as he took my hand and led me in that direction.

"To the camp," he said. "Relax. I want you to enjoy this."

Memories of my first night there were still plenty fresh, so I half expected to be pelted with something as we walked through the guards. He must have sensed my concern because he repeated "Relax" as we made our way down the dirt path between the rows of tents.

About halfway to the river, another path ran off to the left between two of the larger tents. As soon as we started up the path, I heard music off in the distance. A minute or so later we stepped through a dense row of pine trees. I could barely believe my eyes. There, in a large clearing ringed by a circle of pines like those we'd just come through, must have been the majority of those from the camp. All were seated on the ground around a stage positioned in the area closest to the river. A few turned and waved to Gaston, but most others were riveted to the stage.

"Let's sit over here," Gaston said, pointing to our right. "I see an extra blanket we can use."

I was so transfixed by the music I barely heard him. A young girl about eleven or twelve was singing, in what could be only be described as an elegant voice, the dreamy words of "Tell It to the Clouds," one of the more popular new songs of the previous spring. Men playing, from her left to her right, a guitar, a banjo, a violin, and a mouth harp accompanied her. Beautiful notes streamed from their instruments. At one point in the song, the girl stopped singing and stepped back as the guitar and banjo players took over. They were in perfect rhythm, each complementing the other wonderfully. Finally, the girl stepped again to the front of the stage and sang the last chorus, her voice filling the night sky.

As the song ended, she curtsied, then turned and pointed to the musicians. The crowd erupted into cheers. "Surprised?" Gaston asked, leaning close so I could hear him over the thunderous applause.

"Who are they?" I asked. "They're wonderful."

"They're no good, rotten clammers—that's who they are," he said, playfully. "All of them. The one with the violin—he's in charge of boat repairs. The banjo picker—he's responsible for keeping everyone supplied with crowfoot hooks. The harp player is our wagon mender. And that little girl can remove more clam meat from shells in a day than anyone else here. That's the truth. Oh—and I forgot the guitar player. He's our camp doctor. He's 'river taught.' I'd trust him with my life more than I would with any of those croakers up at Bellevue Hospital."

"I'm still in shock, not by the fact they're clammers, but by how beautiful they sound. What a voice she has. And the man playing the violin—I've never heard anything like him before in my life."

While Gaston told me more about the musicians, a tall gangly man wearing coveralls torn through at both knees climbed on stage and motioned for everyone to settle down. "It's time for our sing-along!" his voice boomed.

The words were barely out of his mouth when the applause started up again. He did his best to quiet the crowd. "Hold your horses. If you recall, we nearly had a train wreck last Saturday night."

Many in the crowd laughed at this last remark. Some turned and stared at Gaston, who immediately covered his eyes and lowered his head, obviously embarrassed. He suddenly shouted out, "It wasn't my fault. Somebody pointed at me—I won't mention any names—and I just started singing. How'd I know it wasn't my turn?"

More laughter followed as the man on stage continued, "I reckon we'll forgive you—this time. But I'm going to be keeping my eye on you tonight."

Then, facing the group once again, he added, "Everybody watch me tonight. I'll point to your section when it's your turn. Watch me close—and don't get lost. Now, go ahead and split into your groups."

At that point, a good dozen or so men stood throughout the crowd and walked around while designating which people belonged to which group. When one of these men got close to us, he shouted, "All of you here—you're together."

We glanced around to make sure we understood our affiliation. When the man on stage seemed satisfied, he spoke again. "Tonight we're going to try our best at "She'll Be Comin' Round the Mountain." I'll point to a group to start us off. Then, and you better pay attention so you'll know when to jump in, I'm going to point to the next group—and they better pick it up fast right from there. I might even point to two groups at once, and if I do, you better both sing out right away. No lags tonight. And get the words right this week. Okay—that's enough jabber. Everybody, ready. Here we go."

He pointed to the group seated right below him, and they started right in, singing the first part of the song quite loudly— "She'll be comin' round the mountain when she comes." Their voices weren't all together, but it wasn't all that bad. Then, suddenly, he pointed to another group, and they picked up the words quite smoothly in mid-verse. He finally pointed to our group, and we jumped in as best we could, but not all of us were singing the same words. Especially Gaston. He either didn't know the song or wasn't paying attention. When he should have been singing "We'll be havin' chicken and dumplings when she comes," he was singing "We'll be havin' cheeses and pumpkins when she comes." Several members of our group rolled their eyes and sang a little louder, trying to cover up Gaston's off-kilter lyrics. I kept singing, but my eyes were on Gaston and not on our conductor, who had already pointed to another group. That left me singing by myself—and the only member of my group still standing. When I realized this, I plopped to the ground as quickly as I could, to the roar and laughter of the crowd. Gaston applauded softly and bowed toward me. I tore up a handful of grass and threw it at him.

The song went on and on, but so many groups sang at the wrong time, and with the wrong lyrics, it wasn't long before I wasn't sure we were still singing the same song. The conductor finally threw up his hands and shouted, "That's enough. I've had it. I'll never do this again. You people are terrible!"

Everyone applauded again, this time for our frustrated conductor. Gaston came back and sat beside me. "He says that every Saturday night," he said. "Always acts like he's having a fit, but he really loves this. Oh, he's our preacher—and a darn good one."

"This is fun," I said. "You do this every Saturday?"

Gaston replied, "You're surprised clammers can have fun, too. Am I right?"

The truth was, I really was surprised. I had heard nothing but work associated with life in the camp. It had never occurred to me they took time to rest up and enjoy themselves—and especially not like this.

I started to tell Gaston I was ashamed of myself, but he didn't give me a chance to finish. He cut me off and said, "I felt the same way until I finally got to know them. They're a hardworking people. At the same time, they're full of love and joy. Most people never get to see this side. My life has been touched, blessed, by my time here. Truth be told, I don't think I ever understood just how beautiful life can be until they took me in. It's true most are poor as church mice if it's money we're talking about. But, if we're talking about a lust for living and a joy for the simple pleasures of life, they're as rich as any on the earth."

He took my hand and held it gently in his. Our eyes met, and for an instant I thought he was going to kiss me. I started closing my eyes, but the booming voice of the conductor rang out again.

"I don't know about the rest of you, but I think I could have a bite to eat. Are you hungry?"

"Yes!" rang out as everyone quickly stood up.

"Then what are we waiting for?" the conductor shouted. "Just try to beat me to the table!"

At his urging, everyone moved toward an opening in the trees behind the stage. As we left the clearing, I just couldn't resist. Shaking my head, I said, "Well, you're a man of many talents, but singing certainly isn't one of them."

"I may not have the best voice in the world," he shot back, "but I've got volume. My mother said a person had to have one or the other."

We laughed as he again took my hand in his.

"You definitely do have the volume, but where in the world did you come up with those lyrics? You weren't even close most of the time. 'Cheeses and pumpkins'? What was that?"

"Did you hear anybody say anything to me about that?" he asked, grinning.

He had a point. He was Gunboat Gaston, and nobody— except maybe a preacher—would take a chance offering him any criticism. I had noticed most around us politely acknowledged his presence, but none came over to talk to him. They didn't exactly seem afraid of him, but they did keep their distance. He was an enigma, not just to me, but apparently to everyone else as well. Still, as I stood next to him, I felt security of a type I'd never felt before.

It wasn't long before it was our turn to step through the trees and into another open area, this one back along the river. There, in front of us, two rows of tables ran from where we stood all the way down to the dock at the river's edge. At each table women from the camp arranged serving dishes, plates, bowls, and cups. For the first time since I arrived in Muscatine, the air wasn't filled with the smell of industry. It had been replaced by a tantalizing medley of food aromas.

"Now I've seen it all!" I said, stopping in my tracks and pointing ahead.

"Not yet you haven't. But give it a few minutes. I hope you haven't had your supper yet because we're about to feast."

"My mother always said a woman should eat like a bird in front of a man, but if you'll forgive me, tonight I'm starved—and plan to eat like a horse."

"And I'll be right there at the trough with you," he said, urging me forward.

"Where did all this come from?" I asked when we came to the first table.

"It's a tradition that plays out every other Saturday night. Everyone in the camp brings something to share. I supplied a fair amount of catfish I caught this morning. Others do what they can do. There's only one rule: you can have as much as you want, but don't waste anything. I always found that reasonable enough. When you're ready, grab a plate and help yourself."

I didn't know where to start. There were platters of catfish steaks, heaping piles of fry cake, bowls of corn and beans, and pots of a rich vegetable stew. The next table had buckets of lemonade, pots of coffee, and a drink called "Marble Rock," which Gaston described as a cross between tea and homemade root beer.

I took a piece of catfish and some fry cake. Then, along the edge of the plate, I created small mounds of corn and beans. The lemonade looked good, so I got a cup of that. Gaston, much to my surprise, took only a small portion of the catfish and the fry cake—and a cup of Marble Rock.

We found some soft grass on a ridge about halfway down the row of tables and sat down to eat. From there we could see the others filling their plates and moving off to find their own areas to sit. The atmosphere grew very quiet as all began enjoying their food. Mine was delicious, especially the beans, which were as tender as any I'd ever put in my mouth. The fry bread had a smoky flavor, which complimented the catfish, which had been cooked over a fire of applewood. Gaston suggested I try his Marble Rock, so I took a small sip. It was delicious—and very much like the root beer my grandmother made back in Grandview.

Mindful of Gaston's words that we not waste any of our food, I ate everything on my plate. I could have eaten more, but I thought, under the circumstances, that would have been rude since I hadn't brought anything to share. After Gaston's last bite, he gathered our plates and cups and took them to two women who were responsible for the cleanup.

After he returned, I said, "This was a feast. Thank you for allowing me to share in this."

"I'm glad you enjoyed it. Everyone works hard to put on a nice spread, and it's usually mouthwatering. Tonight was no exception. It would be nice if we could eat like this all the time, but get-togethers like this let everyone dream of what all might have one day."

After pausing briefly, he turned toward me and asked, "Has tonight changed your thinking about the camp—and those who live here?"

"Yes, it has. I don't know how the reputation was made, but I can tell you from today on I'll do my part to see it's erased. These are wonderful people. I see that now, and I'm ashamed I ever thought otherwise."

Gaston didn't say anything in response. Instead, we both lay back on the grass and looked at the sky. It was a beautiful evening. The light was fading quickly, and stars were just starting to appear. Below us and off to our right, a large fire illuminated the area by the dock. The crackle and pop of wood thrown into the flames drew our attention.

"My favorite part of these gatherings is coming up," he said, finally. "We'll need to get closer to the fire to hear everything. It's so nice here I hate to move, but we better—before all the good spots are taken."

"There's more?"

"At the end of these gatherings, one of the old-timers, Josiah Marshand, always tells a story for the children. They do enjoy his tales, but I think it's the parents who like them best of all, especially because they usually end up having a lesson for their sons and daughters. Let's get closer."

I reluctantly left the soft grass, but Gaston was so excited about listening to the tale I wanted to be nearby to see his reaction. We walked over and joined several others sitting on a big log behind the last row of children.

We had just settled in when Josiah Marshand walked between the children and the fire. The glow of the flames cast eerie shadows on his face and his long, white beard, and several of the children gasped.

"Listen careful to me tonight," he began. "What I'm gonna tell you could mean the difference between you growing up to a ripe old age—or you being eaten up alive!"

The children gasped again as he quickly continued. "You see that bridge over yonder? High Bridge? I helped build that there bridge. Way nigh on to back before all you was born. I was just a youngin' myself back in them days, but I still put in a man's work. Well, one week in the late summer that bridge was put up, my back got to hurtin' me something fierce from toting them bricks that make the wall across the sides. Backbreaking work it was. I was so stove up I couldn't straighten myself to save my soul. So, know what I did? Me and three other fellas decided we'd take a cool swim in the river one day after our work was done. We allowed it'd probably soothe our backs enough we could at least sleep without being curled up like a snake. Well, one of them boys was called Toby Snitch. He was bravest and strongest of us all. Why, he could swim across the river here with a hog on his back if he had a notion to. Old Toby Snitch was off swimming by hisself out in the current while the rest of us sorta lolly-gagged in the shallows. We sudden-like heard him screamin' bloody murder, but when we turned to look, he was gone. All we seen was bubbles comin' up to the top. Never saw him again. Next day, wouldn't ya know one of them other boys swam out to the current, and we heard him screamin' just before he was gone. Never saw him again either. By this time we're plumb scared, but everyone else made such fun of us for being fraidy cats we went out again next day—and same thing happened again. This time, it was old Samson Smithers—gone—just like that!"

He snapped his fingers and lunged toward the children in the front row. All screamed and scooted as far back as they could.

"Day after that I was curious about what happened to them boys, so I swum out myself in that current. Before I knowed it, something' took me by the legs and started pullin' me under. I didn't know what it was, but I knowed I better do somethin' quick-like or I'd be a goner. I pulled out this here jackknife and started stabbin' down by my legs. Like this. Well, I seen blood come up, and next thing I know I'm raised up out of the water. I look down, and know what I seen? I was in the mouth of the biggest, meanest catfish ever was! Had a mouth big as that washtub there, and I was swallowed right in it. That fish's eyes were black like pitch and big as saucers. But he takes one good look at my jackknife, and know what he done? He spits me out. Guess I wasn't tasty enough—like them other boys."

Here he leaned closer to the children and said, his voice gentler, "They say that same catfish is still out there—just waitin' for somebody to eat up. And it's said he favors littleuns best of all. Like you. So, if I was you, I'd never, never swim out there without your ma or pa with ya. If you do, you'll likely as sure end up like poor old Toby Snitch. You don't want that, do ya?"

While the children's eyes widened and they shook their heads, one of the fathers snuck up behind them and quickly placed a blanket over the heads of a group right in front. They screamed and shrieked while squirming to free themselves from the blanket. Once free, each darted a different direction while everyone else burst into laughter.

Josiah Marshand bowed deeply and waved to all before he turned and walked down toward the dock. As he did, he received a rousing round of applause.

Gaston smiled as the applause died down. "I love his tales— and he has a lot of them."

I said, smiling, "And now I'm not sure I'll ever put a toe in the water ever again. I'm not so sure that was just an old man's tale. I always heard there were giant catfish that lived around the bridge pierings."

"I've seen some strange things out on the water, things I couldn't explain if I had to. Who knows? Maybe there really are fish that big. There are a lot of things we just don't know and will never be able to understand."

"That's true," I replied. "But I learned quite a great deal tonight."

"What would that be?" he asked.

"I learned a lot about these people. I never understood them at all."

Then, looking into his eyes, I added, "I also learned some-thing else tonight, something I'd like to do."

"And that would be?"

"It would be this," I said, leaning over and kissing him gently.

"You learn quickly," he said when our lips parted. "What else did you learn?"

Clearing my throat, I replied, "I think that's enough educa-tion for now."

He laughed and said, "You're probably right. There's quite an audience here, and a good portion of them are looking right at us. I certainly don't want my reputation spoiled."

"Your reputation? What about mine?"

"You're not the one with the gunboat, remember?"

Then, playfully, he added, "We better leave before they start thinking we actually like each other. That wouldn't do me any good."

"Very funny—and very flattering to me."

"Well, it's like that old expression—'You are the company you keep'—or something like that.

"Then I'm in trouble, too," I replied.

"You are—but in the meantime, think you could stand listening to a little more music? The guitar player has a pretty fair voice, and he usually strums a tune or two before everyone heads off to bed. He plays back over in the clearing on the stage. Interested?"

I was. I was interested in hearing more music, but I was more interested in something else—the man standing before me.

"Shall we?" he asked.

"We shall," I replied, locking my arm with his. "I'll do my best not to wreck your reputation."

As we walked to the clearing, I wasn't too worried about my reputation. But, my changing views on a lot of other reputations had my thoughts in a whirl. Factory owners, workers, Pinks, clammers, Gaston—who were these people?

....

CHAPTER 17

A STRANGE AND EERIE CALM settled over Muscatine through the early days of the next week. Part of this, no doubt, was a result of the steady rain that had pelted down for three straight days.

But it wasn't just the weather causing the change. People were keeping low, playing a waiting game to see which group, owners or workers, would make the next move.

At Blanton, the workers were unusually quiet and reserved as they performed their jobs. I had been moved again, this time to the rounding and grinding stations. Whereas I was once very popular because others felt I might be able to help get them jobs at my uncle's new factory, that same fact was now, apparently, working against me. I was neither part of the workforce nor the ownership. I was neither fish nor fowl. At this time of unrest, I was an unknown and dangerous commodity.

Those in the grinding station were polite enough, but none went out of their way to be friendly. By contrast, the rounders, those who removed the bark from the rough side of the button blank, were, at times, downright mean. One afternoon after a short break, I returned to find a leg had been removed from my chair, which meant I had to work bending over the rest of the afternoon. The backache I had that evening was like nothing I'd ever experienced before, which I imagined was what was intended. They didn't know me, and they didn't trust me. That was a bad combination.

Our evening routines also changed significantly. For reasons the doctors couldn't explain, Viola had taken a terrible turn for the worse. She was no longer allowed visitors while they tried to discover the reasons for the decline, so we stopped going by the hospital on our way home each evening. Mattie wrote another letter to Viola's uncle and urged him to come see her and, if need be, take her back home with him so she could at least be with family during her recovery.

I gave up my walks to the library after supper because they had become too risky. Mattie, on the other hand and much to my surprise, started taking walks, but I was never invited along. She always said she was just getting in some exercise so she wouldn't have to jump a size if she ever had occasion to wear a dress again. I knew that wasn't the reason, but I played along. One night Mattie came back from her walk positively ashen and sat down on the divan without so much as a "Howdy." I asked her what was wrong, but she didn't reply. Instead, she went to her room and closed the door gently behind her. A minute later I heard her quietly sobbing. I thought about going in to comfort her, but she had been so out of sorts lately I thought a good cry might actually be good for her—whatever the cause. Other evenings we occupied ourselves by devouring the paper. Mattie's previous habit had been to peek quickly at the stories and ads, but she now studied every column, as if searching for something.

One evening I interrupted her reading by saying, "Not much news today."

She replied calmly, evenly, "It's when you see the news we can start to worry."

It was then I realized she was reading to make sure there weren't stories about the union or the owners. It was an odd concept to me—reading to make sure stories weren't there. However, I understood what she meant, and deep down I knew she was right.

We also started playing a shell game every night to see which of us would get to start with the front page and main section of the paper. Like me, Mattie had become fascinated by the shell games that took place on Second Street. She brought home from work three small mucket shells and a medium-sized pearl she had "found" at the factory. After a couple nights of practice, she tried out her new skill on me. If I could point out which shell hid the pearl, I got first dibs on the front page. She was pretty good at moving the shells swiftly and in random patterns around the table, but I was still able to point out the shell with the pearl about half the time, which annoyed her to no end. Still, it was a fun and light-hearted way to settle in to read the paper after a long day of work.

Much to her dismay, one evening after what I thought was an extra long period of her moving the shells round and round, I found the pearl immediately. Mattie threw the front section of the paper to me and said, sarcastically, "I hope it's all just society news. That's all you deserve."

I laughed, unfolded the paper, and scanned the front page. My laughter stopped immediately when my eyes caught a story at the bottom titled "Another Unfortunate Accident?"

"Tobias Robinson, supervisor at Riverview Button Company, was found dead last night, the victim of an apparent buggy accident. Police reported finding Mr. Robinson's buggy overturned in a ditch just east of the entrance to Weed Park. His body was found some twenty feet from the buggy. Early reports are his neck had been broken. The police officers at the scene said they had no comment when questioned whether this was just another unfortunate accident or a matter worthy of additional investigation. Mr. Robinson's is the fifth in what appears to be a string of tragic accidents reported in the past week in the Muscatine area...."

I lowered the paper and chose my words carefully. "Mattie, there's a story here about a man named Robinson who was a supervisor at Riverview. They think he died last night when his buggy crashed. Suppose he's any relation to the Robinson that Viola asked me to mention to you?"

Mattie had been reading the comics section. In one swift motion she dropped her paper and snatched the front page from me. She quickly read the story, her lips moving rapidly at every word. When she finished, she threw the paper back to me, picked up the comics, and started reading again, as if nothing had happened.

"Well?" I asked.

"I think it's the same man," she replied softly, still not looking at me. I could tell by the way she was avoiding my eyes she had more to add.

I pressed her for more information. "Do you think it was an accident? Or, do you think...."

"I think you should shut up and read your paper," she said, curtly.

"Now just wait one minute," I said, my voice rising. "This man's dead, and if I had anything to do with...."

"You didn't," Mattie said, cutting me off. She lowered her paper, turned toward me, and added, "I'm sure it was an accident, but I'll also say this about it. It couldn't have happened to a nicer guy. He was a blackmailer—everybody knew it—and he was good at it. Good riddance to bad trash."

She turned back to her paper.

"That's a terrible thing to say about anybody," I said. "That's not very Christian, and you know it."

"Maybe not, but it's true," she replied. "And where he's going, my Christian beliefs aren't going to help him any. That's for sure."

We sat quietly for a long minute—until I just had to ask, "It was probably an accident, right?"

Mattie handed me her section of the paper, grabbed mine, and then said, coldly, "It doesn't matter to me."

"It matters to me," I shot back.

"And that's the difference between us, Pearl."

With that, she went out onto the landing and closed the door behind her, leaving me alone with my thoughts, and the paper stacked in my lap.

I suddenly felt sick. Very sick. I threw the paper to the floor, leaned back, folded my arms, and shut my eyes tightly. I tried and tried to convince myself Robinson's death really had been an accident and that I'd had absolutely nothing to do with it in any way, shape, or form.

In the end, the convincing didn't come....

....

It was in the midst of this, on the Friday of that week, Mattie and I briefly met at the edge of the street outside the factory as soon as the end-of-the-day work whistle blew. We were running short of food again, so Mattie decided to walk down past the markets on Chestnut to see if something might "follow her home." I still didn't approve of Mattie helping herself to food she continued to insist was rightfully ours. I started to scold her, but just the thought of more slumgully stew started my stomach to churning. So, I just shook my head disapprovingly and wagged my finger at her. She responded by screwing up her face and giving me the most sarcastic smile I'd ever seen before saying, "You're a big hypocrite, Pearl. You eat everything I bring home, right?"

I was a hypocrite, and a hungry hypocrite. I would set my principles aside, at least for the short haul, so I could keep up enough energy to work. I wondered just how many others in town were setting aside their principles as well. From what I had seen at Blanton, I guessed the number, sadly, was pretty high.

"Oh, go on. Get out of here," I said, finally, still trying to make my voice sound disapproving—but not too much so.

I also quickly added, "I'm going to go stop by the hospital before I head home and see if I can get the nurse to give a letter to Viola—in case she's up to reading it. I don't want her to think we've abandoned her. I'm also going to see if I can find out how she's really doing. I've got some room on the last page of my letter. Anything you want me to say from you?"

"Just tell her I love her and miss her," Mattie replied. Then, without another word to me, she turned and started down the hill. Some would have found that to be rude behavior, but this was just Mattie and a typical exit for her.

"Goodbye, then!" I shouted. Mattie didn't even turn around.

The most direct way to the hospital was the street running north up the long hill from the factory. The bricks in that street were irregularly placed, with large gaps between some, making it difficult to navigate for both wagons and foot traffic. Mattie had taken me on one of her famous shortcuts the previous week so we could avoid the street. Her shortcut seemed longer in terms of distance, but it shaved off a good five minutes of actual walking time. The shortcut involved taking a dirt path through a thick patch of woods running from the hospital all the way down the hilly slope to Front Street. The only break in the woods was a small wagon road about halfway up the hill that ran at an angle to the loading area on the east side of the hospital. Other than that small opening, the path was sealed off on both sides by thick rows of cedar and ash trees. The path was dusty, but it was also smooth and not nearly as steep as the street. On this day, I was feeling more tired than usual. All I had done most of the day was watch how different designs were "faced" into the buttons. Still, I was exhausted. I rolled up the bottoms of my coveralls so they wouldn't get so dusty and headed straight for the path.

The long shadows of the early evening had already started falling across the path, so I had to be careful where each footstep landed. At one point, my left foot got caught under a root, and I almost fell. Quickly regaining my balance, I forged ahead.

When I got to the clearing where the wagon path intersected, I paused to catch my breath and rub my ankle, which I had twisted slightly when I got tangled with the root. From the right, I caught sight of a large, covered milk wagon pulled by two sorrels slowly making its way toward me as it rattled down the hill. It was driven by an older gentleman wearing a tattered stovepipe hat and a well-worn and soiled duster riding coat.

As he neared me, he suddenly shouted to his horses, "Whoa there! Hold up now!"

The wagon stopped short, and he almost fell off his seat. He then called out, "Ruby, Maude—settle down! Hold fast!"

After wrapping the reins tightly around the handbrake, he jumped down and examined a foot on the horse closest to me.

He looked at me and said, "Just look at this. Ruby's got a bad shoe. I knew that blacksmith didn't know what he was doin'."

He paused and asked, "Missy, do me a favor and come over her and hold back on that handbrake while I take a closer look at this. The road's too steep here. If it slips forward, the wagon will take off and we'll be mashed flatter than a flapjack."

"I'd be glad to," I said, stepping forward. "I've driven teams before, so I know what to do."

I reached up and pushed back on the handbrake with all my strength. "Go ahead," I said. "I've got a good grip."

"You're too kind," he said, kneeling down and lifting the horse's foot up again. "Bless you."

I was concentrating on the brake, but I sensed some movement behind me. Before I could turn around, someone grabbed my arm and jerked me down roughly from the wagon step. There was no chance to move or say anything before someone else placed a cloth sack over my head and grabbed hold of my other arm, wrenching it behind my back.

Cold fear swept over me as the sack turned daylight to darkness. Still stunned, I felt my wrists being tied together behind me as my legs buckled. I could hear voices, but they were muffled and seemed far away. I felt my ankles being drawn together and rope winding around them. I finally fought through the fear long enough to try kicking my legs and swinging my shoulders wildly back and forth to try to break free. As I did, a large hand clasped down over the bag and pressed powerfully against my nose and mouth, cutting off my wind. I jerked my body as violently as I could, but with my legs and hands bound tight, all I could do was shake until I was so dizzy I started falling backward.

Suddenly, I felt myself being picked up and carried. I stopped struggling and strained to hear where I was being taken. After only a few yards, I heard a sharp creak and then the thud of wood against wood, and I was tossed into what must have been the back of the wagon, where I was propped up on a seat of some type. As I was being moved, I could hear the sobs of at least two others. Panic set in again, and I tried lunging forward, hoping to free myself from the wagon and roll down the hill where someone would see me and offer help.

At that moment a hand grabbed the back of my hair through the bag and pushed me back down on the seat. A sharp pain shot all the way down my neck. I started to bolt up again when something hard was pressed to my temple. A long and then a short click followed.

Through the bag I could hear a man say, angrily, as he pressed in even harder at my temple, "Know what this is? It's what's going to happen to you if you don't settle down. The rules are simple. If you scream, you die. If you get loose, you die."

Here he grabbed my hair again and added, "If you jump from the wagon, you'll be dead before you hit the ground. I promise you that. Nod if you understand me."

I was so scared I couldn't move. He pulled violently on my hair and shouted, "Nod—or die!"

I must have nodded because he let go and pushed me harshly again back against the seat.

"And the rest of you," he shouted. "If you cry and I can hear it outside the wagon, I'll come back and kill you all. You understand?"

I could hear him walk heavily to the front of the wagon bed, bang on the back of the seat, and yell, "We're ready. Let's get going!"

The wagon started moving slowly down the hill. As it did, I could hear soft crying and whimpering from across the wagon. I didn't know how many others were there, but it sounded like at least two or three.

My mind raced, but my thoughts wouldn't settle. I had to try something to escape, but I couldn't see anything. I couldn't even tell for sure if the man with the revolver was still with us. I raised my shoulder against the side of my cheek and tried to push up the bag over my head. I had it high enough so I could see feet tied together directly across from me. I tilted my head as far to the side as I could, and two more sets of feet came into view. There didn't appear to be anyone seated on my side of the wagon.

Just then one of the wheels dropped into a rut, and we were all thrown sideways. I crashed to the floor. Raising my head, I could see out of the bag enough to confirm there were four of us being held captive. The man with the gun was no longer with us.

"Quick! Someone help me," I half whispered as loud as I dared. "One of you get down here on the floor. If we get back to back, we can try to untie our hands. Please! Somebody try!" I implored.

"But he said he'd kill us!" a voice called back.

"He'll probably kill us—or worse—anyway, so we don't have anything to lose. We've got to give it a try."

"No!" was the reply. The voice cracked, full of terror.

"We've got to try," I repeated again. "We've got to!"

"I'll do it," a different voice said, one full of tears. "What do you want me to do?"

"Good," I said. "Follow my voice. Get down here on the floor and try to roll so your back is to me. When you do, keep feeling with your hands until you find mine. Then I'll try to untie you— and you untie me. We don't have much time. I'm going to roll now so that my back will be to you. Hurry!"

I heard her fall to the floor and roll so that she was facing away from me. I pressed back against her and felt her hands about halfway up my back.

"You have to get lower," I whispered. "And I'll try to move up a little. Let's try it."

We both scooted slowly until I could feel her hands pressed against mine. "Right there!" I whispered again. "Wriggle your hands back and forth so I can find where the rope's tied."

I quickly used my fingers to trace the rope around her wrists. Nothing. I tried again, this time tugging at the rope as I went. I was about to give up hope when, suddenly, there it was—the knot.

"I found it!" I said. "Hold still."

Using my thumb and index finger on both hands I picked at the knot as hard as I could. My fingernail on my left index finger snapped, and the pain radiated down through my wrist. I clenched my fist for just a few seconds, then started again. The knot finally started to loosen. I poked a finger through it and tugged upward as the knot opened wider.

"Almost there," I said. "Let your hands go completely limp now. Don't pull at all. If you do, you'll tighten the knot again. Then, when I say 'Go,' pull as hard as you can and your hands should come free. Get ready."

Slipping both my index fingers through the hole in the knot, I slowly eased them apart. The knot gave way.

"Okay—now! Pull!" I said, my fingers still curled around the rope.

As she moved, I felt the rope slacken. Her hands were free!

I could tell the first thing she did was remove the bag from over her head because her next words were no longer muffled. "Roll on your stomach," she said to me. "It'll be easier to untie you."

She then sat up and said," I'm going to get my feet loose first. Then I'll get to you."

"No!" I said, rolling back toward her. "Untie my hands first in case he...."

I didn't get to finish the sentence. There was a high-pitched scream followed closely by a loud thwack. The scream stopped instantly. So did the wagon. In a matter of seconds, I could tell the back gate of the wagon was being lowered, and at least two sets of shoes jumped in.

"What did you do?" a voice asked, sternly, gruffly.

"She got loose and saw my face. For all I know, she could have seen all of us. I didn't have any choice. I had to."

"You idiot!" another voice called out. "You have a simple job. What part of tying them up don't you understand? Are you really that useless?"

"But she saw my face!" he said again, drawing out each word.

"What about her?" one of the others asked while kicking me in the side.

"I don't think she saw anything. She's hog-tied pretty good. Must have fallen over when we hit that rut."

The next thing I knew I was pulled up and thrown back into the seat. A hand grabbed me around the neck as I was asked, "What about it? Did you see anything?"

I shook my head that I had not. "That's good," the voice continued. "By now you know why."

Moving away from me the same voiced asked, "What are we going to do about her? Is she dead?"

"Can't tell. She's bleeding pretty bad."

"Then get down there and feel for a pulse! Do I have to do everything for you?"

"Right away," the man responded. I heard his knee hit the wagon bed as he knelt down.

A few seconds later he said, "Her heart's beating. She's still kickin' I guess."

His words were followed by low sobs from the others who were tied up.

One of the men said, "I don't want to hear your tears. You be quiet as mice or you're next."

He then added, "We've got to get rid of this one soon as we can. We need to figure out what to do."

I heard each step down from the wagon. The rear gate shut tightly behind them. Their voices trailed off.

I had been numb the whole time they were in the wagon. I felt so weak, like I had lost control of all my muscles. I was so scared my mouth had gone dry. When I was sure the men couldn't hear me, I asked, quietly, "Can any of you tell what happened to her? How bad is she?"

The girl closest to the front of the wagon said, coldly, "This is your fault. You did this. She's probably dead—and they'll probably kill us all now."

"I'm sorry," I said. "We had to try. Who knows what they're going to do to us. We just had to...."

A tide of emotion caught up with me. In an instant, tears were streaming down my cheeks. I sat back and let my head fall against the side of the wagon. I wanted to say more to her, to try to explain, to try to make her understand. Instead, tears rolled down the side of my nose and fell to my lips.

Just then, the wagon started moving again.

....

We traveled for what seemed about a quarter of an hour. I could tell from the steady clopping of horse hooves we were off the dirt trail and on cobblestone streets as we continued downhill. At one point, the wagon lunged suddenly to the right, and I nearly fell from my seat again. It was difficult to keep concentration, but I tried to follow the wagon's movements. If I was close at all, we were just west of town and very close to the river since I could hear an occasional boat whistle off in the near distance.

The others were still sobbing softly when I heard the driver call the horses to a halt. As soon as we had stopped, the back gate was pulled down, and I saw the toes of dark brown boots that were scuffed and cracked, but the sides were slick with polish.

"Let's go. Stand up," a voice called out to us. "Right now!"

I stood and was immediately pushed toward the back of the wagon, where someone grabbed me around the waist, lifted me out, slung me over his shoulder, and started carrying me like a sack of potatoes. After what had happened earlier, I decided not to fight it.

He carried me into what seemed to be a large, empty building judging from the echo that rang out with each of his footsteps.

"Here we go," he said as he lowered me onto a chair. "You sit here and don't move. Hear me?"

I nodded.

Other footsteps soon followed, and I could hear chair legs scooting across the floor. It wasn't long before a voice said, "We're going to uncover your faces now. Don't be afraid."

"No!—don't do it! Please, no!" one of the other girls cried out. "I don't want to see your faces."

"Now, now," the man responded, his voice full of mock tenderness. "You won't have to worry about that. You'll see."

The sack was suddenly pulled off my head. As my eyes adjusted to the dim light, I could make out six men standing about a dozen feet in front of us—and two more behind. They all had black hoods with thin eye slits and a small mouth opening pulled down over their faces.

They were wearing suits and vests.

I looked quickly at the other two girls who were seated in chairs off to my right. Their faces had also been uncovered. I didn't recognize them. They both appeared just a couple of years older than I. Both wore coveralls. The injured girl was nowhere to be seen.

The tallest of the men stepped forward and addressed us. His voice was soft, almost gentle.

"You're wondering why you're here. I have no doubt you're frightened."

He then walked slowly to a small table just to his left. He picked up a clamming knife with a thin, curved blade. With his other hand, he picked up a small glass bottle.

Turning back toward us, he continued, "Girls, we're going to have a little talk. It needn't take very long. Why, you could be home and having your supper in just a few minutes. But that will depend on you. It will depend on your part of the conversation. My part is going to be very short and direct. Your responses can be the same. At least I hope for your sake they are."

Moving very close to the girl farthest from me, he held up the clamming knife and continued, "I've seen men use these to take the meat out of hundreds of shells in less than an hour. Scoops it right out."

He paused and flicked his wrist to imitate the motion before adding, "I've also seen these used to carve out a woman's cheek like it was going through butter."

He snapped his fingers and continued, "All of you are so pretty. I'd hate to see an accident happen to any of you. But it could happen."

The glass bottle in his other hand was then held up so that we could all see it. "And guess what's in this?" he asked, emphasizing each word. "This is acid, but much more powerful than what you use in your factories. It's dangerous, but I don't think I need to tell you that. I think you already know it. Acid burns are one of the most common injuries these days. Acid can accidentally get on a beautiful woman's face, and the scars run deep. From beautiful to ugly forever, in a matter of seconds. That's a terrible tragedy, and one I hope never happens to any of you."

A couple of the men laughed as he walked back to the table. He put down the knife and bottle and turned again to face us. There was a chair at the end of the table, and he moved it out front and sat down. As soon as he was settled, he spoke again.

Turning to the other men, he said, "Boys, I want you to step forward when I call for you—so that these nice, young women can see what you've got to show them."

"First," he continued, "I've seen women branded on their faces."

Here he motioned for one of the men to step forward. As he did, he waved a branding iron above his head.

"And I've heard of whippings so bad the girls were scarred for life."

Another man stepped forward and cracked a whip on the floor just in front of us. We all flinched and arched back.

"Some have been sold into slavery. The women are taken to other countries, and they never see their families again."

The man standing on the far right threw three sets of leg shackles at our feet.

"You get the idea," he said, standing and walking closer to us. "Now we're going to have a little conversation. It's going to go like this. I'm going to ask you some questions, and you are going to give me honest answers. It can be that simple, and as I said before, it can be very quick. I don't like to have my time wasted. And you know who in my experience wastes time the most? Bad little girls. I see nothing but good girls in front of me, so I think we'll all be having our suppers before night falls."

He then moved over and stood right in front of me. "Let's start the conversation by you telling me your name."

I was so scared my mouth wouldn't move. I tried. Nothing would come out.

"Oh, no!" he said, his voice turning pure evil. "Don't tell me you're going to waste my time. Not you!"

I managed to croak out, "My voice.... I'm dry...water... please...."

He snapped his fingers and pointed to one of the men. He came over, opened a metal flask, and poured some of its contents into my mouth. It was whiskey. I coughed and gagged. The man in charge walked over and lifted my head back up.

"Let's try this again," he said, more seriously this time. "What's your name?"

"Pearl. Pearl McGill," I said, my tongue and throat still burning.

"That's better," he said, smiling sickly. "Now Pearl—where do you work?"

"Blanton," I said, feeling dizzy and faint.

The room started turning blurry as he continued, "And what do you do there?"

Before I had time to think about it, the words were out of my mouth. "I'm working for my uncle."

"And who's your uncle?" he asked, a surprised look appeared on is face.

I struggled for the words, finally able to say, "Sam Henry McGill."

"Don't lie to me," he said, his voice rising. "I happen to know who owns that factory, and it sure isn't any Sam Henry McGill, is it?"

A wave of nausea hit me as more of the whiskey rose in my throat. "No. My uncle owns a button company in Grandview. I'm learning the business to help him start a new factory there. Mr. Blanton is a family friend. He and my uncle put me to work. It's complicated."

The man lightly placed his hand on my shoulder and asked, again softly, "And they wanted you to join the union too, right? Tell me about that."

"My uncle hates unionists. So does Mr. Blanton."

I was becoming dizzier and dizzier. My words suddenly started sounding like they were coming from a long way off. I tilted my head back several times and said, "Please.... Closer. I want to tell you...."

He lowered his head close to my lips, and I added, whispering, "You can ask Mr. Blanton. I tell him when I hear what the unionists are doing. That's my job. Please. Ask him. He'll tell you."

I couldn't continue. I was wringing wet from sweat, and yet I suddenly felt very cold.

The man snapped his fingers again. The next thing I knew I was carried to a room on the other side of the building. Once inside, I was plopped down onto another chair. It wasn't long before the leader came in.

"Tell me again, young lady. And I want the truth. Are you telling me you're working directly for Mr. Blanton?"

"I am."

I paused a long time before deciding to continue, "I'm....I'm a spy—I mean an informer—for Mr. Blanton. I tell him what's going on in the factory. I report to him every week, every Monday. You can ask him. He'll tell you."

My heart was pounding, and I heard a ringing in my ears. I was on the verge of blacking out when he asked, "What have you told him? Tell me."

"It's not my place to tell you. You'll need to ask him. He made me promise not to speak to anyone about this. He meant it."

Here he paused and studied my face closely before

continuing, "Where do you live? What's the address?"

I told him, and he grew more serious, his voice lowering this time, "You better be telling me the truth about yourself. I'm going to check on it. If you're lying, you'll be dead within the week. That's not a threat. It's a promise."

"I'm not lying," I said, mustering up as much strength as I could. "Do all the checking you want. I'm not going anywhere."

We sat in silence a minute before I asked, "What about the girl in the wagon? What about those two out there?"

"Not your concern," he replied. "We'll take care of them in our own special way. Don't you give them another thought."

I knew I shouldn't ask, but had to. "If they heard me tell you.... What then?"

"That's something you won't have to worry about. I promise you that. Just go on about your business and forget you were ever here. *Forget* you were ever here. I hope my meaning's clear."

It was.

He bent down to untie my hands and ankles. "You were just at the wrong place at the wrong time. All we saw were your coveralls. These days, they might as well be flags."

"What happens now?" I asked, rubbing circulation back into my legs and wrists.

"We get you out of here. But it has to look good for the other girls...just in case they're allowed to...."

He stopped, smiled, and continued, deadly serious, "I'm going to call a couple of men in. I want you to pretend you're unconscious. They'll carry you outside. I've got a man out there who will see you home to the address you gave me. It better be right."

He paused, and continued, "Don't be frightened by what I say to them. I might as well take advantage of you ending up here. Maybe I can use you to loosen up the tongues of the others. I'll give it a try."

After looking at his watch, he said, "Time for you to go. I'm still going to be checking up on you. We'll talk again one day, either way this ends up."

With that, he called in two men and quickly let them in on the plan. As they picked me up, I went limp and closed my eyes, not before catching a glimpse of a high school ring on the hand of one of the men. They carried me out of the room and started for the main entrance. The leader called after them, "Weigh her down and dump her in the river. That's what happens to bad little girls."

My eyes opened just enough to see the girl on the far right throw up on her coveralls.

Once outside, I did exactly the same.

....

CHAPTER 18

MY LEGS WERE SO WEAK I couldn't have walked half a block without collapsing, so it was a good thing I was taken home in a buggy. The driver of the rig, a short, pudgy man with a black derby cocked severely to the side, never spoke a word the whole way back. I was so frightened and my mouth was so dry, I couldn't speak. The only sounds I noticed were the sharp, steady clomps of the horse's hooves. When we finally arrived at the foot of our steps, he got out and offered a hand to help me down. I gladly took it. As I slowly and deliberately started climbing the steps, I turned to see him jotting something in a small notebook. His eyes followed me all the way up to the door.

Mattie was reading the paper on the divan when I entered.

"It's about time you showed up," she said, not looking up. "I bet the fruit is brown by now. Probably have to just throw it out. And if that stew cooks any more...."

Her words trailed off as she finally looked over to me. The front of my coveralls was coated with a mixture of vomit and blood. My wrists were still bleeding where the rope had cut into them.

"What in the world happened to you?" Mattie asked, jumping up and flinging the paper to the side. "Are you okay?"

"Oh, Mattie," I cried, rushing to her and hugging her as tightly as I could. The tears poured out in a flood of both relief and anguish. I sobbed and shook as she slowly stroked my hair and tried comforting me. I caught a word now and then, but I buried my face tightly against her neck and missed most of what she was saying. I held to her for several minutes, neither of us moving an inch.

She finally pushed me back to arm's length and asked, this time her voice commanding, "It's time to talk. Let's hear all about it now."

"I have to sit down," I said, nearly falling as I moved toward one of the kitchen chairs. Mattie put her arm around me and helped me to the table. Once seated, I put my face in my hands and the tears came again.

Mattie reached over, pulled my hands down, and said, "Talk to me. It'll do you good."

Once I gained enough composure to begin, my words came in steady bursts, punctuated only by brief pauses to wipe my eyes and nose. As I relayed the events, Mattie just sat there, starting blankly at me. The only time she showed any emotion at all was when I described what the men were wearing. She raised her eyebrows and nodded.

I didn't know how much of what I was relaying made any sense. I stuttered and stammered my way through as many details as I could, but my throat was so dry my voice kept giving out. At one point I bolted to the bathroom and was sick again. When I returned, Mattie was waiting for me with a cool rag. She also brought a bowl of cool water to the table and gently washed the blood from my wrists as I continued.

It wasn't until I reached the point of telling why I had been let go that I realized I needed to stop and go no farther. Mattie still didn't know anything about my work for Mr. Blanton, and this definitely wasn't the time to talk about it. I simply looked at the floor and fell silent.

At that point, Mattie suddenly shouted, "Do you need any more proof than this!"

"Proof of what?" I asked, startled by her outburst.

"You're kidding, right?" She stared at me coldly and continued, "Proof of which side is right... and just. If you don't see it now after what just happened to you, then you never will. Never."

"What I saw was brutality. Senseless brutality."

When I didn't say more, Mattie threw up her hands and

practically screamed, "You're a fool! The worst kind of fool—a blind fool!"

My emotions were still twisted, taunt. Her last shouts were the last straw for me.

"No, you listen to me for a minute!" I shouted back at her. "Now it's my turn."

I was ready to go on the attack, but just as quickly as the anger had welled up, I realized this wasn't the time. I wanted to say I'd already seen plenty on both sides—stealing and sabotage on one, and cruelty and brutality on the other. I knew that would only make matters worse—that Mattie would say the workers did what they did because they were helping themselves to what was rightfully theirs. And I knew what she'd say about the owners. Her mind was made up, and nothing I could do or say would change that. For Mattie, there were no shades of gray.

As I sat there, one thought kept racing through my mind. What happened to me didn't mean the owners were wrong in their overall concerns and beliefs, but it did show me just how wrong they were in trying to resolve their problems with violence. But, did right and wrong really even matter at this point? A sad and pitiful lack of communication was the main culprit for what was taking place around us. Without that, nothing would change. Life would go on for all on the edge of a very high and narrow cliff, one with loose, unstable footing. One false step would mean a fall with disastrous results. What troubled me most was the knowledge that neither side seemed smart enough to realize if one party died, the other would soon follow. The industry couldn't survive without a dedicated workforce, and the workers couldn't survive without continued expansion and development by the owners. This seemed to be lost completely on everyone. What happened to me on this night made me realize the importance of communication more than ever before. Right? Wrong? Both were false trails. Both were red herrings at this point. The word everyone should have been focusing on all along was buried in suspicion, fear, and hate—and that word was *understanding.* Understanding of each other. Understanding of needs and purpose.

It would take epic communication for this to be achieved, but it had to be, and soon, or the area round the edge of the cliff would surely crumble and everything would be lost. This much I knew, and the knowledge made me angry, angry at the hard-headedness and downright stupidity of it all. If everyone would just talk and truly listen to what was said, the real stink hovering over Muscatine would float away with the wind. But until that time, what could be done? What could I do? The questions made my stomach churn. I ran to the bathroom and was sick again.

This time when I returned to the table, Mattie didn't lay into me. Instead, she moved her chair next to mine, put her arm around me, and said, gently, "I'm glad you're fine. Glad you weren't...."

She paused, and I thought I detected her voice wavering slightly. It shocked me. Mattie—our rock—showing any sign of tender emotion was something I never thought I'd live to see. She was tough as shoe tacks, and I had grown to expect nothing less. To see her like this brought back my tears.

After several minutes, she pulled back from me and said, "We'll get through this. It'll be fine."

I wanted to believe her, but for now, I had nothing but doubts.

....

Sleep was hard coming and fitful when it finally did arrive. Several times I woke up thinking about what had happened to me the night before, and each time I found myself covered with perspiration. The heat was so oppressive we had opened every window before retiring, but there was no breeze at all. The combination of the heat and lack of air movement made my sheet cling to me.

I had finally fallen into a deep sleep when Mattie nudged me to get up. In the short haul, it didn't really matter what had happened to me. We still needed to get to work, still needed the payday waiting for us. We hardly spoke as we dressed and then ate a quick bite of breakfast. There wasn't much left to say.

Our walk to the factory was equally silent. We took Mattie's shortcut again, and as we did I looked up the hill toward where I had been taken hostage. The morning sun reflected softly off the leaves of the trees there, so I had to shield my eyes. In the beauty of the early morning, it was difficult to believe such an ugly experience had started there.

When we reached the sidewalk going up to the factory, I turned to Mattie and broke the silence. "Mattie, what's going to happen? What's going to happen to us?"

She responded quickly, almost as if she had been expecting my questions. "You remember how I always said to give up all hope when you enter this building? Not any more. Change is coming, and soon."

Her voice was calm but firm. As we entered the door, she turned and said, "And it starts right now. See you tonight. We'll walk home together."

Before I could reply, she was headed down the hallway.

Thankfully, the workday went quickly enough. Because one of the workers in the shell sorting station had broken a hand trying to dislodge a large, irregularly shaped shell that had gotten stuck between the rollers, I was asked to step in and fill the gap in the process. It was mindless work. We shoveled shells from large piles behind us onto a small platform at the head of the rollers. Others then used long-handled rakes to push them onto the rollers, where they slid and bounced along until a gap of sufficient size allowed them to fall into buckets placed strategically below. Other than the need to remove the occasional stuck shell, there wasn't much more to be done. This station, for me, was "mindless but physical"—with double emphasis on the physical. After about an hour my shoulders throbbed, but we had to keep moving at a brisk pace to make a dent in the large piles of shells constantly being rebuilt behind us as wagons brought them to the factory.

My co-workers in this station were a breed of their own. I had expected men would be doing most of the shoveling, but women outnumbered the men three to one. These women were short, squat, and incredibly strong, and they were the bosses in this station. They gave the command when the pace needed to be changed or a stuck shell needed to be removed from the rollers. The men never spoke, not a peep, all morning long. During break times, men and women went their separate ways. The women allowed me to sit with them during the breaks, but I kept my mouth shut and just listened to them. The talk was the rising price of food in Muscatine. Wages were not keeping up with the increased cost, and they all agreed something had to be done—but they didn't know what. Several theories were offered, ranging from ways to stretch out the food they did have over several meals to ways they could, in Mattie's terms, "find" food for their families. It was soon clear I wasn't the only one anxious about what the future might bring. I knew "misery loves company," but I felt better after listening to them put into words many of my own thoughts.

What affected me most was watching the children do their work. When the buckets below the rollers filled, the children came and dragged them to the next station, the soaking tanks. I felt so sorry for them. Their clothes were sopped with the briny, brackish water, and as a result, they scratched themselves constantly. Most had a deep, wracking cough that echoed throughout the room. Their faces weren't just dirty; they were filthy with mud and shell dust caking their cheeks. Several were missing front teeth, and these were not baby teeth. These were teeth knocked out while retrieving shells from under the rollers or dumping them into the soaking tanks. Two were already missing fingers, courtesy of the rollers. Still another had a crude patch over an absent eye. All were barefoot, and "colorful" wouldn't even come close to describing the words that came out of their mouths as they stepped on the sharp shell pieces scattered across the floor. During the breaks, when the adults would huddle and sink into conversation, the children would run to a small alcove next to the base of the elevator, light up their pipes and cigarettes, and puff away until it was time to return to work. After one of the breaks, I told another shoveler that it was surprising that all smoked so heavily. The reply came back matter-of-factly. Everyone believed the smoke would coat and protect their young lungs and keep them from coming down with everything from pneumonia to dust-lung. The oldest of the lot was only eight-years-old. Eight.

I managed to make it through the day, but I was dragging so badly when the whistle finally blew, I could barely keep my eyes open. Combined lack of sleep and the repetition of shoveling shells all day had me right on the edge of exhaustion. Mattie met me out on the sidewalk after work, and the two of us walked home together, again without much conversation. I was thankful for the added security of her company. Still, every time we spied a wagon off in the distance, we looked at each other and winced, imagining what might be inside its coverings.

When we reached the bottom of our steps, she told me to climb quickly, get inside, and lock the door behind me. She said she was off to find us some supper and would be back as soon as she could. I was so tired I just nodded and started up the steps. Once inside, I went straight for the divan and sat down, not even jumping when a spring found its mark. Within minutes, I was sound asleep.

It was half past ten when I finally woke up. I lit a lamp and made my way to the sink to pour myself a glass of water. On my way I saw a note on the table next to a small plate of fruit and bread. The note read, simply, "Eat and then go back to sleep. I'm off to see some friends. We'll talk in the morning. Mattie."

The sweet release of sleep was what I needed more than anything else so I covered the plate with a dishcloth, blew out the lamp, and got right back on the divan. I was asleep the minute my head touched the pillow.

....

CHAPTER 19

MATTIE WAS STILL NOT HOME when I woke up. I dressed, ate a banana and some grapes, and sat at the kitchen table to gather my thoughts. I wanted to talk to Gaston. It was hard for me to connect my thoughts, but I needed to talk to Gaston. He had told me how to get in touch with him if I ever needed to, and I decided this was the time. I wrote a quick note telling Mattie I was going for a long Sunday walk and then headed as fast as I could down the steps and across town.

When I got to the camp, my reception was exactly what I had expected.

Before I made my way ten feet past the entrance, a tomato came hurtling toward me—only this time I was ready. Stepping quickly to the side, I watched it land with a thud in the soft dirt a few yards behind me. It had been thrown from behind a tent to my left, but I couldn't see who had offered it. I didn't have much time to think about it because I was suddenly aware of several voices, and they weren't friendly, approaching from my right.

I was in no mood for a repeat of my first visit, so I threw up my hands and yelled loudly as I could, "Not this time you don't! I've had this reception before, and I'm tired of it. Next person who takes a step toward me gets a fist right in the eye. Come on ahead if you don't believe me."

All motion around me stopped. When I dared look, I saw to my right half a dozen grim-faced girls, their hands clutching either long sticks or more tomatoes. On the left, an older woman holding a large shovel stepped from behind a tent and into the clearing. We all stood there, motionless, studying each other. My heart was pounding, but I wasn't going to give ground easily. Not today.

I lowered my arms and folded them tightly across my chest. I was frightened right down to my little toes, but I mustered courage enough to purse my lips and put on the meanest look I could manage. As I did, the woman with the shovel suddenly burst out laughing. Those off to my right immediately followed her lead. I instinctively winced and started to duck because I figured I was about to become the butt of either one of their jokes or another act of violence.

The older woman stepped forward, leaned heavily on her shovel, and said, still laughing, "Well, you're not exactly dressed for it, but I'd bet money you'd try to take a poke at one of us."

As all eyes seemed to be studying me, it came to me that I probably did look at least a tad out of place to these women. I knew not to wear my coveralls because that would have immediately branded me a "Cutter." I should have worn the same clothes I had the other night, but I wanted to look nice when I saw Gaston. I thought a simple, pleated black skirt, white blouse, and a very plain, brown afternoon hat would be appropriate. I had powdered my face and lightly touched over my lips with Mattie's new lipstick. All of this set me apart from these women, most of whom, to put it charitably, were one step away from rags.

My appearance had bought me some valuable time, but I knew it wouldn't last. The woman with the shovel seemed to be in charge, so I turned to face her.

"I mean no harm," I said, my voice still shaking. "That's the gospel truth. I've come... I've come...."

She cut me off, "Well, spit it out. Don't have all day. Come for what?"

Finding my voice again, I quickly added, "I have come to buy a scarlet pearl. I was told I could find it here."

"What did you say? What kind?" she asked in almost an angry tone as she let go of her shovel and stepped closer to me.

"Scarlet," I repeated. "A scarlet pearl."

"You sure?" she asked, placing her hands on her hips and staring right into my eyes.

I nodded. She then motioned for the rest of the group to leave. When they had started back to their tents, she stepped forward, took my right hand firmly in hers, and studied it a few seconds.

"You're definitely no cutter—at least you haven't been one for long," she said, finally. "And by the look of you, you're sure as blazes not one of us. Just what are you? I need to know before there's any more talk about a scarlet pearl."

As she continued giving me the once-over, I noticed she wasn't nearly as old as I had originally thought. At first glance, I guessed her to be near to fifty. Now, imagining her without the dirt and grime caked on her face and arms, my guess was nearer to thirty—a hard thirty. Her off-white dress was ripped at the right shoulder, and several large, brown stains dotted the area around her knees. She wore shoes, but they didn't match. One was dark blue; the other was black.

"I'm a friend," I said. "I was told not to say any more than that."

She smiled and shook her head. "He's out of his mind. I just don't know how to place you two together."

She was fishing, but I wouldn't bite. Instead, I said, "That isn't your job. As I see it, your only job is to help me get what I came after. That's right, isn't it?"

She didn't respond to my question. "Didn't I see you here at the get-together? Wasn't that you?"

"Might have been," I replied.

She continued shaking her head. Finally, she extended her hand and said, "I'm Flora. And yours?"

"Pearl," I said, smiling weakly, still unsure of how much I should say to her. I shook her hand firmly, then quickly backed up a couple of steps.

"Sure you are, honey," she replied. "Pearl. That's a good one. Serves me right for asking a direct question."

"No, really...." I started to say when she cut in and pointed down the path under the bridge.

"I'll walk you to water's edge. You'll have to wait there. I'll see about getting that scarlet pearl for you. It could be a long wait—or short as a whistle."

"I'll wait as long as I have to," I replied.

Most of my view of the camp the night of the feast had been away from where the people lived and worked, so our walk now afforded me a much better perspective. As I had noted previously, on both sides of the path a row of tents ran all the way down to the water's edge. What I hadn't noticed before were the large piles of shells, some as high as ten or twelve feet, heaped between the tents. These served as fences or dividers, giving the residents of the tents at least a small measure of privacy from those around them. At the same time, these shells produced a stench so powerful I was forced at one point to pull out my handkerchief and breathe through it.

My escort looked at me, shook her head, and laughed while saying, "You'll get used to it."

If I had a nickel for every time I'd heard that since arriving in Muscatine.... I replied, simply, "I'm sure I will—when my nose dies and falls off my face."

She laughed even harder and motioned me to continue following her. As we walked along, it wasn't just the piles of shells assaulting my nose. I could see large kettles behind the tents on the east side of the path. Flora must have sensed my curiosity because she volunteered that these were used to boil and steam the clams before they were pried open to have the meat removed. The meat was discarded into still other piles behind the shells. I asked what happened to the meat and was told most of it eventually ended up as fertilizer or animal feed. The piles of meat reeked to high heaven, even more so every time the wind shifted. However, the clammers suffered through this because about one in a hundred shells harbored a pearl, which could make the difference financially between a good batch of shells and a great batch of shells. The smell from the rotting meat was a minor nuisance because of the odd pearl that appeared just often enough.

When we reached the riverbank, Flora motioned me to wait while she walked over to have a few words with an older gentleman who was cane-pole fishing. I couldn't hear what they were saying, but the man finally nodded and handed her a folding camp chair.

Flora walked back over to me and handed me the chair. "Here," she said. "Park yourself on this. Better than sitting on the dirt in that rig you've got on. I'll get word out about what you're looking for."

"Wish I could stay and watch," she said, smiling broadly. "I'd give a day's shells to find out how this is going to turn out."

She paused and continued, more seriously this time, "Watch yourself. That's all I'm going to say. Just watch yourself. And I wouldn't recommend coming back here again."

Before I could reply, she turned and was well on her way back up the path. There didn't seem to be anything else to do at this point, so I unfolded the chair and sat down to wait. The older gentleman soon caught a small catfish and pulled it up on the bank. As it flopped and slapped at the ground, he placed his boot on it and pried out the hook. Then, in one swift motion, he scooped it up and slammed it into a bucket behind him.

"First of the day," he said, shaking his head and looking over at me. "Fishin' ain't what it used to be around these parts. Why, just last year I'd have caught a good dozen, and all big as my leg, by this time of the mornin'. Shame. Darn shame."

"The water seems awfully dirty here by the bridge," I replied. "Maybe you should move upstream a little. Might be better there."

"I've tried that, Missy. I figured the same thing. Didn't do no good though. Everything's just getting played out around here. It'll be soon time to pack up and move again, and I'll be glad for it. Been here too long now anyway."

"How long have you been here—at this camp, I mean?" I asked, as he baited his hook.

"Oh, nigh on to three years now, I think. Maybe three and a half. I forget. I forget a lot these days. People say that comes from gettin' old, but I say it's from being plain bored. Don't have no reason to remember things any more. I just sit here and fish every day and help tie up the boats now and again."

He flung his line out as far as it would go and then, without looking at me, asked offhandedly, "And what about you? What do you do around here? Are you useful—or are you like me?"

"Depends upon what you mean by useful. I'm not much good at anything right now, and you wouldn't get much of an argument about that from the folks I work with. I guess you could say my job right now is to learn—as much as I can. There are days I feel dumb as a post."

"Then you're human," he said, smiling again. "We all have those days. I think the good Lord intended it that way. After all, if we knew everything, then what purpose would our journey through life serve? You just chew on that a minute and see what you end up spittin' out."

"You're pretty smart for an old fisherman," I said, trying to compliment him with my tone. "You seem anything but useless to me."

"You flatter me, Missy," he said, pulling up his line to check his bait and then lowering it gently back into the river. "But I'll take it. That's the nicest thing anyone's said to me in months."

"I say what's on my mind, many say to a fault," I added. "And I like to believe I'm a fair judge of character."

I saw him smile again, but he didn't turn toward me. Instead, we sat a few minutes in silence. He finally looked over at me and said, "Even when I'm not looking directly at you I can feel the questions in your eyes, Girl. What is it you're wanting to know?"

"I'm sorry, Sir," I replied. "I didn't mean to interrupt your fishing. Please forgive me."

"They ain't bitin' worth a hoot and a holler anyway."

He pulled in his line, sat his pole to the side, and continued, "Go ahead and ask. I got nothin' else to do. They say I'm too old to go in the boats, so I'm stuck here on the bank. They say I'm useless as horns on a dog. Times were I could outwork those young whipper-snappers any day of the week with one arm tied behind me. But they won't let me get in a boat with 'em. Never thought I'd see the day."

His voice trailed off as he looked out on the river. I guessed he was somewhere around sixty years old, but I had grown to understand looks were deceiving. The backs of his hands were knotted and covered with large brown spots. His face, while gentle, was leathered and creased by what must have been years of work in the sun. Whatever his age, he looked strong enough to be doing any type of work he wanted to do. But here he was— fishing, killing time, passing the days.

"I'm sorry," I said. "Younger people sometimes think they know it all—leastwise that's what my mother always says. They're not always right."

"I think I'd like your mother," he said, a twinkle appearing in his light hazel eyes. He then continued, "And don't you apologize to me. No need to. You're not bothering me. I welcome the company. No one else wants to talk to me."

"That's their loss," I said, moving my chair over closer to him, "and my gain."

He smiled again and said, "You've buttered me up enough now. What is it you want to know?"

"By the way, my name's Pearl," I said.

He nodded slowly and said, "Just call me Hector. That'll do."

"Nice to meet you, Hector," I replied.

"Likewise, Miss Pearl. Now what can I do for you?"

For what must have been a good half-hour, I asked about and he explained the workings of the camp, beginning with the clamming boats. Some had elaborate webs of twine, each strand about six inches apart from the surrounding ones, hanging down from a large metal bar that could be raised or lowered in the center of the boats. The lines coiled around this bar, and Hector said unwinding them would lengthen them to match the depth of the river where the clamming would take place. Each length of twine had a hook tied at the end. The most common of these were three-pronged, and the tines were nearly straight and flared out slightly from the others. Hector said these were called crowfoot hooks. When I gave him a curious look he motioned for me to wait while he walked over and looked along the river's edge. He finally bent down, picked something up, and tossed it to me.

"What does this hook look like to you?" he asked, grinning.

"A crow's foot," I said, rolling my eyes and finally understanding.

"Exactly," he replied. "Person who thought up that name didn't have to think much, did he?"

He explained how the hooks were used. When clammers found a good clamming bed, they lowered the hooks into the water so they could drag along the bottom. Hector said while clams feed, their shells open so they can close around food that floats by.

"Clams can't tell the difference between a pebble and a crowfoot. Feels all the same to them, so when a hook goes across, they snap their shells shut and hang on. Then all that has to be done is to pull them up and take 'em off the line. It's just that simple. What's tough is finding a good bed. That ain't easy as it used to be, especially now that the best beds around here have played out. Boats are going out farther and farther every day now. I remember when a good clamming boat would go out and come back in to unload a good three, sometimes four, times a day. Now some stay out a good two days before they have a haul big enough not to be embarrassed by. Why, up by Washington, Iowa, they're already having to bring shells from Arkansas and Tennessee to keep their factories going. You couldn't find a camp like ours up there if your life depended on it. All gone now—down to Arkansas I reckon."

"That's a shame," I said. "Can anything be done about it? Is that going to happen here, too?"

"Likely so," he replied, lowering his voice and looking down at the ground. "Only way to help would be to stop clamming here completely and let the beds grow again. I don't see that happening. I heard that a bunch of owners have hired old man Boepple to see if he can come up with a way to start new beds fast, but I don't think it can be done."

"Mr. John Boepple?" I asked.

"The very same. Know him?"

"My uncle does. They go back a ways."

"Well, I wish him luck, but he's fightin' Mother Nature, and I never heard of anyone ever winnin' that fight."

I had the feeling our time together would be short, so I kept firing questions. I found out the mystery of the buckets that were constantly hauled from the river up to the tents. These contained water for the boiling kettles to keep them from going dry and burning the shells. I asked about the long rakes stacked together down by the dock. Hector explained these were used by some instead of the traditional line and crow's foot hooks. Basically, a clammer held a rake in each hand while the current drew him through a bed. One was used to scoop up the shells; the other was clamped over the top to keep the shells contained until they could be lifted into the boat. He said some of these "rakers" were so skilled they could tell simply by touch whether they were scooping shells, rocks, or just about any other item that might be resting on the bottom. If they knew it wasn't a shell, they'd simply twist the rake and set the item free before going after more shells.

I also wanted to know more about the piles of shells between the tents, specifically how often they were taken to the factories. Hector said this depended upon whether a clammer worked alone or had thrown in with one or two others. A solitary clammer, he said, would typically take off one day a week to take his shells to sell at one of the factories. If his harvests were rich, this was a good system. However, the time hauling the shells was time he couldn't spend on the river, so he actually lost a day of clamming each week. Others teamed up so that while one person took care of hauling the shells away, the others could still be gathering them up and replenishing their piles. They had to share profits, but during slow times this evened out and kept food on their tables.

"And what about the piles of meat?" I asked, scrinching up my face. "When do those get taken away?"

He laughed and said, "Not often enough, that's for sure! We get paid so little for it that we'd be better off if we dumped everything back in the river—only that would poison the water even more. If you can figure out a way to make good use of the meat, you'll find your fortune. So far, none of us have come up with a single, solitary thing."

There was so much more I wanted to ask. I started in on another question when he cut me off and motioned for me to listen to him.

"Now it's my turn to ask you something," he said. "What do you want with this scarlet pearl? How much do you know about it?"

It was obvious Flora had told him why I was here, which caught me off guard.

"Heaven only knows why, but our paths keep crossing," I explained. "We seem to be linked in some odd sort of way I can't explain. To be honest, I don't know much about him, but I do believe he has a good heart. He told me he'd be there if I ever needed something, and now I do. That's why I'm here. That's why I want to see him."

I paused, then added, "You know him well?"

"I'm not sure anyone does. Keeps to himself mostly. But I agree with you about his heart. He's taken care of us all more times that I could cipher—and he never stays around long enough for so much as a thank you. He's here and gone, and that's the way he wants it. We respect that—because we respect him."

"Any idea where he comes from?" I asked.

"That's not for me to say, even if I did know the answer. If you want to know more about him, you'll have to ask him yourself. "

I nodded I understood. He stood up and walked to a small boat tied about twenty feet off to his left. As he untied it from its mooring, he said, without looking back at me, "Had to make sure you weren't bad. Looks like you ain't. Are you?"

"Depends on the day," I replied. "Today's a good day, I think. At least I hope so."

"I'm bettin' it will be," he said, motioning for me to come over and step aboard. "Can tell it from the smile on your face."

I blushed, and he laughed.

"Where we going?" I then asked, confused.

"Time to get you a scarlet pearl. I'll be the one taking you. Go ahead. Get in and anchor yourself to one of those seats in the middle. We've got a little bit of a ride ahead of us."

"You were studying me, weren't you? I mean before, while we were talking."

"Can't be too safe these days," he said while starting the small motor. "Just making sure. You just sit back and relax now. I'll get us there soon as I can."

The river breeze felt good on my face as we made our way upstream and away from the bridge. Glancing ahead, I noticed how beautiful the shore looked. It was night when I was on the river with Gaston, and I could now tell the darkness had hidden the dense stretches of trees and the dozens of small tributaries that branched deep into the bank on both sides. I could also see smaller camps set up along a few of these. I wanted to ask about them, but the wind and motor would have drowned my voice, so I had to be content with sitting back and enjoying the scenery, not a difficult task at all in these surroundings.

I lost track of the time, but we had been travelling a pretty fair distance when I turned around and could no longer see any sign of High Bridge. Hector must have noticed me looking back because he called out, "Almost there. Just around the next bend."

We eased toward a small tributary to our right. Hector stayed close to the bank as he navigated us cautiously and slowly around large logs in the water ahead of us. It almost appeared from the way they were staggered they had been placed there on purpose—to slow our progress.

At one point, Hector stopped us entirely as he pulled up a long paddle and used it to push us through a spot where the logs created a zig-zag trough just barely big enough for us to slip through. Once we did get through, he eased the boat to the shore and stopped the motor. From under the seat he brought out, of all things, a school bell. He raised it high above his head and let it clang five times. Just a matter of seconds later, off in the distance another bell also rang out five times in response.

"You can get out now," he said.

I stepped carefully out onto the bank.

"Follow that path up through the trees over there."

"You're not coming with me?" I asked. Then, almost in a panic, I added, "How am I going to get back home?"

"Danged if I know," he said, smiling and pushing off.

He started the motor again, swung the boat around, and roared away. "But..." was all I could get out before he was too far away to hear me.

I was in the middle of nowhere, a fact that made me shiver. The trees were so dense I could see only a short distance up the path ahead. The trees were also so tall the sun was nearly blocked, making it appear hours later in the day. Shivering or not, I had no choice but to start hiking up the path.

I hadn't gone too far when I saw a figure coming toward me. My first thought was to look for a stick or rock to protect myself, so I stepped quickly off the path between two large oak trees.

"You can come out now," a familiar voice called out. "I saw you duck in there."

It was Gaston. I stepped back to the path and said, "Well, you could have announced yourself a little earlier. How would I know it was you? You could have been...."

I paused, and he finished my thought for me. "Could have been a scraggly, good-for-nothing fiend."

We both laughed. "Yes, that's exactly what I meant," I said, stepping forward to shake his hand. As he took mine, in one swift motion he pulled me close and kissed me, gently, warmly.

I backed up and started to protest, but he cut me off and instructed me to follow him up the path. He was already several feet away, and I was still standing in my original spot when he turned and said, "Miss my company so soon?"

"No—just wanted my dime back."

Then, I smiled slightly and shook my head. "I'm afraid it's more serious than that. I need your help."

"Then we'll talk," he said. "Let's go this way."

The path took one hard turn to the right and then another back left before we came to a small clearing. In the back corner of the clearing was a small cabin with curls of smoke coming from its chimney.

"Yours?" I asked as we came closer.

"Mine," he said, proudly. "Bet you thought I lived in my boat and used my cannon to hang my laundry on. Right?"

"No, it's just that it's so—so beautiful."

"And I'm not. I know—it doesn't make a lot of sense. Just wait until you see the inside. You'll be more confused than ever."

I smirked and scolded him. "That's not what I meant, and you know it. It's just not what I pictured for you, that's all."

"Then see if this is what you pictured," he said, helping me up three small steps to the landing in front of the door. He opened the door for me and let me go in ahead of him. What I saw before me was even a greater shock. Floor to ceiling bookshelves lined the far wall, and every shelf was full of books. In front of the shelves was a writing desk and chair. To the right, an Aladdin lamp with a tall, ornate globe stood on a nightstand next to his bed. On the left was the kitchen area. It wasn't large, but everything was immaculately clean, including the row of varying sizes of iron skillets hanging neatly above the washbasin. There was an oval dining table and a small Franklin stove.

"You're absolutely right," I said, turning to face him. "I am surprised. Unless you tell me you stole all of this, I'm going to be mightily disappointed in you. As a matter of fact, if this all isn't ill-gotten-gains from piracy or looting, you're the biggest faker since that medicine man who came through Grandview last year."

"Faker?" he said in mock protest. "Can I help it if to most people I'm the second coming of the Black Plague?"

"Yes, you probably can help it, but you won't. I still don't understand all of this. I know it's none of my business, but I've found you out. Aren't you worried just a little about that? Afraid I might tell?"

"And just who would you tell—and what would you tell them? That I live in a house in the woods that's furnished with booty I've snatched up here and there? Think that would change their opinions?"

"Likely not," I admitted.

"And what about you coming out here to be all alone with me. What would they say about that? No, you're trapped, Miss Pearl. You can't tell on me because in doing so you'd be telling on yourself. You know what that's called? My grandfather called it an idiot's truce."

"I've been feeling more and more like an idiot of late, so that name sure fits me. And as far as you are concerned...."

"Watch it!" he said, playfully. "Be careful of your next words. Remember I'm your only hope to get back home."

"Then it will have to be a truce," I said, starting to extend my hand and then pulling it back quickly when I suddenly remembered what happened the last time I tried to shake his hand.

"A little jumpy?" he said, motioning me to sit in one of the chairs at the kitchen table.

I looked at him without expression and said, dryly, "Only around you."

"I take it this isn't just a social call," he said while pouring me a glass of water from the pitcher to his right. "You said you needed my help. What can I do for you?"

"You once told me that what was going on in Muscatine

wasn't your fight—that you were staying out of it."

My mouth was dry, so I paused and took a sip of water, then continued. "You talk big. That's for sure. But, you're not being completely honest. You say you don't care what happens to the owners or the workers, but I know you're in this fight just the same. I've heard the stories of how you've been helping the clammers. Just about everybody forgets about them, but they're front and center in all this. Without them, neither the workers nor the owners would be in business. No shells, no buttons—simple as that. And from what I've seen, the clammers are being taken advantage of more than anyone else—and you've chosen to help them. So, you can't tell me you're not in the fight, because you are."

He didn't say anything. Instead, he smiled and poured me more water. I continued, "It's because you can see everything from the outside—the problems between the owners and workers—that I'm here. That's why I want your advice."

"Go on," he said. "What exactly do you want from me?"

I looked him right in the eyes and said, "You believe you're staying neutral, yet you're doing a lot behind the scenes to make life at least a little better for the clammers. What I want to know is...is it enough? Are you going to look back and be sorry you didn't jump into the big fight—the one between owners and workers—or will you still feel you've done the right thing after the dust clears, whichever way it falls?"

"What are you are asking?" Leaning forward and speaking gently now, he said, "Are you asking my permission for you to stay out of the—what did you call it—the 'big fight'? If you are, you've come to the wrong cabin. That's a decision only you can make for yourself. That's something you'll have to work out with your own heart. I can't help you with that."

We sat for a few minutes in silence. Images ran through my mind—of Viola in the hospital bed, the skirmish near the bridge, the deaths of the Knox boys, my own abduction. I hated violence, and that was the one common denominator among all events.

It had to stop. It had to stop before any type of reasonable and productive communication could take place. But how could that happen? Someone had to step forward and do something to start everyone on this path.

I had been holding my feelings in check for so long I thought I was past most everything. I was wrong. Sitting there and looking at Gaston, I felt my emotions crash. The tears came quickly. He immediately pulled his chair next to mine, put his arms around me, and pulled me close. I buried my face on his chest and wept. I hugged him tighter and tighter as I drew in air between sobs. He ran his hand gently down my cheek, brushing away the tears.

"Let it go," he said, forcefully. "Let it all out. All of it."

As he hugged me, he started slowly rocking us back and forth. I was finally able to catch my breath and stop shaking. I started pulling myself back far enough to thank him when he suddenly jerked sideways, stared out the window, and pulled me roughly from the chair to the floor.

The second we hit the floor the window in the kitchen shattered and shards of glass flew our direction. A sharp crack followed almost simultaneously. He covered me with his body as he said, "Stay down! There'll be one more."

The words were barely out of his mouth when a second spray of glass covered us, followed by a loud crack.

"Don't move," he commanded.

He crawled to the left of the door and grabbed a double-barreled shotgun leaning against the wall. Then, standing and opening the door ever so slightly, he stuck the gun through the opening and, without aiming, fired first one barrel then the other in rapid succession. My ears stung from the concussion echoing in the cabin. He opened the door a little wider, cautiously looked out, and closed it again.

"Get up now, but stay away from the window. Move your chair around to this side."

He cracked the door and looked out as I pleaded, "What's going on? What is it?"

It had happened so fast that I was shocked more than scared. I was suddenly also very angry that my blouse had ripped when I fell to the floor.

Gaston saw me picking at the hole and came over. "Are you hurt?" he asked, removing my hand so he could inspect the rip.

"I'm fine," I said. "At least I think so."

"Well, I'm glad for that," he said with relief. "It's bad enough they're after me, but I'd never forgive myself if anything happened to you."

"What was that?" I asked, rubbing the bruise I felt coming up on my knee.

"I haven't been able to find out who it is, but I know it isn't anyone from the camp. Probably those new people from Arkansas. But, I have no doubt what they're after. This happens about once a week now. They're not trying to kill me. At least I don't think so. If they are, then they're the worst shots in the world. No, I think they're just trying to scare me off. Everyone believes the tributary that runs along here is where I gather my pinkies. It isn't, but they still think it so. I guess the shooters figure if I get spooked out of here, they can slip right into a windfall. The great irony is they're about as far away from the real location as they could be—but still I'm being shot at!"

"This happens every week?"

"It does. They could just wait and pick me off somewhere along the path if they really wanted to, but they don't. Must be some clammers' code that's keeping them from doing that, but I'll be darned if I know what it might be. I guess I should just feel lucky."

He uprighted his chair and moved both of ours still farther on the other side of the table. Smiling weakly, he said to me, "Oh, by the way, welcome to my cabin."

"It's a visit I won't soon forget. That's for sure," I said, using my handkerchief to brush small pieces of glass from the side of my dress. "It's not every day I get shot at."

"Relax," he said, softly. "They'll be gone now. They always

run off right after I fire back, so we're safe now. I know—my nerves are still shaky, too. Why don't we have something stronger than water. Whiskey? Coffee?

"Coffee doesn't sound bad," I replied, my voice still quivering.

"I'll get some started. Sorry for the interruption."

He said it so casually that we both started laughing again.

As he ground the coffee beans, he turned to me and said, "You already had your mind made up before you got here, didn't you?"

He paused and continued, his voice growing more serious. "No, you're not seeking advice. Unless I miss my mark, you're seeking vindication for a decision you've already made."

"It might be," I said. "I'm confused."

"Then let's hear all about it," he said. "Tell me everything. Get it off your chest. I can listen. That much I can do for you."

"You sure about that?"

"No," he said, smiling broadly this time. "But, I'll take a chance."

"Then pull up a chair when you're ready. This could take a while."

"Get started," he said. "I'm not going anywhere—and neither are you until we're absolutely sure those gunhawks are gone. Go ahead. Let it out."

The dam burst, and everything I'd held inside came spilling out—what I felt about the owners, the workers in the plants, the violence that seemed to be everywhere, the need for communication—everything. I even shared with him what details I could remember of my abduction. I did most of the talking while he listened and calmly urged me on. We broke long enough to eat some venison stew he had simmering on the stove. While we ate, I told him about my family. I asked about his, but he wasn't in the mood to share details, and I didn't press him.

We talked long into the evening. And as we did so, I learned he was right: I had already made up my mind.

....

CHAPTER 20

I GOT BACK HOME JUST after ten and hoped Mattie would be asleep. Gaston had brought me back across the river and set me to shore just a little farther to the west than he had the time before. He offered to walk me home, but given that it was Sunday night and most people would already be in their beds, I convinced him it was safe enough for me to journey alone. After a brief and tender kiss goodbye, he pushed away from the shore and back out into the current. I had stood there and watched him until his outline faded into the darkness of the river.

I turned my key in the latch as quietly as I could and tried to slip inside without being heard. But there, sitting at the kitchen table, was Mattie, staring daggers at me.

"Where in the world have you been?" she lit into me. "I've been worried sick. After what happened the other day, I was waiting for the worst. And here you come waltzing in like a queen. You should be ashamed of yourself."

"I'm sorry," I replied. "Truly I am. The time just got away from me. That's all."

"That's all, my foot!" she shouted back. "You scared me half to death. Look at me—I'm still shaking."

"I should have said I might be away all day. I just didn't know. I had no idea. It just turned out that way. Please forgive me."

"I shouldn't forgive you," she said, drumming her fingers on the table. "You have no idea what I've been through today. While you were off to goodness knows where, you know what I was doing? I went to the hospital to see Viola—only to find out her uncle came and got her. She's gone. She still wasn't improving, so

he took her back to Washington. I didn't even get to say goodbye."
She bit her lip as I saw tears welling up in her eyes.

"And then you," she continued, tears now streaming down her cheeks. "For all I knew, you could have been floating down the river. Don't ever do this again. Promise me right now!"

"I promise," I said, walking over and sitting across from her at the table. "And I'm sorry about Viola. I just hope and pray she now gets the care she needs. You said her uncle's a great doctor, so she's in good hands. That's what's most important. We'll go up there some Sunday and see her—soon."

We sat in silence a good while, each with our own thoughts. I was sad I didn't get to see Viola before her uncle came, but I was also comforted in the knowledge she'd now be with family and getting loving care.

Mattie was still wiping away tears, but I'd lived with her long enough to know she wasn't going to let me off the hook so easily. She was sad and worried about Viola, but that wasn't going to distract her from trying to find out where I had been. When she finally turned to face me, I could tell from her eyes the inquisition was coming, so I decided to head her off.

"You said you were worried I might have been floating down the river. Well, I was—in a manner of speaking." That got her attention, and she leaned forward and motioned with her hand that she wanted me to continue.

"That is, I went for a boat ride. A long way off, too."

I could have tortured her and drawn the story out, but I didn't. There was something I wanted to tell her, and I knew it would be better sooner than later. Before she could interrupt with questions about the boat ride, I went through the whole story. I told her about the clamming camp and what I had seen and learned there. But, I didn't mention the method of contacting Gaston; I knew I should keep that to myself. My camp visit shocked her, and she started to scold me again for even being around the clammers, but I diverted her attention by telling her I had gone there to see Gaston. I might as well have pushed her hand into a bag of snakes. Her reaction certainly couldn't have been filled with more surprise.

"Gaston?" she asked, her mouth falling open. "You mean Gunboat Gaston? The man responsible for more mayhem around here than whiskey? Have you lost your mind completely?"

I didn't answer her. Instead, I continued my story. I was almost finished telling her the bits and pieces I was willing to share about my earlier time spent with him when Mattie suddenly stood up, placed the back of her hand to her forehead, and very dramatically shuffled to the divan and pretended to fall down in a faint. She landed on a sharp spring and groaned loudly. I laughed, but the minute I did I knew I shouldn't have. Mattie jumped from the couch, rushed over to me, and started shaking my shoulders roughly.

"Just what is the matter with you?" she asked, her voice rising. "Are you so tired of living you're out looking to get killed? Don't you know he'd just as soon slit your throat as look at you?"

I brushed her hands away and scooted my chair back, distancing myself as much as I could from her. "You wait just a minute," I said, now going on the attack myself. "You're going to listen to what I have to say about him—and you're going to listen good. Sit yourself down."

I was careful what I shared, but I did my best to show him as someone deeply concerned about the present situation—and especially about the welfare of those living in the camp. Mattie shook her head repeatedly as I continued. At one point, she interrupted me and said, "If I don't pull it all out first, I better shake the straw out of my hair. I'm the one who was in the dark. You aren't as country as you appear, girl."

I smiled. "Maybe not—but I've got a few things to learn. And I'm going to need your help."

When I had given all the details about Gaston I was going to, I paused for a minute before saying, "I went there today to ask for his advice about something that's been eating away at me for a long time now. Instead, he let me talk until I figured most everything out for myself. My whole world changed today."

She sat back down, but not before giving me a look that bordered on disgust and mistrust. I still wasn't sure how best to approach the subject, so I decided to dive right in.

"Mattie, listen to me without saying anything until I'm finished."

I paused briefly, then continued, "You and I have talked a lot about what's going on with the owners and workers. You've been as obvious as a butcher knife about your views, and you've made no secret of where you think I should stand on all this. I told you over and over until I was practically blue in the face my beliefs are that both sides have plenty of right and wrong within them. I still think that. I still think both sides need to listen to each other—and that's how this is all eventually going to get settled. But having said that, now I know I can't sit on my hands and do nothing while this unfolds. It's time for me to get into the fray, and I'm finally ready."

After all the pestering Mattie had given me, I expected her to say something. Instead, her eyes grew Wide, and she let out a low whistle. "Can I say something now?" she asked, her voice rising.

"No," I replied.

I added, "I want you to know I've made this decision for a practical reason. The owners would never take me seriously, mostly because of my age and inexperience. However, I don't think that would be an issue with the unionists. My voice could be heard with them, and I think they'd respect my attempts to bring everyone together. After all, I've worked alongside some of their members in the factory, so I know something of what they've been through and what they're fighting for. I'm going to join up with the union."

Mattie didn't wait for permission to speak. She practically leapt across the table and started kissing me up and down my cheeks. I finally backed away and started laughing. Mattie started crying.

"I've been praying for this," she said, choking back tears. "I've wanted to tell you so much. I've wanted...."Her voice trailed off.

"I know," I said. "I could read between the lines in our talks, but I could always tell you stopped short. From now on, you don't have to. I'm in it for the long haul."

"I just don't know what to say," Mattie said, her tears easing. We laughed again and sat back down.

"There's one more thing I have to tell you, and you're not going to like it much. I don't want it between us. You need to know it before you decide whether I'm worthy of your confidence."

It was time for bluntness, so I laid it out as quickly as I could. "When I first got here, I had two jobs. I was supposed to learn as much about the business as I could to help out Uncle Sam Henry. I was glad to do that. I knew it would help him. But, I also had a second job I didn't share with you."

I paused, looked away from her, and continued, "I was also supposed to keep my eyes and ears open to see if I could find out anything about the unionists and workers who were stealing from the factory—and pass that along. What I'm trying to tell you is that Viola wasn't the only informer around here. I didn't mind it much at first. But, being with the people in the factory and seeing them scratch and claw every day just to stay alive wasn't something I expected. I couldn't spy on them and live with myself, so I quit doing that. I still meet every Monday morning with Mr. Blanton, but now I tell him only what I'm sure he already knows. He doesn't know I've had a change of heart, and I can't tell him or I'll lose my job. It's a charade I'm going to have to keep playing."

I expected at least a mild show of outrage from Mattie, but all she did was fold her arms and smile back at me.

"What? What is it?" I asked.

"I hate to tell you, but I already knew about that. You're not breaking any new trail here."

"What do you mean you knew?"

Walking over to the divan, she lifted the cushion and pulled out my ledger. I gasped as she held it out to me.

"You're not much of a sneak," she said, finally tossing the ledger over to me. "Never have been. But you're going to get better at it. A lot better. I'll teach you everything I know."

"If you knew all about this, then why didn't you say something before?"

"I've known you a lot of years. I didn't think it'd take long for you to understand what folks here are being put through. Basically, I was betting on your heart—and you didn't disappoint me."

Before I could respond, she added, "I've got a piece of advice I hope you'll take. Don't tell anyone else about your meetings with Mr. Blanton."

I nodded. "So where do we go from here?" I asked. "I'm ready to get started."

"You're an answer to a prayer," she replied. "With Viola gone, we've had a gaping hole on the union's Executive Committee. I'm one of the membership officers. Viola and I were serving together on the committee, but she had skills I didn't have. She was our recording secretary. She wasn't bad at it, either. Plus, she had letterhead stationary she'd stolen from every place she worked, so there wasn't any type of communication she couldn't send—or any type she couldn't fake. But, with her gone, we need someone who writes well. Really well. You're the best writer I've ever known, and this position has your name all over it. That is, if you want it."

I didn't hesitate. "I'll take it—with pride and honor."

"Good. Then we need to meet with a couple of people, so I can clear it with them. We'll see them after work tomorrow. That sound okay to you?"

"Tomorrow won't come soon enough for me."

Mattie paused here, turned stone-cold serious, and said, "There's one more thing. Once you turn this corner, there is no turning back. The owners aren't the only ones with enforcers. If you ever do anything to hurt the cause, there'll be nothing I can do to help you. I don't think I need to spell that out. I just had to mention it."

"I know," I said. "I take no offense. I understand."

"Then," she said, hugging me tightly, "welcome to the fight. I'm glad you'll be along because this fight is one we're going to win."

"It's one I want us all to win," I added.

....

Mr. Blanton skipped his Monday morning talk with everyone which, given the present atmosphere, didn't come as much of a surprise to anyone. He did ask me to come to his office for our meeting, and I was so nervous my stomach was flopping. He didn't seem to notice.

I told him I was convinced a supervisor on the top floor was stealing bottles of hydrochloric acid and selling them to other plants. I didn't know if he was actually selling them to other plants—although I had heard that was so in conversation during breaks—but I had several times seen him sneaking small bottles of the acid into his pocket. I wouldn't have said anything except he seemed to take great pleasure any time a worker in that station accidentally came in contact with the acid and got burned. It was clear to all he didn't care about their safety, so I didn't mind one bit putting the mark on him.

I also let him know that Dillard Soams, who had been moved to the soaking tanks, was adamantly and violently opposed to the unionists—and vowed to get them if he ever found them out. Mr. Blanton was especially pleased by this news and said Soams would be receiving a nice raise. Actually, Soams never said this, but his wife did just have twins, and they badly needed an increase in income. I was glad I could help him out with that.

Mr. Blanton wasn't very happy I didn't have news about the unionists. I said no one was talking—no one was willing to risk losing a job, especially because the price of food had really shot up around town. It was just a little white lie, but it was a lie, nonetheless. Still, I wasn't going to lose any sleep over it. Mattie was obviously having a very bad influence on me.

The rest of the day rushed by. Mr. Blanton had me moved to the shipping station because one of the girls there had nearly cut off her finger on a box-cutting knife. Since I was already familiar with the workings of the station, I spent most of the time day-dreaming. I managed to get through the day without incident and rushed outside to meet Mattie as soon as the whistle blew.

"We're all set," Mattie whispered to me as we quickened our pace down the sidewalk. "Follow me—and keep up."

We trudged up the hill, and when we came to Third Street, instead of turning right toward home, we went left and continued about two blocks to a brick, three-story house on the south side of the street.

"Let me do the talking," Mattie said as we walked up the steps. "If you're asked anything, be short in your answers. He hates long-winded people. He must have despised me until I finally figured that out."

"Whose house is this?" I whispered.

"I have no idea," was Mattie's reply. "We try not to meet in the same place twice. That way we don't have to worry as much about spies watching us coming and going. We just get an address and show up at the appointed time."

That made perfectly good sense to me. I nodded and waited behind her as she rang the bell.

Soon an elderly woman wearing a light, lace shawl greeted us, and after asking our names, instructed us to follow her. We were led to a spacious back porch that overlooked not just the river, but our factory as well. The irony wasn't lost on Mattie. She pointed out the window and shook her head.

I hadn't noticed when we entered the porch, but a man was seated off to our right. He rose and greeted Mattie warmly, first shaking her hand and then hugging her. He looked to be in his early thirties. His complexion was dark, and his ears bowed out prominently. He also had a deep and wide part in his hair that ran all the way up to his forehead.

Mattie turned to me and said, "I want you to meet Mr. Charles Hanley."

Then, turning to Mr. Hanley, she added, "And I'd like to introduce you to Miss Pearl McGill."

He shook my hand and said, wasting no time, "Let's get right down to it. Please be seated."

As soon as we were, he continued, "I've heard a great deal about you already, and if Mattie vouches for you, that's good enough for me. So, I have only two questions I'd like to ask. First, do you write well?"

Mindful of Mattie's advice, I answered, plainly, "I do, sir. Very well."

"Good. Second, are you a religious girl?"

This question caught me completely off guard. I looked at Mattie. She nodded, so I looked him directly in the eyes and said, "Sir, I am."

"Good again," he said, finally smiling. "You're now our recording secretary. See you both tomorrow night. We'll let you know where and when."

He stood without another word and bowed slightly toward us. Mattie stood up and grabbed my arm, immediately trying to usher me out of the porch. However, I stopped and stood firm. Against Mattie's previous advice, I turned back to Mr. Hanley and said, "If you don't mind me asking, just who are you?"

He smiled and looked at his watch before answering. "Didn't Mattie tell you? I'm the attorney for the Button Workers' Protective Union. Actually, my official title is Counsel for the Defense. I guess you could say I'm the first line of protection if something goes wrong."

A stunned, "Oh" was all I could muster in response. Mattie yanked on my arm, and back through the house we went, letting ourselves out the front door. Once on the porch, I said, still foggy about what had just happened, "Did I dream that, or am I the new recording secretary?"

Mattie laughed. "It really happened. He's a man of very few words, as you'll come to find out."

"I already get that," I said, shaking my head. "He'd have to have his mouth taped shut to be any more stingy with words. He didn't even ask me why I wanted to be part of this. How come he didn't do that?"

"He didn't have to. I already talked to him about you a long time ago."

Here she paused, before adding, "I knew long before you did that you'd fight with us."

"You're pretty sure of yourself, aren't you?"

"I have to be."

We walked a fair distance down Third Street without a word. Finally, I couldn't contain my curiousity any longer. "What did he mean about tomorrow night? Another meeting?"

"We're going to meet up with a few more of the executive board members. We've got a lot of work to do and very little time to do it. You won't feel a moment's peace from now on."

"I'm ready," I said again without hesitation. "Let's get to work." We quickened our pace and walked the rest of the way home in silence.

....

CHAPTER 21

THE NEXT EVENING WE ATE a quick supper of slumgully stew and green apples, not a good combination for someone with an already nervous stomach. While we ate, Mattie filled me in on what she thought might happen at the meeting.

"I'll introduce you to everyone when we get there, but it's best if you keep pretty quiet tonight. You have a lot to learn, so remember what you're always telling me: 'Much silence makes a powerful noise.' That's good advice."

I understood. She added, "I might as well tell you now we've been talking about organizing a strike, and my guess is most of the meeting will be about that. Listen with an open mind to what everyone has to say about it. It's definitely time for this kind of action."

"Why talk of a strike before trying to get together with the owners to talk things through?" I replied. "That doesn't make sense to me."

"I expected that to be your first reaction. Just hold your horses and listen to what everyone says tonight. You'll see why this is on the table. Please, hold your tongue and wait."

"I'll try," I said, shaking my head.

"That's all I'm asking."

Then, looking at her watch, she said, "Goodness—we better hurry. Forget the dishes. We'll do them later. Let's get changed. Nothing fancy. Get out of those coveralls. Lately, people with coveralls might just as well have a bull's eye on their backs."

We were soon heading east on Second Street past all the familiar shops. When we were just about to the intersection above the train station, we turned north a few blocks, stopping at a small frame home set back a fair distance from the street.

"This is the address," Mattie said, putting her arm out to stop me. "Remember, listen and learn."

Mattie led me up the sidewalk.

A buck-toothed girl of about twelve or thirteen greeted us at the door. She asked our names and immediately checked a list on the entry table to her right. She invited us to follow her down a long hallway that ran through the middle of the house to a porch out back. This porch didn't have the view of the one we were in the day before, but it was twice as large.

As we entered, all rose from chairs around a large table to welcome us. There were nine present. Everyone smiled and waved or nodded to Mattie and looked a little suspiciously in my direction.

"I want to introduce all of you to Miss Pearl McGill," Mattie said, adding a flourish of her arm. "She's lived with me since coming to Muscatine and works with me at Blanton. I've known her since we were kids. She's good people. I can also tell you this much—she's one truly gifted writer, so we're darn lucky she'll be taking over Viola's duties."

All nodded politely, and someone off to the left shouted, "Here-here!"

Mattie suggested introductions of the other executive board members were in order, so after Mattie and I were seated, around the table they went.

An older gentleman to my left introduced himself as Oliver Wilson, Business Agent of the Button Workers' Protective Union. As soon as he stopped speaking, several others, at the same time, said, "He's the boss!" Everyone laughed, and Mr. Wilson playfully asked them to pipe down. "That's not really true," he said. "Fred Ray is our President, and he is the real boss. However, it looks like it's my fate to be at least somewhat in charge of the negotiation side of things for the time being."

Charles Hanley, whom we met the day before, was next to Mr. Wilson. He mentioned we were already acquainted, so he suggested we move along to the next person; Mattie was right—he didn't like to waste words. Seated to Charles' right was J.R. Hanley, his father, who introduced himself as "second counsel for the defense, almost as good as my son." This also produced polite ribbing. Hanley Sr. had the same pronounced ears as his son, but his face was marked by a thick, bushy mustache and large, piercing eyes. Still, seeing them together, it was plain the apple didn't fall too far from the tree.

The rest of the group consisted of workers from button factories spread all across town. Some were in supervisory roles, which again brought home to me that not all supervisors were fitted with horns. Others were regular station workers who decided, for a variety of reasons, that building a union would help better their lives and the lives of others. These were, from Mr. Hanley's left all the way around the rest of the table, the following folks: Miss Marva Jane Simmons from the Hawkeye Button Company; Mrs. Oleta Franklin, from the Pioneer Button Company; Mr. Vernon Jones, from the Empire City Pearl Button Works; Miss Hilda Snyder, from the Muscatine Button Company; Jack Fredericks, from the U.S. Button Company; Isaac Phillips, from the Automatic Button Company; and John Alexander, from the Grau Button Factory.

I knew the union had been making inroads in many factories in Muscatine, but I had no idea their reach had traveled this far. There were factories not represented in the room, but this group represented the full range of the different types of factories, from those that were primarily cutting stations to those that were finishing plants—and everything else in between. I could hear pride in their voices, a pride that obviously provided a unique bond for them.

After the introductions, Mr. Wilson stood up, lit his cigar, puffed a few times, and then addressed us all.

"Let's get started. I'm going to call this meeting to order. As I do, there is something that needs to be said."

Here he paused and stepped over to where I was seated

and stood directly behind my chair. He placed a hand on my shoulder and his voice was solemn now. "This young woman has large shoes to fill. I just learned that Viola is still ill and won't be returning any time soon. I know we all love Viola dearly and wish her nothing but the best as she recovers. She was always a tireless and selfless worker—and that will be difficult to replace. If Pearl here can do but half of what Viola did, I'll be satisfied."

He paused, patted me lightly on the shoulder, and added, "For the other half of her duties, I'm going to be asking an awful lot, and it is only fair she knows this right up front."

Mr. Wilson still hadn't addressed me directly. As he spoke to the group, I might as well have been invisible. When he returned to his chair, he pointed at me, and said, "You'll definitely do."

I looked around to see the others, including Mattie, trying to hide their smiles. Apparently, they knew what was coming next.

"You're also here," he continued, speaking directly to me this time, "because you're going to be the new face of the union. You're going to be—what did you call it, Charles?—our 'poster girl.' Look at her, everybody. She's pretty and has that look about her that just shouts 'wholesomeness.' She comes from a good family with solid roots here in southeast Iowa."

He cleared his throat. "And did I mention her uncle owns a button cutting business, so she knows both sides of the issues at hand?"

This last remark produced what appeared to me to be a nervous buzz around the table. "Don't worry," he quickly added. "She's on our side of the fence. Put any qualms you might have to the side."

"That's right," Mattie joined in.

Mr. Wilson continued, again speaking more to the group than to me, "Pearl is working in Blanton's factory to earn the funds that will enable her to have additional schooling—to enter one of the most noble of professions—teaching. She'll be shaping the minds and hearts of the future workers of Iowa."

Here his voice rose as he added, "Pearl, and so many fine

young men and women like her, are the future of our nation. They're willing to work hard and give an honest day's work. All they ask for is fair treatment and compensation—and we have to see they get it. Whether in the button industry or the garment industry or the steel industry, workers deserve the opportunity for better lives. They must not be held back by owners who cheat them, abuse them, maim them, and then just throw them onto the scrap pile like the mounds of drilled shells we see all over this town."

He turned to face me. "In short, we want you for what you stand for. Look at you. How could any decent human being deny you these possibilities and opportunities? I don't see how they could and still look themselves in the mirror. So, we're going to use you at every opportunity we can. When the time is right, I'll help see that you get to join the right groups and meet the right people. This is a tall order, so I'm asking you right now if you'll allow us to use you. I'm asking for your consent. Understand this: If we can get all of this for someone like you, then the rewards will soon enough reach the lowest worker in the darkest, dankest factory in this industry. In creating the possibilities for you, we'll create the reality for the rank and file of the button industry. So, Miss Pearl McGill—what say you to this? Do we have your consent?"

All eyes were directly on me, but he didn't let me answer. He added, lightening his voice, "Of course, we need you first and foremost as our new recording secretary. There's much for you to do in that area. We won't use you beyond that until it becomes absolutely necessary. And, if we do, the union will take care of you in every way. I give you my word on that."

I was speechless. While he spoke I felt a mixture of being flattered, suspicious, and downright frightened. That he and others could see me as an inspiration was beyond my scope of thinking, but I did understand his logic and reasoning. I'd be, as Mr. Hanley Sr. described, the "poster girl" for the union. I'd represent the humanity behind the changes so many asked for and deserved.

My first instinct was to say I would not do it. There were others aplenty who would be much better representatives. Dillard Soams from our own soaking stations at Blanton immediately came to mind. He was working to save enough money to open his own furniture store where he could design his own chairs and tables. And there was also Sheila Kuempel, who hoped to earn enough to start her own restaurant one day. However, the more I thought about them, the more I realized they might not make the best publicity material because of looks alone. Dillard was missing two of his fingers and had a long acid scar on his left cheek. Sheila lost a front tooth when a shell suddenly spun off the sorting bars, and, for reasons no one could determine, her hair had recently started falling out. I wasn't what most people would have called pretty, but I did have all my fingers, teeth, and hair. I had at least that much going for me.

This wasn't the time to say, "Mr. Wilson, I'll think about it." I made the decision to turn the corner, and now there was no turning back. I was in this fight up to my eyes. To deny his request would have been like saying I was there for them—as long as there was no risk for me. I knew danger would be part and parcel of the work needed to be done, and I had vowed to myself I wouldn't shy away from it. I hadn't been brought up to back away from a fight if I truly believed the cause just. And now, looking around the table at those representing a cause that could potentially influence the lives of nearly three thousand souls in the button industry, I knew I could give only one response—the one from my heart.

"I'll play my part—with pride."

The words had no sooner left my mouth than Mr. Wilson stood up, followed by the others, and started applauding, loudly this time. I appreciated their show of support, but it was still mightily embarrassing. At the same time, Mattie blotted away tears, which almost set me over the edge

As soon as all were seated, Mr. Wilson immediately said, "We thank you, Pearl—and are grateful you'll be with us."

Pausing only for a moment, he reached into his briefcase, pulled out a thick stack of papers, and spread them out on the table before him.

"Now that we've taken care of that, we have one other piece of business needing our attention tonight."

A low rumble spread around the table, and most snapped upright in their chairs. I was still basking in flattery and suddenly felt very much in the dark. However, I didn't feel this way for long.

Mr. Wilson looked around the group, exhaled loudly, and began, "It's time for us to talk strategy. Charles has come up with a plan that has strong merit. Charles, lay this out for us."

"Thank you," he replied, pushing his chair back. "I'd be happy to. My suggestion is potentially the path of least resistance, the path that just might get everybody to the same table right away. What we would do is let it out that we've set a strike date, that on this date workers would walk out in droves which would, in effect, force the factories to close up business. The owners already know that for a long time now we've considered asking for a strike, so this would play right into their fears. In short, this would be one really big hand of poker, and we'd be running a bluff. But, we have one huge advantage. They don't know we're not yet ready for a strike, but they do know one could happen— and soon."

He paused briefly, took a drink of water, and continued, "So, here's how it would play out. You would tell the trusted people in your factories to spread it around that the union is calling for a general strike on 'X' date. We'll get to the timetable in a minute. Then, after the word is out, Pearl, as directed by Mr. Wilson, will send a letter to all owners suggesting it is now time for all of us to meet and discuss a specific list of items of greatest concern to us."

He leaned over and picked up a piece of paper in front of Mr. Wilson before adding, "I've taken the liberty of putting this list together, based upon the discussions we've had in this group. Remember what I've said before. We better have a specific list ready to go—to keep everything on track—and we need to go from top priority down the ladder. I've also mixed in a couple of items we know they also want to improve so that we don't look like we only care if one side of the forest gets cleared. I've also included an item or two that we know they'd never go for in a million years. In legal negotiations, these are called 'throw-aways,' and getting them off the table will make them feel like they're more in control than they really are. And, for them, getting rid of these just might take the sting out of giving us something else."

Turning to me, he said, "Here's your first official task. Take notes for this part of the meeting. Here's some paper and pencils."

"I'd be glad to," I replied. "It has been a long time since I've done this. I'll do my best to keep up."

"Just let me know if I go too fast. Speak up if I do. Everyone ready? Here's the list. Oh—one more thing before I start. Note these are not presented as demands. They are presented as discussion items. If we make demands they'll just be thrown back in our faces."

The others nodded in agreement. He cleared his throat and began.

"One, we'd like to talk about issues of safety in the factories. This is one that should be of interest to them as well, if we can present the discussion in the right way. Sick or injured workers reduce production and cost them a lot of money each year."

"Two, wages and methods of determine them. This won't be an easy discussion. We all know they take advantage of and cheat their employees at every turn through everything from doctoring weight scales to increasing the number of what constitutes a gross of product. I heard one owner is now requiring his blank cutters to produce two dozen above gross for them to get paid for a gross. That's criminal."

"Three, work hours—the length of the work week. From their perspective, the more work they can get everyone to do without increasing wages is very much to their advantage. This won't be an easy area to address."

"Four—and this is one of our 'throw-away' items because they'd never agree to it—we'll tell them we'd like to talk about bonuses for workers if production runs higher than planned. There are furniture factories out in California where workers get extra wages if the overall production for a month is above what was expected. However, that will probably never play here in Muscatine. Still, we'll put up a weak discussion and let them rant and rave, and they'll be very full of themselves when we agree to take it off the table. "

"Five is another 'throw-away.' It's a good idea, but they'll never go for it, not now, probably not ever. They'll say it screams of Socialism. We'll say it shouts humanity. Whatever we each call it, it will never get the discussion it deserves. Basically, we'd like to suggest small weekly contributions from each worker— matched by ownership—to be placed into a pool to be used to help defray medical expenses of those injured while on the job. Too many people lose fingers, limbs, and eyes –and some even die—because they simply cannot afford to see a doctor. Of everything we're fighting for, this concerns me more than anything."

"Sixth, and finally, we'd like them to recognize our right to have the union and agree not to punish those who join it. We shouldn't have to meet in secret out of fear, like we're doing right now."

When he finished with the list, he said, "Let's open this up for discussion. What do you think?"

Mrs. Frank was the first to respond. "These demands—or 'discussion items'—are long overdue. We need to force the issue. We just can't keep going on and on like this, with nothing changing. The people I work with at Pioneer are fed up; they're tired of being little more than slaves to the owners. We must stand up for our rights now!"

"I agree," Mr. Fredericks said. "U.S. Button Company is a powder keg, and unless we can show some progress soon, it isn't going to take much to touch everyone off. If workers go off half-cocked, it will destroy everything we've worked for to this point.

Let's give them something to hang their hats on."

Mattie joined in. "I agree with Jack. We can kill two birds with one stone here. The strike threat and the list should get the owners to the table, and, at the same time, the workers will see action taking place and should be more willing to wait and see what happens."

I had been instructed by Mattie to do little more than watch and listen, but I had to jump into the discussion. "The last thing we want—and the last thing that would help right now—would be riots. If the workers in all the plants are of the same mind on this, that something has to happen soon, then this is the answer."

Mattie gave me a look that suggested I stop, but I continued. "The key to all of this is going to be how the list is presented. Mr. Hanley was right when he said the list should be presented as 'discussion' items. We must be very careful about that. Communication is the weapon that will get what we all want. If that door is closed, then the riots will happen and we'll all be doomed."

Charles smiled and motioned for me to go on. "There are two sides to this. The owners have to make a decent profit to keep the factories open, pay for maintenance of their machines, and plan for future growth and change. If they can't do that, then they'll be forced out of business and we'll all lose our jobs. Everyone loses if that happens. It would be wise for us to remember something Viola said a time or two: 'You can catch more flies with sugar than manure.' If we really want to change any of that, we can't go into these discussions slinging manure. The plan and the list are sound, so I say we get started."

"So do I," Miss Simmons said, slapping her hand on the table. "Let's take a vote. All in favor, say so."

All did—and then broke out into heartfelt cheers.

"Let's not get too excited yet," Charles said, bringing us back down a notch. "We've got a very long way to go."

"But this is the spark we've all been waiting for," Mattie replied, raising her fist in the air.

"Amen to that," Mr. Frank added.

"Then one more thing," Charles said. "I suggest we let it out our strike date is exactly three weeks from tomorrow. That should give us enough time to get our list to the owners and give them enough time to decide this really is the time to get together and talk. Do you agree with this timetable?"

All did, without additional discussion.

As I looked around at our group, I saw genuine joy and promise. There was no way of knowing how all of this would play out, but if heart had anything to do with it, this group was going to present a formidable front.

....

On our way home we were so wound up we wanted to keep talking about the meeting, but we knew it was dangerous if anyone overheard us. We kept most of our sentences to very few words, like "Believe it?" "No, you?" "Can't wait!" "Me, too!"

Anyone who did hear us probably thought we had a touch of the sillies, which, I guess, we did have. After we were safe inside our living room, I exploded with questions. Mattie had to ask me to slow down and collect myself.

When I had enough breath to keep from stuttering, I asked her, "You knew all of this was going to be discussed tonight, didn't you? And this business with me was your idea, wasn't it?"

"Maybe I did mention you'd make a good poster girl. I hope you'll be proud of that. We're putting our faith in you and what you can do for the cause."

"Mattie, what happens to me—to us—if I do end up that poster girl? If that happens, that means a strike has really started. What then? I heard Mr. Wilson say I'd be taken care of 'in every way,' but what did he mean by that? You have any idea? I didn't think about that until later, and it's got me worried now."

"Like you, I hope we don't end up striking," she replied. "But, if we do, we're going to put everything into the fight we can. That includes your efforts—and mine. You're now on the executive board of the BWPU, which means if we do strike, the union will pay you a good wage to keep working for them as recording secretary. I'll keep my position and be paid, too. We won't get rich, but we also won't have to move out of these luxurious quarters or give up our superlative diet."

"Seriously?" I asked, in disbelief. "They'll keep us on wage? For how long?"

"For as long as it takes. If that happens, let's hope that isn't long."

"When do you think I'll be called to help with the letter we're going to send to all the owners?"

"Soon," Mattie replied. "Very soon."

....

CHAPTER 22

THE NEXT WEEK FLEW PAST, what with work at the factory during the day and union duties at night. We met each evening in a different location, for safety reasons. I spent most of my time as recording secretary preparing the letters containing the list of discussion items to be sent to the owners. Every other night we had a general meeting of the executive board. There were two main topics of discussion we always came around to before adjourning. The first was how we could increase membership in the union. Mattie was in charge of this area and led the discussions during this portion of the meetings. She was especially interested in our reactions to some of her plans, and we gave them freely. The other item was how we might convince the owners it was in their best interest to consider seriously the list of discussion items. Our talks in this area were lively and loud voices were raised, but in the end all were respectful. We hoped and prayed we could rekindle at least a touch of this respect and consideration when the owners would eventually be brought into the discussions, but we were not going to hold our breath.

All seemed to be going very well until Saturday morning, February 25, exactly one week before the "official" strike date we had set. Mattie and I had just started down our steps on our way to work when we saw people below running every which direction. This much activity usually meant a fire close by, but we didn't see or smell any smoke.

When we reached the street, Mattie grabbed the arm of a coverall-clad young woman as she ran by.

"What's going on?" Mattie inquired. "A fire?"

"Worse than that," the young woman shrieked, gasping for breath. "All the factories are closed up. We got no more work. What are we going to do now?"

"Closed up?" I asked. "Why?"

"All I know is everyone's being turned away. I got to get home now to see my husband. Got to figure out what to do."

With that, she broke Mattie's hold and bolted up the street.

"What was she talking about?" I asked Mattie.

Mattie raised her eyes to the early morning sky. "I hope it isn't so."

"What?" I asked, getting more concerned by the second.

"We talked about the possibility of this about a month ago. There were rumors the owners were considering a lockout to try to break the union. They might have done it."

She paused. "You get to the factory quick as you can and see what you can find out. I know where to find Charles Hanley. If anyone knows what's going on, it'll be him. If you find out it is a lockout, let's meet back here in a couple of hours, and we'll talk about what we should do. If it isn't, well, I'll get to Blanton's as fast as I can and make up some excuse for being late."

....

A steady stream of men and women rushed past me from the other direction as I made my way to the factory. I tried stopping a couple of them to get information, but no one would stop. The terror in their faces told me what I was seeking.

When I finally reached the steps to the factory, a guard stepped in front of me and pointed to a large sign on the door. It read, simply, "Closed Until Further Notice."

"You'll have to leave, Miss. No one's allowed in. Go along now."

"But I'd like to see Mr. Blanton," I said. "Please tell him Pearl McGill is here."

"Doesn't matter who you are," the guard replied. "I've got orders...."

Just then Miss Fitch opened the main door and said, "You can let this one in. Come right this way, Miss McGill. Mr. Blanton told me to watch for you."

The guard backed off to the side and allowed me past. As soon as we were inside, Miss Fitch said, her voice full of genuine concern, "Oh, it's a tragedy! In all my years I never thought it would come to anything like this. What's going to happen?"

Mr. Blanton stepped out of his office, handed some papers to Miss Fitch, and, without a word, motioned for me to follow him back inside. He closed the door behind us.

"It's a sad, sad day for the industry," he said, sitting heavily in his chair. "Never imagined I'd see the day."

I sat down across from him and studied his face. He was ashen, and small beads of sweat were streaked across his forehead. His clothes were wrinkled, as if he had slept in them.

"What is this all about? What's happening?"

He kept tapping a pencil on his desk and swung his chair so he could look out the window. Without turning back toward me, he began.

"I've got a message I want you to give Sam Henry. He needs to know what's going on. Can you do that for me?"

He didn't wait for me to reply. Instead, he continued, "Looks like the rumors were right: the unionists were planning a strike. We found out last week and got together for a meeting to decide what we could do to put an end to this foolishness. Owners of forty-three of the big factories and a fair number of the small ones decided we'd simply shut down and teach those unionists a lesson—teach them which side of their bread gets buttered. We'll let them starve a while and see how they like that. If it comes down to a choice between their precious union and food on the table, we think they'll snap to their senses."

He paused, shook his head, stood up, and walked to the window, peering intently below. I asked, "But won't this hurt the owners as much as the workers? You won't be making any money either. I don't see how this can help either side...."

He cut me off, brusquely, "I went along with it because if we're going to take action, this is the time. It hasn't been the case so much for us here, but many of the other factories have over-produced product. Best for us to hold onto this surplus so we don't saturate the market and drive prices down. Don't get me wrong—the factories are all in competition, but we'd be shooting ourselves in the foot if we reduced profits for everyone. And the economy out East isn't good right now. That means the clothing and textile factories are suffering, too, so our market has shrunk, at least temporarily. It won't kill us to shut down for a while. But it just might kill off the union. We're calling this a shutdown, but it's really...."

His voice trailed off, and he turned around and looked at me like a man who had just realized he'd said too much.

"It's really what?" I asked, calmly, hoping he would continue.

"Tell your uncle it's a lockout. What I said before about the market is true, but this union...."

He went back to the window before continuing, "Do you know what we found out at the meeting? The union is going to demand a one hundred percent salary increase for all workers. Can you image that! One hundred percent! They're crazy, I tell you. And on top of that, they want a union officer to be right there with our supervisors in every workstation in every factory. Why, if that happened, every time someone got a hangnail the whole plant would be forced to shut down. I can tell you this— this is not going to happen here. Not by a long shot. Let's starve them out and see how they feel then."

What he had mentioned certainly wasn't on the discussion list we had prepared. One hundred percent raises? Union supervisors?

"Are you sure that's what the unionists were going to ask for?" I asked. "What makes you think that?"

"Some of the other owners at the meeting told us. They heard it from their informers. I'm sure it's true."

I had to choose my words carefully. "But what if that isn't

what they want at all? Wouldn't it be better to meet with them to find out for sure before shutting down the factories? Wouldn't it be better for everybody? What if those owners are wrong?"

"Doesn't matter. The lockout won't hurt us. And as far as those unionists are concerned, once they get an inch, they'll want the whole mile. We've got to nip this in the bud. This is the time to take a stand."

"But what would it hurt to make sure? What would it hurt to see what they have to say?"

He smiled. "Pearl, you've got the innocence I wish others still had. Yes, in an ideal world it would be best if we all knew what would help the other fellow—because each could probably profit by that. But don't you understand this is different? If we sit down with them, by that act we admit a union exists. Right now, we don't recognize the union, and we don't intend to. Now, if some of the workers step forward to talk for the others, we might be able to get something sorted out. Maybe. But they better not say they are there on behalf of the union if they know what's good for them."

Clearly, his mind was made up. Nothing I could say at this point would make a dent in his reasoning. I had to get this information back to Mattie, so I started to get up from my chair.

"Wait just a minute before you go. I want to say something else. You've been a good soldier for me, Pearl. I'm not forgetting that. It may be a week, possibly two, but some of us are going to ease into operation again, at least on a limited basis. All of us decided when we fire up production again we'll do it with people who renounce the union and sign a loyalty oath to us. The others can go to hell. If we have to, we'll also hire replacement workers. We want people who want to work—and who will be faithful and loyal. I want you back here. I'll send word to you when the time comes."

"I appreciate that, Mr. Blanton," I replied. "I really do. But I don't think I should...."

He cut me off. "I know what you're going to say—that you'd

be worried about your safety—about being seen with those who come back to work. I won't blame you if you go back to Grandview until all this blows over. I'll support whatever you want to do."

When he paused, I quickly interjected, "Sir, I don't see how this can be good for anyone. I just want to see everybody listen to each other and get this over with. I'd like to help with that."

"Whatever you decide, be careful. This could get really ugly. Don't get caught in the middle."

If only he knew.

"I'll send word to you when the time is right," he said as I started for the door.

I thanked him again—and thanked Miss Fitch as I walked through the office. Once outside, I looked back toward Mr. Blanton's window. He was standing there, staring off into the distance.

....

The streets were full of people rushing in all directions as I made my way home. Three thousand workers suddenly had no place to go, and it was obvious they didn't know how to react, didn't know what to do. Some clustered in groups at intersections. I paused near one of these groups long enough to hear they were all throwing out speculation as to why the factories had closed their doors. Their thoughts ranged from retaliation against the union to the factories closing their doors to make safety upgrades. The person who uttered this last possibility was razzed and shoved out of the group by the others. It was clear the owners had won the first skirmish, and confusion was spreading like wildfire.

At the intersection of Front and Chestnut, a police officer, frantically blowing his whistle, chased about half a dozen men carrying what appeared to be sacks of flour. A woman across the street shouted to no one in particular, "They've robbed the mercantile! Stop them!"

The thieves wore work coveralls. It hadn't taken long for the panic to start turning into violence. If the factories stayed closed, it wouldn't be long before few would be able to afford food. Suddenly, the men running with the sacks of flour didn't seem so absurd after all. I stepped to the other side of the street and quickened my pace.

Mattie was seated at the kitchen table when I walked in.

"What'd you find out?" she shouted, jumping up. "Tell me."

As quickly as I could, I relayed what Mr. Blanton had said. When I was finished, Mattie said, "It all makes sense. It fills in some gaps in what I heard this morning. We're in trouble now. They beat us to the punch, and that will take the wind out of our sails."

She shared with me what she had learned from Charles. He also knew the owners touted this as a shutdown, but the fact of the matter was this was a lockout, plain and simple, and it was done to destroy the union. Charles had already received word that button factories all across the region were still operating at full tilt. This meant what I'd heard earlier from Mr. Blanton about the economic conditions out East was not true.

Charles told Mattie the owners were smart to call this a shutdown instead of a lockout because they wouldn't have to publicly address any issues brought forth by the union. Instead, they could whine and moan and have a field day in the newspapers about rough economic conditions and how difficult it was for them, under the best of circumstances, to keep their doors open. By claiming financial woes, they would, essentially, be asking for sympathy and understanding. If they could make people believe this, then the union members would seem like uncaring ingrates, all of whom were interested in nothing but their own welfare. In short, the unionists would end up looking like a pack of spoiled, rotten brats, which is exactly what the owners were aiming for.

"This creates another problem," Mattie added. "We'll have to come out into the open a lot earlier than we wanted to because we'll have to rally the workers now more than ever. If we don't get a strong union put together—and soon—we'll be cooked. We have to get busy, and I do mean right now."

She continued, "Charles said something else. As of this morning, you and I are officially on the union payroll. That's one less thing to worry about."

"So what's next?" I asked. "What did Charles say he wanted us to do?"

"The executive board is going to get together for a planning meeting this afternoon."

Mattie looked at her watch. "It's a little early, but I suggest we grab a bite of lunch now. We're going to be very busy this afternoon."

My stomach was churning, but I knew she was right. We ate quickly, and as we did, not a word passed between us. Neither one of us, like most everyone else in town, knew what to say. The owners had won the first skirmish.

....

Our meeting place was a newer, large home just west of the main downtown district on Front Street. Mr. Wilson, Charles, and his father were in a private meeting when we arrived, so we were asked to sit in the parlor until called for. The other members of the board came in one by one, each in various stages of shock and disbelief. We talked among ourselves, trying to guess what would happen next. It wasn't long before we were called into a wide dining room and asked to sit at two tables that had been pushed together. Mr. Wilson was first to address us.

"I don't have to tell you this changes our plans—and especially the timetable. I've got to give the owners credit; they're smarter than I would have thought. Still, this lockout isn't a complete surprise to us. We considered the possibility and made contingency plans that should carry us through. Here's what we're going to do."

He pointed at Charles, then at me, before continuing, "These two have a lot of work to do today. I want you to take care of two things before you turn out the lamps tonight. First, fliers and posters need to be designed and written in a way that will make people feel bad if they don't join the union right now—that if they don't, they're risking everything. And I'm going to give you some extra help. Marva Jane, Oleta—work with them on this. Think about everything you've heard those at your factories say and get their feelings into these fliers. I've got a good friend in the printing business here in town, and he said he'd run them off for us as soon as we get our ideas to him. If you finish this work by tonight, fliers can be printed up and posted all over town by tomorrow afternoon. We need to stop the panic we've seen in the streets this morning."

"Then, you've got some letters to write and get into the mail."

He pulled a sheet of paper from his vest pocket and continued, "This is the list. The first letter will go to Mr. Samuel Gompers, President of the American Federation of Labor."

This announcement produced quite a stir from the others.

"Yes, that's right," Mr. Wilson added. "The American Federation of Labor. We've already visited with them, and it looks like they are going to let our Button Workers' Protective Union join forces with them. We'll soon also be charter chapter 12854 of the AFL. The AFL is not a group to mess with lightly, which the local owners will find out soon enough. If they want to play rough, they haven't seen anything yet."

"Hallelujah!" Mr. Fredericks shouted when he heard the news. "It's about time!"

"It's exactly the time," Mr. Wilson responded. "This affiliation will give us power that will scare the owners right down to their socks. There are times when it's best to fight fire with fire— and this is one of them. Two more letters also need to be sent out, one to John Lennon, the AFL National Treasurer, and the other to Emmett Flood, the National Organizer. Mr. Lennon will come out here to stand shoulder to shoulder with us."

He paused. "And the best part is this: Mr. Lennon is also

going to bring us some emergency operating funds, so you'll all get paid regularly."

This brought nervous laughter and soft applause from the group.

"Mr. Flood will also come here. He's going to work with Mattie to help us build up membership and organize speeches and rallies. Which reminds me—Weed Park is probably the best venue for the larger gatherings we're going to have, and it's not too early to be scouting it out and deciding upon how we can best use that location. Let's get right on that. Mattie, if you need help with your work before Mr. Flood gets here, Hilda and Vernon can give you a hand. Plan on them working with you from now on, if that's okay with everyone."

We all nodded our approval, so he went on, "Pearl, here's an added treat. Actually, it's a nice treat for us all, but you'll be the most directly affected in our group. You're going to send a letter to the Women's Trade Union League in Chicago. They're expecting to hear from us—just not this soon. We need someone to be our liaison to that group, and you're going to be it—because you're our poster girl. Because so many of the workers in the button industry are women, they offer special support services we can draw upon. They've earned a reputation for going into strike situations and helping set up support services, like medical care, food, and housing, for those in need. Depending on how long all of this plays out, we're going to need their help most of all."

Mr. Wilson handed the sheet of paper to me and said, "The addresses are on the back. Get to work as soon as possible."

I started to get up from my chair, but he placed a hand on my shoulder. "There are a couple more things you should know about. The first is more a matter of semantics than anything else, but it may prove useful to us in the end. As we've said, the owners are calling this a shutdown. We know it's really a lockout. Semantics, right? Well, I've got a third word to throw in that hopper—strike. If this isn't settled, we're going to call for a strike to fight fire with fire. The word *strike* presents a certain measure of fear, and we'll make use of it. The second piece of news is that a telegram has already been sent this morning to Governor Beryl Carroll—asking him to step in and see if he can bring all parties together to talk. I don't know if he'll try, but we had to ask him—and had to let him know what's going on here. I've met the man only once, but my impression was he's tough, but fair. I don't know how he's going to respond. We just have to wait and see."

He paused one last time. "And it wouldn't hurt to pray."

The prayer would come without us being asked to do so. The sudden lockout was enough to make sure of that. At the same time, none of us was much interested in playing the waiting game. We wanted action, even if we didn't know at this point exactly what it could or should be.

And we wanted that action now. In turn, each of us rose from the table and prepared to do our work. It was time, and we were ready.

....

CHAPTER 23

FOR THE NEXT WEEK THE executive board met briefly before we each split off to begin our work of the day. It was too much of a risk for us to meet in one location regularly, so we were asked to memorize a schedule of rotating meeting locations. All were within easy walking distance, so this was not a problem. My main responsibility each day was to work directly with Charles to create what seemed like an endless stream of letters to keep people informed and to ask for various types of help and support. I seldom saw Mattie after the update sessions. Her work took her out to visit with the workers in an attempt to get them to join with the union. She was very good at her work, and Mr. Wilson praised her for it just about every morning.

In the middle of the week four representatives from the Chicago office of the Women's Trade Union League visited us. These women were specialists in organizing support efforts for those affected by the lockout, and I learned a great deal from them. First, they visited the owners of the main stores in town and convinced them if the button industry remained shut down for long, stores might be forced out of business. The argument was strong enough they ended up getting free meeting space, housing, and food for the workers. They were all strong, determined women, and I quickly grew to admire them. So, when they officially asked me if I'd like to serve as the local liaison to the WTUL, I was honored to accept. They invited me to come to Chicago when the opportunity presented itself to attend training sessions for young women interested in helping deliver their brand of support services for communities facing situations like ours. I thanked them—and told them I would get to Chicago as soon as it would be appropriate.

Later that week Mr. Wilson called us together for a special update. He told us Governor Carroll had acted swiftly after being contacted and had agreed to do his best to act as an intermediary. In a secret meeting held the night before, Governor Carroll had invited Mr. Wilson and Mr. Hanley Sr., representing the union, and several from the ranks of the factory owners to try opening discussion. According to Mr. Wilson, their talk was kept in very general terms and was strained but peaceful enough at first. However, at the point when Mr. Hanley asked them to recognize the workers' right to belong to the union, the owners stormed out of the room. After the owners departed, the Governor, who remained neutral and open-minded about the issues at hand, Mr. Wilson, and Mr. Hanley decided the main tasks to accomplish were now two-fold. First, more effort needed to be placed into finding support of all types for those currently out of work, both for their sake and for the sake of the Muscatine businesses. And second, it was imperative all sit back down at the table as quickly as possible, and the Governor said he would personally work on this.

On top of everything else taking place, the factories were, one by one, starting to reopen with replacement workers and those who had renounced the union and agreed to sign loyalty oaths. Mr. Blanton had told me a little about this, but I had no idea it would happen so quickly. When those locked out of their jobs saw the replacement workers, some called them "scabs," taking up their old posts, the tension boiled and rippled to every corner of the town. By the close of that week, the violence we all feared started.

Fights broke out every morning at factories all across town between those who had lost their jobs, most of whom were unionists, and the replacement workers. Guards placed at the main entrances of the factories were no match for the mobs of displaced workers who showed up with rocks and clubs to greet their replacements. The police were called as soon as a fight would erupt, but they couldn't be everywhere at once. The unionists quickly discovered if the police didn't show up within ten minutes, they probably weren't coming at all, which gave them free rein to continue the beatings they were dishing out.

It didn't take long for some of the displaced to get more creative in expressing their anger. They got their hands on hydrochloric acid and used it to make bombs which they threw into the homes of scab workers. There were no reports of anyone being injured in this manner, but the knowledge that this might happen kept lamps low and curtains drawn tightly shut at night.

The factories were also vandalized. Trash piles outside the buildings were set ablaze, and rocks and bricks were heaved through windows. Some even managed to cut off the water supply to the buildings, which shut down whole factories. No water—no production.

Another popular method of getting their message across was through pelting the replacement workers, while they were on their way to the factories, with rotten tomatoes and eggs. The egg and tomato-throwers formed small armies that hid behind bushes and trees while waiting for their prey to come into view—and then charged out and struck. One morning even the mayor of Muscatine, who was walking to a factory with a group of replacement workers, was hit squarely in the middle of his forehead by someone flinging a particularly nasty egg. The blow knocked the mayor down and almost rendered him unconscious.

It didn't take long for the owners to decide they had taken enough of this. Several of them called upon the mayor and asked for help. Still sporting a knot the size of a walnut in the middle of his forehead, the mayor didn't need much convincing. Something had to be done right away. He contacted the sheriff and instructed him to hire some enforcers, men he knew had helped clean up similar problems in Chicago and St. Louis. When the sheriff asked how many he should hire, the mayor reportedly said, "Two dozen or so ought to do it. Get them here as fast as you can."

Enforcers arrived in two days. They were actually professional strikebreakers who came with the reputation of being nothing more than bullies and thugs. It was no wonder, then, they were proud of being called "Sluggers," a name that had stuck to them and which they had richly earned for their efforts in St. Louis and Chicago. Most telling was the fact the Pinkertons wanted nothing to do with them. If they didn't care for their methods, that spoke volumes to us.

As soon as word spread of the Sluggers' arrival, the streets started to empty, especially at night. At first people hoped for safety in numbers by walking in groups, but that soon changed when the mayor rushed through a new city ordinance stating it would be unlawful for more than three people to gather together on the streets at one time. The penalty for violation was a stiff fine and confinement in the city jail. The ordinance demonstrated in a very public way which side the city officials were on in this fight. It also meant new challenges to Mattie's work as coordinator of gatherings and rallies.

Once people no longer walked in large groups, the threats and beatings increased dramatically. The Sluggers waited in the shadows near street corners for unsuspecting passersby. Poor souls thought to be unionists were pulled into alleys and beaten, at times to the point of needing care at Bellevue Hospital. During daylight hours, the Sluggers stood boldly outside stores in the main sections of town and chased away anyone who even remotely looked to them like they had worked in the button industry. Many asked why groups of locked-out workers couldn't stop this, but the fact was the Sluggers had the protection of the police, which complicated matters beyond easy solutions. Therefore, two separate battles raged on every day: one between the unionists and the replacement workers, and the other between the Sluggers and anyone they felt belonged to or was in sympathy with the union. Muscatine was on the edge of a bloodbath.

One late afternoon about a week after their arrival, the

Sluggers crossed a taboo line.

I had just returned home after completing my work for the day and stopping by the library to pick up a new book the librarian had been holding for me. Mattie suddenly rushed in and shouted, "Get your shoes back on. We've got to go—now!"

"Whatever are you talking about?" I asked, reaching for my shoes.

"Hurry up. I'll tell you as we go. Come on! We've got to get down to the station!"

As we hurried along, Mattie relayed the story to me. Earlier in the afternoon, the Sluggers had kicked and slapped down an eight-year-old girl, Olga Magnusson, right in the middle of Second Street. Olga had been with her parents, both of whom had been locked out by the Hawkeye Button Company. Apparently, the family hadn't been quick enough to get out of the way of the Sluggers as they made their way down the sidewalk and ended up suffering the consequences, especially young Olga, who lost three of her front teeth and suffered a deep gash above her right eye. The event had been witnessed not just by displaced workers passing by, but also by a goodly number of shopkeepers and others as well. All who had seen the incident were horrified, but they were too frightened to come to the aid of the family. While the Magnussons nursed their wounds, word of the event spread across town like a rifle shot, and groups demanding revenge formed immediately. It was one thing for the thugs to harass and pick on adults, but they crossed the line when they brutalized a child.

Pausing in her telling of the story, Mattie turned to me and said, "This has to stop."

I was in shock. I had heard enough stories about the Sluggers to believe most anything except that they would attack a child.

By the time we reached the station, the crowd had grown to several thousand. I had never seen this many people in one place in all my life. All were pressed toward the main platform and were straining to hear a man addressing the assembled group.

Mattie leaned over and said, through the buzz of the crowd, he was George Turner, a supervisor at the U.S. Button Company and part-time boxer at a local club.

As he spoke, his loud, dramatic voice projected well into the crowd.

"I don't know about you," he said, his voice booming, "but I've had enough of this. First we get locked out of our jobs—just because we're concerned about our safety and well being. Then we get attacked and beat up just because of who we are and what we do for a living. We're told we can come back to work if we promise to roll over and take everything the owners shove down our throats. They want slaves, nothing more. Then they tell the merchants not to sell anything to us so they can starve us out."

Here he paused. His voice started to crack as his emotions raged to the surface. He wiped his eyes and continued, "And now they've beaten little Olga Magnusson within an inch of her life because her parents make buttons!"

The tears streamed down his cheeks. When he finally regained his composure, he added, "This could have been my little girl. Your little girl. Sure as life, they'll be next if we don't do something."

Shouts of "That's right" and "Let's get 'em!" rang out from the crowd. Mr. Turner, apparently oblivious to these, continued, his voice rising again. "Remember what the Bible says, 'An eye for an eye.' That's what we need now—Biblical justice. And I can tell you how we can get it. We can get it by getting rid of the Sluggers. I say we march over to their hotel and give them a taste of their own medicine. The only thing they understand is violence, so let's give it to 'em. I normally don't cotton to this, but I see no other choice. The safety of our families depends on what we do tonight. If we don't act, it's the same as giving them permission to attack our families any time they feel like it. We can't let that happen, can we?"

The crowd around us roared, "No!" A chant of "Get the Sluggers! Get the Sluggers!" rang out in a chorus that started at the front and moved quickly back to where we were standing.

"Then what are we waiting for?" Mr. Turner shouted above the chant. "Follow me!"

The crowd turned, and we were suddenly no longer in the back. We were now in the front of a mob determined to dole out justice to men they thought the lowest form of humanity. The crowd parted just long enough to let Mr. Turner make his way through. As he passed by, I noticed he had a small pistol in his hand.

"I don't want to watch this," I said to Mattie as we were swept forward with the crowd. "Let's go home."

"Not a chance," Mattie replied, practically screaming so that her words could be heard. "I agree with George. This has to be done—and now. We're all a part of this, whether we like it or not. If we don't show support, we might as well pack up and leave town. If we get separated, we'll meet at home. Watch yourself. Run if the police get near you. Don't forget the new ordinance."

I didn't agree with her, but it soon became apparent I couldn't have dislodged myself from the mass surrounding me if my life had depended upon it. We were pressed in with the determination of vengeance, and there was no way out. I held to Mattie's arm as long as I could, but it wasn't long before we were separated.

The crowd was so thick I couldn't tell which direction we were moving. I guessed it was toward Front Street, but I wasn't sure. I was like a shell being forced down the sorting rollers, waiting to see where I would fall. When those around me suddenly pressed to the right, a small opening to my left offered me the chance I had been praying for. With all the energy I could call up, I darted through the opening and into the clear. Exhausted, I sat down on a bench at the side of the road and lifted my feet so they wouldn't be trampled by those still marching by. Even so, my legs were still battered, so I inched up and sat on the back of the bench, placing my feet firmly on the seat and out of harm's way. At least I thought that was the case.

Off to my left three quick shots rang out. I ducked and held tightly to the bench as those around me screamed and fought for cover. When I looked back up, a line of police officers was running toward the front of the crowd. Following them was a group of Sluggers, who started indiscriminately punching and kicking those in their path. I was startled by their brutality and instinctively tried to run back toward the station. That was when a fist landed a glancing blow to my right cheek, dropping me like a stone to the ground. I wasn't as much hurt as stunned—and tried to crawl to the back of the bench, seeking safe haven. As I did, one of the Sluggers was knocked off his feet, and he crashed down heavily on top of me. Our eyes met, and he raised a fist to hit me. A large rock lay on the ground at the end of the bench, and in one motion I grabbed it up and drew it down on the side of the Slugger's head. He looked at me, surprise filling his eyes, and fell back, his body suddenly motionless. I tried to lean over to make sure he would be all right, but I was picked up by someone next to me who said, commandingly, "Move. The police are coming." The person grabbed my hand and pulled me deep into the crowd.

My jaw began to throb, and I felt like I was going to throw up. I wanted to sit down, but the people crushing in around me made this impossible. I had no choice but to keep standing and move with the crowd. After what seemed an eternity, we stopped and all became eerily quiet. I poked my head up and saw we were in front of the Commercial Hotel. It wasn't long before George Turner's voice rang out once again.

"This message is for the Sluggers," he shouted. "We want you gone from this town, and we mean now. If you don't, we're going to burn you out!"

The crowd shouted approval. Off to my right, I could see half a dozen men with blazing torches standing on the sidewalk. They were waving them in circles over their heads.

"See those torches?" Mr. Turner called out. "You've got exactly five minutes to get moving or we're throwing them in. This isn't a bluff. This is a warning—and we mean it."

A thunderous roar spread through the crowd.

"You don't have the guts," one of the sluggers suddenly yelled back from the safety of the interior of the hotel. "There isn't an ounce of courage in the whole lot of you. Go home if you know what's good for you."

"We'd rather watch you roast!" Mr. Turner called back.

With that, he made his way to the men on the sidewalk and grabbed a torch from the one on the far end. He walked slowly and deliberately back to his original position and held the fire high.

"You talking about courage!" he screamed. "Anyone who beats an eight-year-old girl and a bunch of old, defenseless women is nothing but a coward. That's what all of you are. Dirty stinkin' cowards! You've got four more minutes and I'll show you what courage is. Stay in there and burn alive if you don't believe me!"

Suddenly, a man ran onto the porch of the hotel. As he did, he frantically waved his arms back and forth over his head.

"Let's stop this!" he shouted. "Doesn't need to happen. I know all of you are angry and probably rightly so. I heard what happened this afternoon, and I'm sorry about that."

"And just who are you?" Mr. Turner called out to him. "What give you the right to butt into this?"

"I'm Sheriff McDaniel," he replied, "and it's my duty to step in here."

As soon as he announced his name, a murmur spread through the crowd. Just as quickly, someone called out, "Ain't your fight, Sheriff. It's ours. You've done no good for us; we'll take care of this ourselves."

"If this building is torched, I'll arrest everyone I can get my hands on for premeditated murder because that's exactly what it will be. Murder, plain and simple."

"Then what are we supposed to do?" another voice called out. "We're not going to put up with them any more. Who knows who they'll beat or kill next."

The crowd roared again and inched toward the sheriff. Someone off to the right threw a rock. The sheriff ducked at the last minute, and it crashed through the window behind him. A cheer rose in the crowd.

"Wait!" the sheriff yelled, again waving his hands above his head. "You don't have to do this. If this stops now, if this doesn't go any farther, I promise you I'll have them all out of town by tomorrow morning. You have my word on it."

"And what does your word mean?" Mr. Turner asked, moving toward the sheriff. "So far, your word has meant nothing."

"I give you my word," the sheriff replied, speaking directly to Mr. Turner. "And I'll keep it."

"How do we know that?" Mr. Turner asked, his voice clipped, cold.

"Because I'm willing to admit before everyone here that I've been wrong. I've looked the other way, and I shouldn't have. These men have no business here. They don't belong. If you'll leave it up to me, I'll get them out of here before anyone else gets hurt. That's my duty and my responsibility—and I promise you I'll see that it's done."

The sheriff walked directly over to Mr. Turner and stood before him. He wasted no time holding out his hand and motioning for the torch. Mr. Turner didn't respond. Instead, he stood rigidly, motionless in front of him. The crowd grew silent, waiting to see what would follow.

"Give him the torch, George," a woman's voice finally called out from behind him. "If you don't, then we're no better than the animals they are!"

"Give it to me," the sheriff repeated, this time calmly. "I'll keep my word."

"Don't let us down," Mr. Turner finally said, slowly handing him the torch.

"I won't," the sheriff replied, dropping the torch to the ground and stomping out the fire. He motioned for the others holding torches to do the same thing.

"Everyone, go home. I'll take care of this. Clear the area."

I was surprised by the quiet as those around me slowly

moved away. Everyone seemed spent, drained. The crowd was so large it took some time before I could get across the street and over to Chestnut. Once there, I stopped and looked back toward the hotel. The sheriff was standing alone on the porch, his hands clasped behind his back. He sat down in a chair near the rail and dropped his head against his chest, as if he were praying.

Looking past the sheriff to the patch of open ground on the other side of Front Street, I saw a small group of people standing there, none of them moving. I recognized Flora from the clamming camp and realized the others were also clammers. My breath caught as I scanned the rest of the front row. There, in the center, was Gaston. Our eyes met, and I started to wave, but stopped when he suddenly turned to the side. At first my heart sank, but I quickly realized he had done that to protect me. Two deputies stood just to the right of his group, and he was making sure they wouldn't be able to make any connection between us. After a minute or so he turned and looked one last time in my direction. As he did, he smiled, turned, and walked back toward the river.

Mattie was already home when I got there. "That was close!" she said as I entered and plopped myself on the divan. "Can you imagine if the hotel had been set on fire? We would have had roasted Sluggers!"

"That's not funny," I scolded her. "Shame on you. Just think about how many people might have been killed or seriously hurt. Violence isn't the way to get anything accomplished, and you know that."

"Maybe not," Mattie cut in, "but I'll tell you one thing it would have done. It would have put a fast stop to the rein of terror that's turned this place into a ghost town. When people are afraid to walk the streets, what kind of life is that? Answer me that!"

"The sheriff said he'd get them out of here. That'll be legal and proper, the way it should be done. Cooler heads must get involved in all this. If that doesn't happen, then we will see more violence—and our cause may be lost."

"Lighten up," Mattie implored. "We just had a major victory. It might not have happened in the way you'd like, but it was a victory nonetheless."

I left the divan and walked to the kitchen for a glass of water. Looking out the window behind the sink, I could see large groups of people milling around below, from Second Street all the way down to the river. The sheriff had wanted all to disperse, to go home and simmer down. It was obvious that wasn't happening. Off to the far left, a large bonfire raged, its sparks floating high into the sky. Closer up the hill, I heard the sound of glass breaking, not once but twice in rapid succession. The violence wasn't over. I feared what it would bring, but who was I to say anything? I had been as guilty, and maybe more so, than anyone else this night. I thought of the man I had hit with the rock. It happened so quickly and had been self-defense, but I was still ashamed of myself. I wondered what had happened to him after I was pushed away through the crowd. I prayed he was recovering well. I wanted to tell Mattie about this, but I knew it would only fan the fires so I kept my mouth shut.

"It doesn't end here, you know," I said, turning to face her. "It'll get a lot uglier before it starts getting better. Tonight didn't solve anything."

"Maybe not for you," Mattie replied, standing and coming over to join me at the window. "but take a good, long look at what you see down there. You tell me tonight wasn't good for those people. Tell me that."

"What I'm telling you is this is just the beginning, and we may not like what comes next."

"I'm keeping an open mind," Mattie said, sarcastically, sitting back down again.

I let her have the last word. There was nothing else I could say that would have made a dent in her thinking. We didn't say more and turned down the lamps and went to bed. Before I fell asleep, I heard an explosion that sounded like it had happened down by the river. I didn't have the energy to get up to look. I closed my eyes—and was soon fast asleep.

....

My words were prophetic, but I took no pleasure in it.

The Sluggers were gone—but the State Militia replaced them.

The sheriff, good to his word, had made swift arrangements to get the Sluggers out of town. A large group of concerned citizens remained at the hotel, helped the sheriff escort the Sluggers to the station, and kept an eye on them until they boarded the early morning train to Chicago.

We found out later the mayor and sheriff met again later in the morning and made a decision. The violence of the previous evening had been a warning for them of what still could happen unless order was restored to Muscatine. Just before noon they decided, with the backing and urging of the factory owners, to contact the Governor and request the State Militia be brought in to help restore order and keep the peace. In their plea they didn't just point to the events of the previous evening. They included details of the vandalism at the factories and the fights between the displaced workers and their replacements. They had the nerve to add the confrontations that had been caused by the Sluggers. The mayor even threw in the fact he was assaulted one morning, although everyone doubted he mentioned it was an egg that had conked him on the forehead. Whatever he said to the Governor worked.

By late afternoon three companies of Militia arrived. They set up camp at Reservoir Park, which meant we were able to sit on our landing and watch them as they marched past and up the long hill. They looked all business in their crisp uniforms and high boots, with bayonet scabbards attached to their ammunition belts. Each man was armed with a rifle.

We were anxious for details, so the afternoon newspapers sold out as quickly as they reached the streets. The Governor had declared Martial Law for Muscatine. Under the provisions of Martial Law, the citizens of Muscatine were required to follow a very strict set of rules, especially involving public behavior and curfew.

People would initially be allowed on the streets only between the hours of seven a.m. and six p.m. Anyone without special written permission caught out at any other time would be subject to immediate arrest and confinement at the Militia camp.

Violence of any type would not be tolerated and would, result in immediate arrest. We imagined this would put a swift end to the skirmishes outside the factories.

If these rules were violated, the Militia had jurisdiction over punishment, and we heard that could be severe. Still, if anything good could be said about Martial Law, it was that the sheriff and local police no longer had control. If the State Militia could be impartial, then maybe the laws would be enforced fairly. That's what I kept telling myself and anyone else who'd listen.

The presence of the Militia and being under Martial Law had, at the same time, both a frightening and a calming effect on us all. We were frightened because we realized just how far all of this had already gone. At the same time, a calm settled over the town as people once again felt safe walking up and down the streets.

The newspapers were full of speculation about what would happen next. None of us knew anything for sure, but gossip ran through the town like rainwater through the gutters.

At this point, all we could do was wait and see—and for some of us behind the scenes, keep doing our work.

We didn't know where our work for the union did or did not fit into the regulations of Martial Law, but we chose to keep at it just the same. Martial Law wouldn't last forever, and we had so much to do. We kept a low profile and stopped handing out fliers, putting up posters, or doing any union business out in public.

"I can't wait to see what happens next," Mattie said as we watched the last of the soldiers march up Third Street toward the camp. For me, waiting was just fine.

....

CHAPTER 24

THE THREE COMPANIES OF STATE Militia remained in Muscatine only four days. That was just long enough to make everyone realize violence and force were not going to rule the day.

At the same time, the owners had badly misjudged how the unionists would view the presence of the Militia. They thought the workers would be terrified. That was not the case. The mayor and the city police acted clearly on the side of the owners, but having the Militia around quickly placed enforcement of the law into the hands of a fair and just neutral party. Therefore, the presence of the Militia and the resulting implementation of Martial Law backfired on the owners and set the workers free to resume their fight.

When the Militia pulled out, the town settled into a badly needed period of calm. Life around town appeared to go back to normal—except the lockout was still in place, and the displaced workers were still bitterly angry. Even in this tenuous state of calm, the lines remained clearly drawn between unionists and owners. Discussions between the groups were needed, but neither side wanted to be the first to step across those lines.

The owners had made an error in judgment. They had mistakenly believed they could "wait out" the unionists and "win the war of time." Most workers were hanging on financially by way of a hope and a prayer, so the owners thought it wouldn't take long for workers to throw in the towel and return to work under the owners' conditions. What the owners hadn't anticipated was the aid provided to the workers by members of the Chicago chapter of the Women's Trade Union League, who had swooped into

Muscatine like cavalry to the rescue. The network of support services they helped build all across town provided food, clothing, and, in some cases, shelter for a number of those locked out. This aid allowed the unionists to dig in their heels for the long haul, if necessary. Once the owners found out about the efforts of the WTUL, they knew the battle had shifted dramatically.

Neither side could afford a prolonged stalemate. The longer the lockout continued, the greater the chance the industry as a whole could be damaged or destroyed. If that happened, there would be no winner, and owners and unionists alike would lose their livelihoods. Still, neither side wanted to make the first move for fear it would be taken as a sign of weakness or failing support in its membership.

Several weeks went by without a meeting being scheduled. Finally, to the relief of all, Governor Carroll again stepped forward and called for a meeting. Because the invitation had come from an outside party, both owners and unionists jumped at the opportunity.

On the Wednesday of that third week, Mr. Wilson called together the members of the executive board to discuss strategy. We knew we had to be ready for the meeting with the owners, which was to take place the next afternoon. If this meeting failed, we were certain another opportunity would not present itself again soon.

Mr. Oliver suggested that he, Charles, Mr. Lennon, and I would represent the union at the meeting. When protests erupted from the others, all of whom wished to attend the meeting, Mr. Oliver reminded them their employers didn't know they were members of the union, let alone the executive board, and depending upon which direction the meeting took, their safety might be called into play.

We met long into the night and, in the end, felt we were as ready as we'd ever be.

....

Mattie did her best job of exaggerated pouting when I finished dressing and came over to sit down next to her at the kitchen table.

"It wasn't my decision. I was invited only because I'm the recording secretary. Somebody has to keep a record for us. If it were up to me, I'd send you in my place."

"I could take those notes," Mattie replied, her voice sharp. "I should be there, and you know it."

I paused to let a little tension subside, then said, "Why don't you come along with me? When we get there, I'll tell Mr. Wilson I don't feel well and you've agreed to take my place. I know how much this means to you and how you've worked for this day. Go get dressed. Let's go. There isn't much time."

Mattie picked up a grape from the bowl at the center of the table and threw it at me, hitting me square in the chest.

"What was that for?" I asked.

"It was for being right," she replied. "But I don't know how someone always as right as you are can live with herself. You're the one who has to be there. I couldn't take those notes—but you can. I'd just scribble out chicken scratch that nobody would ever be able to decipher. On top of that, I'd probably get mad right in the middle of everything and start a totally new war. It's best I don't go."

"That's one of the reasons I love you, Mattie. Your concern about others always wins out. You're not nearly as tough as you make out."

"Well I'm still tough enough to be mad at you, even if I do know you're right. So, you better get yourself out of here before I take you up on your offer or, better yet, take a switch to you. Now get out of here. Take your notes. Leave me here in agony all afternoon while you go off to the most important meeting the union has ever had."

My hand was on the doorknob when I heard her chair slide back from the table. I paused long enough for her to rush up behind me.

She hugged me tightly, then added, "Remember what I've always told you. Keep your mouth shut and listen."

....

The meeting was held in one of the rooms at the Commercial Hotel, the same place where the Sluggers were almost set ablaze. That seemed fitting.

As I entered the room, I was startled by the sight of two familiar faces. James, the dime-thrower from my first introduction to Muscatine, was speaking with two men off to my left. Then, as I scanned the rest of the room, my eyes locked with Mr. Blanton's. He walked over to me and asked, in a questioning tone, "What are you doing here?"

"Good evening, Sir," I replied, formally. "If you'll recall, the last time we met I told you I was hoping everyone could get together to talk this out. I was just fortunate enough to get a chance to be involved. I hope you understand."

It was plain he didn't. His face beet red, he exhaled sharply as he turned and walked away from me. A wave of guilt and nausea hit me as I watched him fume across the room. To Mr. Blanton, I must have seemed like Judas.

I was greatly relieved when James came over to greet me.

"Well, Miss McGill. You've certainly come a long way from Grandview. Still have your purse?"

I looked down, and as I did, he laughed—and so did I.

"Just playing with you," he said. "Never gets old, does it?"

Before I could respond, Mr. Wilson called over to me, "Pearl, please come here a minute." As I turned to leave, I smiled at James and said, "There'll be another time, Dime-Thrower."

He recoiled in mock horror and let out a little gasp as I walked away.

Mr. Wilson was standing next to a middle-aged man with striking features, especially his deep olive green eyes. "Pearl McGill, I'd like you to meet Governor Beryl Carroll."

Then, turning to the Governor, he said, "Sir, this is the young woman I've been telling you about."

"I'm honored and pleased to meet you, Governor Carroll," I said, moving my hand out to shake his. He seemed surprised by the gesture but took my hand and squeezed it gently.

"The honor is mine," he said in reply. "Thank you for being here."

Before I could respond to him, another man came over and whispered something in his ear, and then Governor Carroll called everyone to the table.

As we settled in, Governor Carroll said to the group, "I think introductions are in order before we begin. I don't think we all know each other, but we should—because this group just may stay together for future discussions."

Smiling broadly, he said, "Most of you know me. I've been called lot of things in my day, many of them not at all very flattering, but I'm still called Governor Carroll by most."

We all laughed and the tension lessened somewhat, which I'm sure was what he had hoped for. Then, from his left and continuing around the table, each, in turn, introduced himself. Those representing the union were seated together—and those a part of ownership followed.

"I'm Oliver Wilson, Business Manager for the BWPU. I'm also authorized to represent President Ray in all proceedings. Good evening to all."

"Charles Hanley, Attorney for the BWPU. Good evening."

"I'm John Lennon, visiting from Chicago. I'm the National Treasurer for the American Federation of Labor."

I was next. I introduced myself as recording secretary for the BWPU. Most nodded politely toward me, but the expression on Mr. Blanton's face made it clear to me I wouldn't be going back to work for him any time soon.

"Robert Sawchuk, Black Hawk Button Works. Hello."

"J. S. McKee, McKee Button Company. Evening, all."

"I'm Thomas Menker from the U.S. Button Company."

"Joseph Hagermann, the Hawkeye Button Company. Hello to everyone."

Mr. Blanton was next. He stared angrily at me before addressing the group. He didn't give his name. Instead, all he said was "Blanton Button Company." He then looked down at the floor.

"Good evening, everyone. I'm Asa Baker of the Muscatine Button Company."

James nodded toward me, then said to the others, "I'm James Baker, Business Manager for the Muscatine Button Company. I'm assisting Asa." Then, after pausing just for a second and pointing to Mr. Baker, he added, "And I'm his son, too."

That brought additional laughter from the group and further lessened the tension in the room.

"Looks like I'm last. I'm Edward Robison, representing the Pioneer Button Company."

When the introductions were completed, Governor Carroll said, "Very good. Now we can get down to business. But, before we do, I'd like to say a few words that I hope you'll give your best consideration."

Pausing briefly to look around the table, he continued, "I have two rules I ask to be followed at meetings. The first is that everyone listen, genuinely listen, to what others are saying. From my experience, there are always at least two sides and generally more. In any discussion, we must respect the opinion of the other side. That doesn't mean we have to agree with what another person says. It simply means we have to respect the right for that person to believe that way, even if the views are vastly different from our own. Right and wrong aren't part of the process of listening. Right and wrong are judgments of value we place later on what we've heard. And these judgments are best made when we truly listen and make these determinations based upon the total and complete facts, which we can only have in our possession if we do our best job of listening to the other person. Consider this as we begin our discussion tonight."

He did not wait for a reaction. "My second rule is very

simple. No discussion should be considered an end in itself. Let's not consider our talk tonight to be the last words on any subject we might broach. Let's just talk—and listen—to what everyone has to say. If we can do that, we will have accomplished a great deal, and we can all leave here tonight with dignity and honor."

Governor Carroll ended his introductory comments by saying, "To expedite our conversation this evening—and with the blessing of all present—I'd like to be the one to present the discussion topics and act as moderator. Is that acceptable to the group?"

All approved and Governor Carroll presented the first item, reading from a small open notebook on the table in front of him.

"First discussion point tonight is this matter—'that a joint committee of owners and workers should be established, for the mutual benefit of both parties, to negotiate disputes.' Now, I want to stay out of these discussions as much as possible, but this may be one of the 'can't see the forest for the trees' areas, so I'm going to make a recommendation myself. If there are no objections in principle to this first item, then I say it would be a terrible waste of time to go through all the work of choosing these people when we have this fine group, with fine representation present, already together. So, for practical purposes, I suggest all of you become this committee. What say you all? Would this be acceptable to you?

There were a few shrugs of shoulders, smiles, and curious looks around the table, but all quickly agreed we could initially be this group. However, representatives on both sides suggested that in the future the committee membership might need to be changed to provide different or additional representation. It was also suggested the Governor continue to be the moderator when membership changes were considered—to help ensure representation remained fair for all. He agreed to this without hesitation.

I thought the discussion of this item was finished and stopped taking notes, but Mr. Sawchuk suggested that concerns workers might bring up should be dealt with first, if at all possible, at the individual factories involved—and that our committee then be available for consultation or to serve as a "board of appeal" if resolution couldn't be found. Mr. Lennon spoke against this, saying Mr. Sawchuk's suggestion wouldn't change a thing and that concerns would still be handled only at the discretion of the owner at the factory where the concern was expressed. However, both Mr. Blanton and Mr. Oliver spoke in favor of Mr. Sawchuk's amendment, stating that our "board of appeal" would be there to serve as a motivation for everyone, owners and workers alike, to resolve the concerns locally if at all possible. I didn't feel this went far enough, and I silently agreed with Mr. Lennon that it wasn't much of a change. Still, we could take it as a small victory that at least owners would no longer have the final and complete say when concerns were examined.

Governor Carroll presented the next item on the list: "That a joint committee of owners and workers should be established, for the mutual benefit of both parties, to examine safety issues in the factories."

Given the concern all felt about this area, I expected a long discussion to follow. Instead, and much to my surprise, both parties readily agreed the issue of safety should be looked into immediately. Mr. Wilson had said before the meeting he didn't want us to get bogged down in the specifics of this area—that he just wanted to get the item approved for future study and action. Mr. Wilson's logic here was good. He did something else I thought was very smart toward the end of the discussion of this topic. He carefully chose one example to present. It wasn't what he chose but how he presented it that had me shaking my head in admiration.

"Gentlemen," he began, "I would like to make just one specific suggestion here. One of the greatest concerns felt by the workers can be attended to, I think, without it costing you a dime. At the present time, if workers want to wash their hands to remove shell dust and chemicals, this has to be done in most factories down in the soaking tanks. The result has been many cases of what the workers call 'shell poisoning,' which is probably what we would all call blood poisoning. If you gentlemen would allow it, we would find a way to pay for the purchase of barrels that could be placed in the immediate area of the soaking tanks. These barrels could be filled with clean, fresh water used only for washing hands. Then, when the water needs to be changed, it could be transferred to the soaking tanks so there would be no waste or additional cost to you. If we can purchase these barrels, would you allow them?"

The owners agreed in principle with the suggestion but said they weren't sure the best place for the barrels would be near the soaking tanks. I imagined Mr. Wilson was smiling inside because he had said before the meeting he hoped the owners, if they went along with this, would recommend a more sanitary location. The discussion ended with the owners saying they would study potential locations and then make a recommendation for placement of the barrels. All seemed very happy with this, so we moved quickly to the next item.

The next area of discussion was not so pleasantly received. Governor Carroll must have been anticipating this because he lowered his voice and read very slowly, "Weekly work hours should be reduced for all workers, and the number of hours should be made standard across factories."

The words were barely out of his mouth before objections arose. Mr. Hagermann was the first to speak against it.

"We might as well cut our own throats. Profit in this business is earned by product, not by the number of hours worked. If we reduce the work hours, that reduces product—and the profit that comes with it. It's an exacting formula. If we lose profit, workers lose wages."

On the surface it was a sound enough argument from a financial standpoint, but it didn't get to the real heart of the matter, which was the improved quality of life a reduction in hours would provide. This topic was intertwined with safety and health issues, and it was going to be difficult to extricate one from the other.

Mr. Oliver did his best to speak for what an improvement in quality of life would do to the production and morale of the workers. He went so far as to say that the workers might produce a higher quality of work if their health, safety, and working conditions were improved.

As passionate as both Mr. Hagermann and Mr. Oliver were in presenting their views, everyone seemed to be unmoved even a hair from his original position. Just when I thought we'd have to table this discussion and move on, Mr. Hagermann caught us all off stride when he turned to Mr. Menker and said, "Tom, go ahead. We have to tell them sometime. Maybe now will help."

Mr. Menker first poured himself a glass of iced tea, looked slowly around the table, and spoke, directing his words especially to Mr. Oliver and Charles.

"We're going to trust you and ask that what I'm going to say be kept just within our group for the time being."

Here he looked at Governor Carroll, who nodded and said, as if he knew what was coming next, "I'll see to it."

Then, turning to face all of us, Governor Carroll added, "I don't want a word of this to leave the room. If it does, you'll have to answer to me."

Mr. Menker then continued, "To put it bluntly, the shell beds are playing out faster than anyone could have imagined. Harvests are way down, and they're getting worse all the time. The better shells, like ebonys, are all but gone. We now get an overabundance of Pimplebacks and Pigtoes, and as you probably all know, they don't make the best buttons."

He paused again, took a sip of his tea, and added, "This is why we need to keep production and profits up. We need a positive revenue—to allow us to plan for the future. If we run out of shells, and barring a miracle, it looks like that day is coming, we'll have to switch to some other material, possibly metal, possibly wood. There are many possibilities the industry is looking into, but that's a curtain we just can't see behind right now. We have to have the funds to support this research—or we'll all be out of business."

"Don't take my word for it," he continued. "Ask any of the clammers who bring shells to the factories. They see this every day when their boats come back half full now. Why do you think they haven't joined in on all of this? The button workers' jobs might be saved if we end up going to other materials, but the clammers will be out in the cold—and they know it. If things stay as they are, they'll all soon go the way of the buggy whip maker. This could end up being the fate for all of us if we don't plan ahead starting right now."

His remarks echoed what Hector had said to me at the clamming camp. This may also have been one of the reasons Gaston had been so insistent this wasn't his fight.

Mr. Menker exhaled loudly, and said, "That's why we have to say 'no' to reduced hours. We hope you'll understand. As Mr. Hagermann pointed out, it's very simple. If we reduce hours, we reduce product and lose profit. If we lose profit, especially right now, we'd have to reduce pay to the workers and couldn't pay our shares of the research monies. We're in trouble, and if we're in trouble, it falls to all."

The other owners were silent, grim-faced while he spoke. I looked quickly at Mr. Oliver and Charles and saw they had leaned toward each other and were whispering. Charles turned back and spoke to the group.

"We're aware," he said, his voice sincere, firm. "We appreciate your honesty and candor. And we understand at least some of the challenges ahead. We just didn't know how far this had already gone. The area of work hours per week is important to the quality of life, and health in particular, for the workers, but I'll speak for the group. We'll agree to take this discussion topic off the table—for now. We'll revisit it when all of us have a better understanding of where we're going. Agreed?"

I looked around, and the owners, to a man, appeared greatly relieved. One, Mr. Brown, even clapped lightly in approval.

Charles then said, "Obviously, we'd like to help in any way we can. Let's keep that on the table, too. We have skilled workers in the factories who might be able to help by sharing their expertise as plans for the future are made."

"I appreciate your understanding and offer," Mr. McKee responded. "However, I'm afraid if this becomes too public right now, we'll have a full-scale panic on our hands. We're aware of the knowledge and skills in the workforce, and rest assured we'll draw on that when the time is right."

The mood of the group turned more somber and less and less combative as each item was presented. The atmosphere also became more businesslike and formal. Personal opinions and anecdotes were still shared as we moved from item to item, but even these became more informational in tone.

We sailed through the discussions of sanitation, which, as Mr. Oliver was quick to point out, was separate from the issues of safety. Mr. Oliver presented one area in particular. He said the workers were very concerned about toilet facilities at the factories. When Mr. Menker asked if this was really a problem, Mr. Oliver responded, "Please go over to Grau and use one of the toilets there. If you say they're fine, we'll drop the subject." Mr. Menker said he'd take his word for it, and all agreed this was an area for additional study and action.

A waiter brought in another pitcher of iced tea and a large pot of coffee. After these were served, Governor Carroll presented the next item: "All workers would be allowed to actively participate in the weighing, counting, and other means now and in the future used for determining wages." The discussion of this item wasn't very long, but it was pointed on both sides. Charles talked of the need for fairness and above-board tactics on the part of the owners. In response, several of the owners said they'd be a lot more interested in discussing this area if they could be assured we'd help combat the problem of theft in the factories. Basically, they said they needed a way to offset "shrinkage," their term for workers stealing goods and selling them to others. I had seen and heard of more than a few examples of this at Blanton, so I understood their point of view. In the end, both sides agreed to table the discussion and make the topic a major item of consideration at a future meeting.

The conversation was now so smooth and respectful it was easy taking notes. That is, this was the case until the issue of the medical care pool was introduced. Judging by how swift and strong the reaction of the owners was to this, Governor Carroll might just as well have said he was going to burn down the town and shoot all the dogs.

"Socialism!" was both the response and rallying cry of the owners to the idea of the pool. They stated quite strongly that in a democracy each man was responsible for earning his own welfare and future. The emphasis here was on earning. Clearly, they felt giving away medical care would run contrary to everything they held dear. When Mr. Oliver tried to suggest healthy workers would be able to turn out more product and, therefore, generate more profit, the response was that profit would be eaten up by the money put into the medical care pool. Thus, the owners decided it would be what they called a "zero growth" investment—and definitely not in their best interest. At the same time, they believed a medical care pool would not be in the best interest of the workers because it would be giving them something for nothing, making them feel like they weren't strong enough to take care of themselves. This, according to the owners, would lead to destruction of their self worth. It was difficult for me to take notes at that point because the logic of the owners started to escape me. No matter how hard I tried, I just couldn't get a handle on how having healthy workers would be bad.

This area was one of our "giveaways," so when Charles finally got into the discussion, he gave only a half-hearted attempt at convincing the owners this was a good idea. It was a good idea, at least from our perspective, but we knew it was one that would never get beyond a good argument at this point. Finally, Charles agreed to table the discussion of the medical care pool, which seemed to please the owners even more than when the work hour discussion had been placed on hold.

Before we moved to the next topic, Charles tried to lighten the mood by joking with them.

With a very serious look on his face, he said, "So, if you're opposed to that for now, I suppose you'd also be against a plan whereby the workers and owners would share in the profit if the workers reached a certain plateau of performance and product output."

He quickly added a wide smile and laughed softly, but it was too late. The owners had already started to react. To a man, they could be heard muttering the most colorful words I'd heard since my father dropped an anvil on his shoe.

"Guess not," Charles called out loudly enough to regain their attention. "Don't worry—that's not an item we wish to discuss. I was just kidding. Really."

Some of the owners finally realized what he was doing and smiled back. Others, Mr. Blanton in particular, looked as if he might have been on the verge of throwing something at Charles.

The Governor stepped in and changed the subject, directing us back to the rest of the list. The next item, thankfully, was one where both sides immediately agreed change would be a positive step, so it took only a short time to discuss. This had to do with the way the daily "fill-in" workers were hired when needed to replace those who could not report to work. At present, Muscatine Shorty somehow had a monopoly in this area, and each side thought he was working for the other. All laughed heartily when this misperception came to light. Then a few told stories of how Muscatine Shorty took advantage of those he placed in the temporary positions: he abused women; he took part of the workers' pay in exchange for finding them jobs; he encouraged theft of factory property, which he then sold back to the owners. Both sides quickly agreed they'd work together to find a way to hire these fill-in workers—to the mutual benefit of everyone—except, of course, Muscatine Shorty.

Mr. Oliver had asked that the list of discussion items be presented in this order for a reason—so that the bad taste in the mouth created by some of the items be allowed to dissipate as much as possible before certain other topics were explored. His reasoning was that by appearing to give in on some of the more emotional topics, and agreeing on others, it would be easier to make inroads in areas of more lasting value to us when they came up for discussion. As I continued taking notes, I realized his plan was working. He was a master at navigating the discussions, and I grew to admire him more and more.

We came to the last of the items, and Mr. Oliver's reasoning would be sorely tested. I tightened my grip on my pencil because I knew what was coming next—the issue of recognition of the union.

At this point, Governor Carroll read slowly and carefully from the notebook in front of him. "That owners not discriminate in employment or pay on account of union membership."

To say we were stunned by what followed couldn't begin to approach what we were all soon feeling. We simply couldn't believe it when the owners didn't argue, didn't raise an eyebrow. Possibly it was because the Governor followed up by presenting it as first and foremost a grapevine for the workers, to keep all in good communication. Or, maybe it was because owners knew unions were being formed all across the nation and would be in Muscatine soon enough anyway. Maybe they knew it was a battle they couldn't win in the end. It might have been because of the strikes currently taking place in the garment industry, strikes which had brought that industry to the verge of collapse, and the fact they were afraid the same would happen in Muscatine if some sort of compromise couldn't be reached. Whatever the cause, they agreed in principle to offer the union recognition, which was the greatest outcome the executive committee could have hoped for.

I looked again at Mr. Wilson, and he appeared for all the world like a kid who had just stolen the entire contents of a candy jar and gotten away with it. He started to say something, then stopped and shuffled and restacked the papers in front of him.

As he did, I noticed his hands were shaking.

Charles was nearly as jumpy himself. Mr. Lennon, more blank-faced than either of them, sat back and folded his arms across his chest. None of them smiled.

With discussion of union recognition concluded, the last item on the discussion list—"That all workers currently affected by shutdown be reinstated as soon as possible"—suddenly became a non-issue. By virtue of the owners recognizing the union, the workers could now return to work as full-fledged union member without any penalty for their affiliation. That is, they could as soon as the "shutdown" was over. To Charles' credit, he didn't use the term "lockout" when this was discussed since he knew calling it that would only have angered the owners. Whatever it was called, as soon as it ended, all would be able to return to their old jobs. The owners said very little in this discussion, repeating only that the original shutdown had been a result of overproduction and reduced demand. There was no need to argue the real motives. What mattered was workers would soon, we hoped, be going back to their jobs.

At this point, Mr. Oliver chose to give his final thoughts on the matter, and I, for one, was so glad he did.

He began, "This union does not have to be the enemy, as unions are seen to be in many industries in this country. We want to be your partner in what lies ahead. We'll pledge to bring good, solid, respectful leadership here. We promise to work with you to build the future, not tear down the walls of progress. We ask only for fairness and respect in return, and we'll strive to earn that."

Warm smiles followed. It was a fitting end to the proceedings, one that provided a much-needed framework for our next meetings together.

Governor Carroll wasted no time. "I believe we've accomplished enough for a first meeting. I'm proud of you. This has been a good start. This is something to grow on, to build upon. Let's take small steps—and eventually finish the whole journey together. We can all leave this room tonight with our heads held high. We can go back to those we represent and say, truthfully, that we want to continue working toward a positive resolution for everyone. With the blessing of all, I adjourn this meeting. As we do, all of you move around the table and shake hands."

No one spoke as we did. There were a few smiles, but most just gave polite nods. Even James remained very formal and shook my hand stiffly as we passed each other. When I ended up before Mr. Blanton, he didn't make a scene, but he refused to shake my hand; he continued to move to the side without even making eye contact. As he did, he said to me, "I'll be talking to your uncle." It was clear I had hurt him deeply, and I doubted there was anything in the world I could say to make it cut less.

When we were all back in our original places, Governor Carroll said, "We can be proud of what we've done here. Gentlemen—and Lady—until we meet again, I wish you all well."

With that, we prepared to leave. The owners, as a group, left first. As soon as they were across the lobby, we did the same.

Once we were outside the hotel and down the front steps, we looked at each other, disbelief on our faces.

"What just happened?" Charles whispered, just loud enough for all of us to hear. "Did they really recognize us?"

"That's what I heard—if my ears are working," Mr. Wilson replied, shaking his head.

"Gentlemen—and Lady—what you just heard was victory," Mr. Lennon added. "Victory."

He paused, and continued, "Frankly, I'm shocked, but I can guess in part why they did it. I think they came in scared to death we'd not give up on the medical pool fund. Right now, that's one of the major negotiating points in the garment industry out East, and it looks like it's really going to happen there. It's a good and fair idea, but it's also going to cost those owners a fortune. These men are aware of that—and were extremely worried tonight. I think they were probably so relieved they lost focus and let other things go. I don't care why it happened. I'm positively giddy that it did!"

Mr. Wilson added, "I never thought I'd live to see the day. Honestly. I thought they'd continue to fight tooth and nail against the union. We finally have a real chair at the table. No more secret meetings. No more meeting in different places every time we want to get together. That's what I've wanted all along. And now it looks like we've finally got it. Amen!"

"I also got what I was after," I said, adding my joy as well. "My dream all along was that everyone would start listening to each other. I know we'll never agree on everything. I've had enough of the straw knocked out my hair in my time here to know that would never happen. But, if we can continue talks like this, more good than bad is surely to follow. If that happens, then we all win. Before we get too excited for ourselves, we need to remember that we need the owners just as much, if not more, than they need us. We have to make sure we spread that idea. We've got to see an end to this 'Us versus Them' way of thinking. The sooner we do that, the better it will be for everyone."

We walked down the sidewalk and into the street. The meeting had surpassed our wildest dreams. In purely tangible areas, we hadn't gained all that much; however, we established the seeds for continued discussion of safety concerns and wage determination. On top of this, people could return to work. Those areas would have been more than enough for the first discussion, but they paled in comparison to what was now dominating our thoughts. We had left that room with our union moving from a shadowy apparition forced to float from one hiding place to another—to official status as the voice of the workers. This same thought must have come to everyone at once because we all, one by one, suddenly stopped in our tracks and turned back one last time to look at the Commercial Hotel.

Charles started it by raising his arms and shouting, "Yippee!"

Immediately, we all added our own shouts of joy. Even Mr. Wilson, a very conservative and modest gentleman, called out, "Praise be!"

In honor of Viola, I added one of her favorite expressions, "Holy buckets!"

We turned to face each other—and burst into laughter, followed by hugs all around. We hadn't won the war outright, but we had established a presence that could grow and prosper in the light of day. Union members would now have a safe haven, a beacon to follow when rough days appeared ahead. That much we had won. On this night, victory was ours.

"Let's get some sleep," Charles said, finally. "Then we'll meet at my house first thing tomorrow morning. I can say that out loud. My house. And don't sneak around and walk in circles around the block to make sure no one is following you before you get there. Just come on over. How does that sound?"

"It sounds beautiful," I said. "It also sounds like the future is suddenly a lot brighter. This has been an incredible night—and I'll never forget it. Never."

"None of us will," Mr. Lennon added. "And thank you. Thank you for your help and support."

His words felt good, but I felt I had to respond. "Gentlemen," I said, again addressing the group, "I feel like I've just walked into all this right at the end, and I'm feeling more than a little guilty about that. Don't get me wrong. I feel lucky and blessed. I just wish I could have been with you from the start."

"Don't kid yourself," Mr. Lennon cut in. "This isn't the end. This is just the beginning. So, hop aboard, Miss McGill. It's going to be one heck of a ride."

"And I don't intend to miss it."

"One more thing," Charles added. "We need to report what happened tonight to everybody as quickly as we can. We need to let everybody know they can return to work. Pearl, when you get home, tell Mattie I'd like her to get on that right away. Tell her if we can do it, we'd like a meeting announced for tomorrow night at Weed Park. That's the best location I can think of right now because there will be enough room for all."

Then, smiling, he said, "We also need someone to give a

little speech tomorrow night, to talk about what we did tonight and what's coming down the road."

I noticed that all eyes were on me. "You're not serious, are you?" I said, backing away from Charles. "You want me to do that?"

"You're our new poster girl," he replied, smiling again. "This will be a good time for you to get your feet wet and for everyone to meet you. Can you come up with a few words to share with them?"

I was flattered and frightened at the thought of it. I had read the Scripture to our church congregation a few times back in Grandview, and once I even sang in front of the whole town at the Watermelon Festival, but I had never addressed a really large group before. I was torn.

"To be honest, I have no idea whether I can do it, but I'm willing to do the best I can."

"I know you will," he replied. "I have faith in you. We all do."

Everyone grew quiet again. We were all exhausted, spent. After a much quieter round of goodbyes, we started our separate journeys home.

As I walked along Front Street, I looked up and noticed the sky brighter and clearer. I took a deep breath—and my thoughts quickly came crashing back down to earth. The Muscatine air hit me with full force. I pulled out my handkerchief and covered my nose—and started laughing again. Some things never changed. Still, we had just proved anything was possible.

....

Mattie was waiting for details.

Instead of greeting me, she immediately blurted out, "I want it all, and don't you leave out a single detail. Sit over here next to me and get started."

I did my best to relay the events, but I was growing more and more tired by the minute. Plus, my mind kept racing to the fact of my speech the next evening, and I had no clue what I was going to say. Mattie didn't like it, but I gave only the highlights of the discussion, promising I'd give the rest of the details after I ate some food and got some rest. I did tell her that Charles had asked her to get the word out as quickly as possible to as many as she could about tomorrow night's meeting. She said she'd get everyone there if she had to pay for their streetcar fare or drive them to Weed Park in a buggy herself. She was so wound up I wouldn't have bet against her. I also told her I'd be giving the main speech and would appreciate any advice she might have. She just laughed and said, "This is something I have to see!" I was already nervous enough, so that wasn't what I needed to hear.

Even though the hour was growing late, Mattie suggested, and I agreed, this called for a celebration of some type. We were trying to figure out what to do when Mattie jumped up from the table. "I just remembered something. I've got something I've been saving for a special occasion, and I can't think of anything that could come up to top this. I've got coffee—and a can of asparagus!"

"But I hate asparagus," I said.

"So do I," she replied, grimly.

We giggled and leaned back in our chairs. There would be no slumgully stew this night.

The asparagus sandwiches tasted awfully good under the circumstances. The coffee was better than ambrosia.

"We've still got a long way to go," I said, sipping my coffee. "But this is definitely a start. I won't forget this night long as I live."

We sat in silence, basking in the warmth of change.

....

CHAPTER 25

I WORKED ON MY SPEECH nearly all day, taking a break only for a walk down by the river. I told myself I was there for inspiration, but the truth is I was hoping to see Gaston, hoping to be able to pass some of my ideas by him. I had no such luck. I even walked past the entrance to the clamming camp, but I decided it wasn't a good idea to go inside.

From the camp I made a long loop back up to Third Street and decided to take it over to Chestnut. There were fewer businesses and, therefore, fewer distractions that direction, which gave me more time to mull over possibilities for my talk. I knew what I wanted to say; I just didn't know how I was going to say it. I walked until my feet hurt, then hobbled the rest of the way home and took a badly-needed nap.

Mattie came home about four-thirty. She had a large bag of tomatoes and a small round of a very pungent cheese.

"Did you buy those?" I asked, knowing the answer before she even responded.

"Well, define buy," she replied. "We've got a big night tonight, so I thought we could use a special supper," she added. "I'm going to make us a big batch of fried green tomatoes. My grandmother always said tomatoes were brain food. I could use a double dose about now."

I just shook my head and smiled. Mattie Flynn was definitely one of a kind.

The fried green tomatoes were tender and delicious. They didn't make me feel any smarter, but at least I had a full stomach to power me through the evening.

After clearing our plates, we dressed quickly and walked down to the streetcar stop. Weed Park was too far to walk, so we had to ride there.

By the time we arrived at the entrance to the park, the crowd was several hundred strong, and more were pouring in. It took quite an effort for us to make our way through to the gazebo where we had been instructed to meet the rest of the executive board. When we finally made it there, Mr. Wilson was on the top step. He greeted us warmly and suggested we sit with the others and relax with a glass of lemonade. Before we were even halfway through the lemonade, Mr. Wilson walked past all of us while saying, "We need to start. There isn't much daylight left, and I don't want us here too long after dark—no matter how safe we're all feeling now. Let's not take any chances."

Charles seconded his ideas and urged us all to get ready. "This is it," he said, boldly. "Oliver is going to give a few opening remarks; then it's up to you, Pearl. Are you ready?"

"As ready as I'll ever be," I said. My knees were shaking, and sweat caused my dress to cling to my back.

"Hey, don't worry," Mattie said, trying to comfort me. "What's the worst that could happen? Well, you could fall off the gazebo. Or maybe you'll faint. Or you could get sick right here in front of everyone. Or...."

"I get it," I said, cutting her off before she really did make me sick. "Thanks for your support. That's just what I needed to hear."

"Pearl, I've known you since you learned to talk, and I never remember you missing an opportunity to flap your gums. The crowd may be larger, but I doubt much it'll give you any pause once you get rolling. So, drink the rest of your lemonade and get ready. You'll do fine. I'm not worried."

Still my stomach churned.

Mr. Wilson, standing at the edge of the gazebo, motioned for quiet and thanked everyone for coming out to the park. I expected him to give a long and detailed account of the meeting held the previous evening, but he didn't. Instead, he spoke very briefly about how important it was for everyone to stand together and how we should all support each other.

I had just sipped the last of my lemonade when he announced to the crowd, "Ladies and Gentlemen, I would now like to introduce to you our very own Pearl McGill, recording secretary for the Button Workers' Protective Union. Pearl is from the town of Grandview, just to our west. She's working here to earn the funds to fulfill her life-long dream of becoming a teacher. She's a wonderful young woman, one who cares deeply about what happens to all of us. She's been kind enough to offer her skills in the pursuit of creating a bright and prosperous future for those whose lives are tied to the factories. We're lucky to have her with us."

He made a grand gesture with his arm, pointed at me, and added, "Please join me in welcoming Pearl McGill, who has a few words for us tonight."

Polite applause greeted me as I made my way to the railing. I was still nervous, but once I saw the eager faces of those crowding around the gazebo, I remembered why we were here. In an instant, I was ready.

"Human dignity," I began. "What exactly is that? It means different things to different people. Can it be bought? Most people wouldn't say so. Can it be earned? That depends on who you ask. For those who work in our button factories, they'd say it is something very much earned—is very much the product of individual achievement. And what have we achieved? We've made Muscatine the Pearl City—the Pearl Button Capital of the World. The world knows about the quality of the work we do here. We can all be proud of that."

I paused briefly, looked around the crowd, and continued. "But what price do we pay for pride and dignity in our work? Every one of us who has worked in a factory knows the answer to that. Our wages are kept at pitiful levels. We are cheated every way imaginable when those wages are determined. We are made and kept sick through unsafe and unsanitary working conditions that we wouldn't wish on our own worst enemies. Let me ask you something. How many of you have lost a finger or an eye or have lung disease or have shell poisoning or another illness born of the factories? Let me see a show of your hands. Go on—raise your hands. Look around you. Look around. You're not alone. This is why we have to stand up and fight to get the dignity our work deserves. If we don't do something, and soon, what happened recently in a garment factory in New York could happen just as easily right here. Almost a hundred and fifty workers died in a fire at that factory. A hundred and fifty! And that fire could have been prevented with simple safety precautions. We can't let that happen here. We won't let that happen here. Fear and intimidation have been used against us. Who can forget the Sluggers we suffered here recently? And how many have been threatened with the loss of a job if they joined the union? This, too, has to stop—and it will stop."

Many in the crowd applauded loudly. Off to my left a man with a booming voice shouted, "You tell it, Sister!" I paused, before adding, "I was brought up to believe we should earn everything we get in this life. I still believe that and especially since I started working side by side with some of you in the factory. We'll work for everything we get, but we have to be given something first before we can do that. Do you know what it is?"

The crowd grew quiet as all seemed to be leaning forward, straining to hear.

"We have to be given a chance. That chance has to be given to us by the owners. When it comes down to it, that's what all we've been asking for all along. A chance. We have built the Button Workers' Protective Union to help gain this chance to better our lives, our homes, our jobs. Our union is going to help all of us—each and every one of us—get this chance. And we'll fight for this with every breath we have. Listen to me. Your...chance...is...coming!"

There were wild cheers from the crowd, followed by rousing applause. I let this go for a long minute, then waved my arms for quiet again.

"Now before I go on, I want to say something about the owners."

This topic was met by a chorus of boos and some very colorful language. I quickly tried regaining control by shouting above them, "Please listen to me. The owners, too, have rights and needs. They need a fair profit to help with the development of the industry. That may be difficult for some of us to see from the machines we work every day, but it is, nonetheless, very true. It also costs more money than most of us could imagine to maintain the current machinery while purchasing new machinery to move from steam power to electricity. They have plenty of other expenses as well just to keep the factory doors open. I know about these and understand the need for profits more than many because I grew up in the industry. Still, since arriving in Muscatine, I've seen so much more I didn't know existed on both sides. And what has opened my eyes is just how much needs to be done for the workers in this industry. That's you. Each and every one of you!"

My words about the owners had not been well received. Grumbles and exaggerated hisses spread throughout the crowd. I knew I had lost them, at least momentarily, and had to get them back—and fast. "If you'll bear with me for just a little longer, I now want to tell you what is already being done for you—and how and why our chance is now within grasp. Last evening the Executive Committee of the Button Workers' Protective Union met with representatives of the factory owners. Let me share with you what was decided. I know this is why many of you came here this evening, so I won't make you wait any longer. In those discussions, we agreed upon the following."

In making my list of items to share, I thought long and hard about what should, and should not, be mentioned at this point. I had learned a great deal from studying the way Mr. Oliver presented his list of discussion items. After thinking about that, I decided it would be wisest to build upon the positive gains—and not dwell on areas that had been tabled. Everyone needed to hear about the areas that provided the most in the way of hope and a new dawn of discussions and negotiations with the owners. With this belief first and foremost in my thoughts, I addressed the crowd.

"First, we all agreed a special committee composed of both workers and owners should be in place to negotiate any and all concerns and disputes that might arise. This group will serve as something of a 'board of appeal' if matters are not addressed to the satisfaction of all at your individual factories. This means— we will be heard!

"Second, another group is being formed to look into safety in the factories, an issue we are all mightily concerned about. I want you to know this group will make improvements happen, some of them small, some of them much larger. I want to give you an example. Too many of us end up with shell poisoning because we don't have a clean place to wash up. We're working with the owners to set up barrels of clean, fresh water that can be used by everyone. That may seem like a small change, but it represents what we can do when we work together. And, if these water barrels prevent even one case of shell poisoning, that's something we can all hang our hats on."

The crowd cheered for this last item. I had them back. Wasting no time, I continued with my list, providing a brief summary of the other major areas: our discussions of sanitation needs, new ways of determining wages, and the changes that would likely be coming in the hiring of fill-in workers. Each item was met with a roar of approval from the crowd.

My nervousness was nearly gone, but the smiles on the faces of those nearest the gazebo had me on the verge of tearing up.

"I have two more announcements to share with you," I said, pausing for emphasis and to make sure I had the attention of most. "I could give a long-winded piece of background here, but I'm not going to do that. Instead, I'm just going to give it to you in plain English. I am so proud to share with all of you that the owners have now, at long last, officially recognized our Button Workers' Protective Union!"

The roar that followed was deafening. Fists were pumped in the air. Many joined hands and danced wildly. Still others clapped long and loudly. What sounded like a pistol shot rang out near the back of the crowd, and many quickly ducked and looked around before returning to their outbursts of sheer joy and long-awaited relief.

"I have one last announcement," I shouted, trying again to gain at least some measure of their attention, "and it's the icing on the cake. Everyone—listen to me again for just one more minute. I'm sure most of you have already heard something about this today, but I can now give you the official word. For this, I'll read you my notes from the meeting: 'All workers currently affected by the shutdown will be reinstated as soon as possible.' This means all of you who have been locked out can now go back to work!"

It didn't seem possible for the celebration to get any wilder, but it did. The crowd erupted into cheers the likes of which I'd never heard before.

When the cheers finally subsided, I saw my opportunity and spoke again, projecting my voice as loudly as I could.

"The Button Workers' Protective Union has already worked long and diligently on the behalf of all. Now that it has been recognized by the owners, its members no longer need to keep their membership in secret. We can all now show our support openly."

I paused. "But, in order to continue this important work, the union will have to be supported—by all of us. It will continue to fight for change, for improvement of our health, welfare, safety, wages, and our futures. For this to happen, we need to expand our membership. I would like to direct you to the other gazebo to your right. There are several tables there where you can sign on—tonight—to join us in this great cause of representation and solidarity. Our ranks will show ownership we mean business— that we expect to be treated fairly and with dignity. This dignity is now within our grasp. We, the union and its membership, will keep working to get us all that chance. We promise that to you."

Pausing one last time, I said, "The winds of change are here—all around us. And we will ride that wind—to better lives for us all. Thank you for listening to me tonight."

The cheers and shouts rang out again, but, of course, they weren't for me. They were for the change we now hoped and prayed would be coming sooner than anyone had imagined possible.

I looked down, and Mattie was rushing up the steps toward me.

"You were wonderful!" she said, choking back tears. "I'm so proud of you!" Stop just for one minute and enjoy this. See what we've done - what you've done."

"I see hope more than anything," I said, scanning the crowd again. "And we can't let them down. We've got to keep going, got to keep moving ahead. We've got the momentum. That's clear enough. But, we can't rest. Not for a second."

I gently wiped a tear from Mattie's cheek before adding, "It's going to be a rough road ahead. Probably rougher than any of us could ever imagine."

"We'll make it," she replied. "I don't care how rough it gets. What we're doing is right. When things look dark, and I know they will at times, we'll just have to remember an old expression Viola said to me once: 'Even the worst path has holes just on one side.' I don't think I ever understood that until now. Maybe, just maybe, Viola isn't as addled as we thought."

We looked at each other—and both burst into laughter.

"Well, I'm not sure I completely understand that," I said, laughing again, "but I think I get the sentiment. We'll move ahead cautiously, but we will move ahead—and won't let anything stop us. That's good advice, and we'll take it."

....

As Mattie left to watch over the membership tables and just as I was stepping down from the gazebo, out of the corner of my eye I saw him standing next to the trunk of a large weeping willow tree. He was dressed in a dark-blue suit and matching vest. He looked so different and relaxed I barely recognized him. It was Gaston.

He was still applauding politely when I reached him.

"Just what in blue blazes are you doing here—and dressed like that?" I asked while trying to hide my joy in seeing him. "Long way from the river, aren't we?"

"Thought I'd see how the other half lives for a change," he replied, smiling, reaching out to shake my hand.

I ignored his hand, stepped forward, and gave him a quick hug.

"Shouldn't do that," he said, stepping back. "Sure wouldn't do you any good if people realized who you were holding onto." He smiled. "Remember—I'm crazy and dangerous."

"What are you doing here?"

He paused briefly, then spoke, slowly and deliberately, "This still isn't my battle, but I might be able to help my friends in the camp a bit more here on shore than I can with my canon out on the river. I aim to try."

He looked at the ground. "You see, you and I have something in common. Both our families are on the owners' side of this mess, so we have a pretty good idea of what needs to be done."

I must have appeared even more confused than I was feeling because he quickly added, "My name's Baker. David Baker. I believe you and my brother are acquainted."

"James?" I asked. "Then how.....?"

He put his index finger to his lips and shook his head. It was clear he didn't wish to talk about his family, so I didn't press him. He said, "I'm afraid what I have to do now will take me away from here for quite a while. I'm leaving tomorrow morning for Tennessee. I hear the clammers down there think they've come up with a way to protect themselves and preserve their jobs, and I'm going to see what I can learn from them. It might be a wild goose chase—or it could turn out to be something that would help here. I have to go and find out."

We stood in silence until I stepped forward and kissed him on the cheek. Before he could say anything, I said, "I know— I know. You're crazy and dangerous, and we shouldn't be seen together. Somebody already told me that. I'm not a very good listener sometimes."

He smiled and replied, "Well see each other again. I'm sure of it."

"Promise?"

He didn't answer me. He didn't need to. We hugged again briefly. He then said, "You take good care of yourself, my Pearl."

"And you, too, my David. Come back to me safely."

He turned and walked down the hill toward the river.

I jumped when Mattie suddenly appeared behind me and said, over my shoulder, "I still don't approve, but you really do care for him, don't you?"

"I do," I said, turning to face her. "Maybe someday...."

I didn't finish my thought. It was one I was going to keep to myself. Mattie seemed to understand and didn't pester me. I was shocked she didn't, and I appreciated it.

"In the meantime," I said, turning our attention toward the crowd, "we've got work to do. You're supposed to be helping sign people up for the union. Why aren't you over there? And I've got to find Mr. Oliver. Have you seen him?"

Mattie cut me off, laughing, "The straw is totally gone from your hair. I can't call you 'Country Girl' any more. And you're right. We do have plenty we need to do. Let's go. Come on. Let's get at it."

She locked her arm with mine, and we made our way into the crowd.

"You know, Mattie," I said, "I think I'm going to enjoy this."

"Me, too," she replied, tightening her grip. "Feels good, doesn't it?"

"Like nothing I've ever experienced before. That's for sure."

We waved at the Executive Board, all of whom were now standing along the railing of the gazebo. They waved back, their excitement glowing in their faces. As I looked at them, I felt both their joy—and a sense of what was to come. At that instant, I knew my life would never be the same. This was going to be a long battle, and we were planted firmly right at the front lines.

I felt so grateful to be part of the good fight.

....

April 30, 1924, 9:53 P.M., Buffalo, Iowa

ARTHUR BOSSEN WAS ENJOYING A *cigar and reading the evening paper in the parlor when he heard a blood-curdling scream—followed by what he thought to be the sharp crack of a gunshot. He rushed to the window and drew back the curtains. As he peered outside, two figures ran down the sidewalk in front of his home. They were running away from the streetlamp, so he could not make out their faces in the moonless night.*

Arthur reached for his front door, opened it, and stepped onto his porch as men and women rushed from all directions toward the yard of his neighbor, Charles Moore. Arthur walked toward the assembling crowd. Off in the distance, to the southwest, dogs were barking. One suddenly yelped loudly—as if in pain—and the others went silent.

As Arthur approached the group, he heard someone shriek, "My God—she's been shot!" Arthur joined the circle of those gathered around the body of a woman lying on the grass near the Moores' back porch. He recognized several of his neighbors—Mr. and Mrs. Moore and their son, Charlie; Frank DeHaven; and the town Marshall, Carl Rauch. Moving closer to the figure on the ground, Arthur was stunned to see it was the pretty school teacher who lived in the neighborhood. Marshall Rauch knelt down close to her and asked, "Mrs. Vance—who done this to you?"

Mrs. Vance coughed up brackish blood that oozed from the corners of her mouth. She reached up, grabbed Marshall Rauch's shirt, and gurgled what sounded to Arthur like "Car..."—before her hand fell back, her head tilted sideways, and she was motionless.

"Someone get the doctor!" Mrs. Moore cried out.

"Don't bother," Marshall Rauch said, standing and wiping his forehead. "She's gone."

All stood, stunned and silent, over the lifeless body of Ora Pearl McGill Vance.

....

EPILOGUE

THE EYES OF THE NATION focused on the small Mississippi River town of Muscatine, Iowa, in the spring of 1911. The conflict taking place there between owners and workers produced ripples reaching every corner of the nation. Whether one was pro-owner or pro-union, all knew the decisions rendered there would have dramatic influence upon everything from future prices of goods and services to working conditions in nearly every sector of industry. Although newspapers at the time often offered stories of general unrest in industry's workforce, nothing shared with the reading public compared to the events unfolding in the Muscatine button industry. Pearl McGill was, by circumstances and choice, front and center in the conflict.

The initial settlement reached that May was only the first step in what was to be a long and very bumpy journey. The settlement wasn't as important for what it actually produced as for the hope it symbolized. Neither side could claim a clear victory from those initial discussions. Both resigned themselves to something of a short, unsettled truce while realizing changes, both those desired and those fraught with uncertainty, would be coming to both camps.

On the unionist side, the most significant gains involved improvements in safety, a study of sanitary conditions in the factories, discussions of what would constitute a "fair means" of determining wages, and the creation of a structure for sharing workers' concerns with ownership. In addition, an increasing number of owners finally realized the union wasn't going to go away, so communication with its representatives would be necessary, if not essential. All knew these changes would not appear overnight, but progress was started and that, in and of itself, was a major victory.

For ownership, the gains from the negotiations were more difficult to define. Although improving safety and sanitation conditions could result in higher worker output and, therefore, increase badly-needed profits, the owners did not want it to appear as if the workers had forced these issues, even if that was the case. They still wanted at least the appearance of major, if not total, control over the vital issues surrounding the industry. As a way of ensuring this, they saw to it that newspapers printed stories slanted toward owners' benevolence and interest in the workers' welfare: stories that showed the improvements in working conditions were instigated by the owners themselves. At the same time, the conflict in Muscatine proved to be a cautionary tale for ownership in other industries, causing many of them to be proactive in their actions to head off work stoppages and strikes that could have led to their destruction.

However, the settlement was not to last. Change came slowly, and in some cases, not at all. By September, the Button Workers' Protective Union called for a general strike, one that lasted through the next spring. More discussions followed during this period, along with another dose of open conflict, including one incident during which a Muscatine police officer was killed. When the strike finally ended, neither group felt satisfied with the results. The strained relationship between the owners and workers continued through to the early 1930s, when still another strike was called. Looking back with a historical perspective, we can see how the initial discussions and the seeds planted during the strike of 1911-1912, called by some the "Button War of Muscatine," provided the platform for the much-needed and long-awaited improvements that finally came about during the 1930s.

Ironically, the changes born in the early 1930s came at the time the freshwater pearl button industry was all but finished. Within a few years, factory after factory closed its doors as plastic replaced shell as the primary material used in button production. The shell beds had all but played out, and plastic was a cheaper and more durable alternative. In the switchover from shell to plastic, the clammers disappeared completely. At the same time, while many of the same production principles remained, the number of steps in the process of creating a button was dramatically reduced. As a result, only a fraction of the number of workers once employed in the industry were needed. In a short period of time, a whole way of life for thousands of workers came to an end and a parallel, but still new, industry was born. However, it, too, had limited days ahead. Eventually, competition from foreign manufacturers made it all but impossible to keep the doors open for those factories still in business. Today, Muscatine, once called "The Pearl City" and "The Pearl Button Capital of the World," a city that at one time produced over a billion and a half buttons per year, is home to a scant few button companies. Only one of those, the McKee Button Company, remains of the original "finishing plants" from the heyday of the industry. And what became of the pungent odor in the air surrounding Muscatine that bothered so many when the industry was at its peak? Many swear one can still smell it while standing on the Mark Twain Overlook, a bluff just east of the downtown district, when the wind blows in just right from the southwest over the millions of discarded shells still buried around the town.

And what happened to the clams? Sadly, by the early 1920s overharvesting drove dozens of species into extinction. Early efforts to reseed the original beds of remaining species were not successful. Because clams play an important role in filtering and cleansing of rivers and waterways, this failure was a double tragedy. The loss of clam beds is one of the reasons the condition of the Mississippi River has deteriorated through recent decades.

Researchers eventually discovered they could create new clam beds through the migration of certain fish that carried clam larvae (glochidia) in their gills. These fish, such as smallmouth bass and banded sculpin, serve as hosts for clams during their larval stage of development. Researchers have learned that by increasing the numbers of these fish and protecting their habitat, they can indirectly increase the clam population. To help create additional clam beds, some fish hatcheries now raise these special fish and attach the clam larvae to them before releasing them into the rivers. The long-term success of these efforts will not be known for decades, but researchers are hopeful.

Clams will never be used in the mass scale production of buttons again. However, they might be able to help clean up our rivers and streams, thus ensuring a cleaner environment for future generations.

....

Great changes also came to the lives of many of those involved in this story.

John Frederick Boepple, a German immigrant and master button maker, was responsible for the creation of the pearl button industry in Muscatine when in 1887 he discovered a rich bed of shells in a section of the Mississippi River close to the town. His discovery led to what historians today call "The Great Button Boom," a period of swift growth and development of the freshwater pearl button industry. Mr. Boepple opened the first button plant in Muscatine in 1891. Very much a traditionalist in his beliefs, especially as that related to button production, he felt that preserving "strong hand-crafting skills" was much more important and desirable than finding new ways of mechanizing production. So, while his buttons were created with great care and were also, according to many, highly superior in quality, it wasn't long before he was unable to keep up with competitors who had chosen to switch over from hand-operated machines to the latest mechanical tools powered by steam and electricity. Forced out of the business he had started and loved so much, he was eventually hired by the Fairport Biological Station to use his vast knowledge to determine how to preserve and rebuild the shell beds, which were being rapidly depleted. In late fall of 1911, while he was wading in the river and studying the configuration of a shell bed, he stepped on a sharp shell, cutting his right foot badly. Blood poisoning set in, and he became gravely ill. He lingered for several months, finally passing away on January 30, 1912. It is one of the most tragic ironies of the history of the industry that the man who discovered the shell beds should in the end be killed by a shell. Karma? Fate? Poetic justice? Those affiliated with the industry had their own views on this. However people felt, John Frederick Boepple was the father of an industry that touched thousands upon thousands of lives before it ran its course. For that, he will always be remembered—and respected.

David Baker, aka "Gunboat Gaston," left for Tennessee to study the innovative conservation efforts being put into place there by the clammers in that region of the industry. He never returned to Muscatine. It was rumored he was shot and killed while trying to mediate a fight between two groups of clammers, each claiming rights to harvest shells on a remote section of the Tennessee River near Savannah, Tennessee. His brother, James, eventually took over the family business, and it was said by all who knew him that he gave constant attention to improving the working conditions of those in his employ.

Mr. Blanton was so furious with Pearl, believing her to be a "turncoat," he never spoke to her again. The lockout and resulting strike also upset him so badly he became obsessed with trying to keep his workers under tight control. This took a toll on his health, and he died of a heart attack in his office at his factory in the summer of 1913.

Mattie Flynn continued her efforts to establish better working conditions for those in the button industry and, as a result, was soon blacklisted by ownership. Shortly after the strike ended, her services were no longer needed by the union, and she was dropped from their payroll. Because of the blacklisting, she was unable to find employment in Muscatine, not just in the button factories, but in any other businesses. She eventually moved to Chicago, changed her name to escape the hold of the blacklisting, started an employment agency, and had a long and successful career helping those in need find gainful employment in all sectors of industry. Through the years, and behind the scenes, she never gave up the fight to improve the lives of workers everywhere. In 1942 she died as a result of injuries received in an auto accident. She had been on her way home from a meeting to establish special childcare centers for children of parents working in defense plants aiding the war effort. A proud and courageous woman, Mattie Flynn never gave up the good fight.

Viola Alexander never fully recovered from the concussion sustained in Muscatine. For three months after being taken to Washington, Iowa, she drifted in and out of consciousness, finally succumbing to a stroke. She was twenty-three years old.

Pearl McGill decided to accept the invitation from the Womens' Trade Union League to come to their offices in Chicago after the initial settlement in Muscatine. There, she was taken under the wing of the WTUL. They helped polish her speaking skills, taught her how to organize rallies, and schooled her in the basics of fundraising. As a "poster girl" for the rights of workers —and representing the Button Workers' Protective Union, the Women's Trade Union League, and the American Federation of Labor—she was most valuable and could provide the greatest contribution by giving talks and speeches. It wasn't long before she became a popular and dynamic speaker. During this time, she spoke to every group she felt might be able to help the cause— from large church congregations in Boston to groups of factory workers in New York City to gatherings of locked out workers in St. Louis to dozens upon dozens of other groups in cities across the country. She became so consumed with her efforts to gain rights for workers that ownership, in a wide variety of industries, soon saw her as a serious threat and a formidable foe, one to be watched closely. Warnings and death threats followed her nearly everywhere she went. However, these did not slow her or lessen her resolve. Still, her new, high profile started working against her, and she knew it would be better for herself and the unions if she could find another way to contribute to the cause.

After much deliberation and soul-searching, she found that other way—serving again as a patsy, an industrial spy. She made her high profile a non-issue by creating new identities and names for herself and then securing entry-level jobs in several different industries. In each instance, she worked just long enough to gain valuable information about conditions in the factories that could be used by the unions in their negotiations with ownership. Her work for Mr. Blanton had prepared her well for this role, and she was quite good at it. Eventually, however, and before serious harm came to her, she received word owners somehow had been tipped off to her endeavors. They quickly tried to discredit her work by labeling her a "Socialist," a "Communist," and the worst type of instigator and troublemaker, but the names never bothered Pearl. What did bother her were the injustices she saw every place she went. Her heart was still firmly in the fight, but she knew at that point her work with the unions had run its course. She would no longer be able to continue her speeches, and her spying days were definitely over. From a practical standpoint, she knew it was time for her to step away, at least temporarily, from her work with the unions. It was time, finally, for her to go about trying to achieve her first true dream—and what had brought her into the button industry in the first place: a teaching career. Shortly thereafter, Pearl moved to Cedar Falls, Iowa, hoping to earn her teaching certificate at Iowa State Teachers College. However, even after all the work she had done for the unions, her financial situation was still tenuous at best.

In February of 1914, while hanging on by a thread financially, Pearl heard that Helen Keller was coming to address a group of teachers and students in Cedar Falls. Pearl knew of Ms. Keller's tireless work in support of workers' rights and felt her a kindred soul; as it turned out, Ms. Keller had heard of Pearl's work as well. She wrote Ms. Keller a letter and made plans to meet her when she arrived in town. Pearl later said their meeting was most inspirational and enjoyable. While the visit lifted Pearl's spirits, which she badly needed at that time, she was still facing the prospect of having to drop out of school because of her financial difficulties. That is—that was the case until she shortly thereafter received the following letter from Ms. Keller:

Dear Miss McGill:

I have thought of you many times since we saw you at the station in Cedar Falls, and my heart goes out to you in your brave struggle for education, so that,I am moved to try to help you. Will you accept the en-closed check as a token of my warm sympathy and comradeship? I long to give back to others all the help and happiness that have been bestowed upon me, and it makes me happy to have this opportunity to do something for one whose courage and devotion to a noble cause are such an inspiration to me. I wish you every success in your work. I look forward confidently to your being a teacher, not only in a class room, but in the great school of the world. It is splendid to think what you can do with your fine mind and fearless heart to lessen the terrible ignorance of men on the most vital questions of our daily life-- the questions of bread, of right thinking and right living.

With affectionate greetings, in which my teacher joins me, I am,

Sincerely your comrade,

Helen Keller

Kansas City, Missouri,   114 Fenway.

February nineteenth   Boston,

Mass

* (Note: Ms. Keller's letter courtesy of Jean Burns)

Enclosed with the letter was a check that would cover the cost of Pearl's entire education. With that financial support, Pearl earned her County Teaching Certificate—and subsequently landed her first teaching position.

As she had in everything else she had put her heart and mind to in her life, Pearl excelled as a teacher, bringing to her students a joy for learning that opened the world for them. She , remained in the classroom for ten years, touching and inspiring hundreds of students.

Sadly, Pearl McGill's life was tragically cut short. Pearl was murdered on the evening of April 30, 1924 in the town of Buffalo, Iowa. She was thirty years old.

Pearl's pioneering work with the labor unions will remain her legacy. The story of her early life and decision to put her own dreams temporarily aside to fight for the rights and dignity of others would become an inspiration to many who would follow. Pearl wasn't just a "poster girl" for a union; she was the face of hope and the future for the thousands of workers still suffering the terrible working conditions in factories all across the land. That this young woman from the tiny town of Grandview, Iowa, could have such an impact upon the labor force of the nation resonated with those still immersed in the fight. Through the years, word of her efforts inspired so many that some eighty-two years after her passing she was posthumously inducted into the Iowa Labor Hall of Fame, a proud branch of the Iowa Federation of Labor.

....

AFTERWORD

No story of the life of Pearl McGill would be complete without at least a brief discussion of the end of her life. Her death, and more particularly the manner and circumstances of her death, have been shrouded in mystery for decades—and the complete truth of what actually happened may never be known. However, what evidence does exist indicates the initial newspaper accounts of her passing were at best incorrect, and possibly downright fabricated.

What we know to be true is that Pearl McGill was murdered near 10 P.M. on April 30, 1924 in Buffalo, Iowa. She was shot once with a .32 caliber bullet. Once past that fact, the truth gets as muddy as the stretch of the Mississippi River flowing just a stone's throw from the center of that town.

As I began my journey to write this story, I was already aware of the publicity surrounding her death and believed, like most others, that the accounts were accurate. It didn't take long for me to learn otherwise. In conducting my research, I kept uncovering pieces of a puzzle that simply didn't fit together—and even found some gaping holes where missing pieces should have been but weren't. The more of these pieces I collected, the more I became fascinated with trying to put together the complete puzzle. During my search, I visited nearly two dozen archives, record centers, and government offices. I tracked down the original coroner's report filed for Pearl's death, original news accounts long lost to the shelves of history, original eyewitness accounts, original maps and geographic information of the era, original police reports, and even the long-lost coroner's inquest filed shortly after the murder—a vastly different document than the basic coroner's report. I also was able to interview relatives of the principal characters. I even visited the town of Buffalo on three different occasions to "walk off" the purported events of the crime; the main homes involved are all still standing, and the streets remain virtually unchanged. After studying all the information I had gathered during my research, I found several interrelated areas that, when assembled, could help shed light on what happened that terrible and fateful night.

Marriage Background:

While David Baker (Gunboat Gaston) remained firmly in her heart even after his death, Pearl eventually had to move on emotionally. While teaching in Buffalo, Iowa, Pearl met Edward Vance, a local button cutter and brother to one of her dearest friends. After a courtship of just a few months, they were married on April 21, 1917. Their marriage soon became what friends and relatives alike termed "tumultuous" and "dysfunctional." Edward was prone to fits of depression and paranoia, which resulted at times in forced confinement for medical treatment. He would eventually receive these treatments at several hospitals, including the State Hospital for the Insane at Mt. Pleasant, Iowa. After seven years of this relationship, Pearl filed for and was granted a divorce; the court records show she was granted the divorce in June of 1923 on the grounds of "Cruel and Inhumane Treatment."

Some months before Pearl was murdered, Edward had proposed a reconciliation with her. She declined.

Initial Speculation in Newspapers:

Just hours after Pearl's death, newspaper reporters converged on Buffalo and created a sensational account of murder and madness that both captivated and put an entire region into panic, panic that spawned a desperate manhunt and resulted in the citizens of Buffalo huddling for safety in their homes.

The first news accounts stated, quite authoritatively and in bold headlines, that undoubtedly Edward Vance murdered Pearl.

They did this despite the fact no evidence to support this speculation had yet been gathered. One particularly imaginative scribe wrote that Pearl was reading her Bible and eating peach slices at her kitchen table when her ex-husband, who had been hiding in the kitchen closet, suddenly leapt out and assaulted her—then chased her down the street before shooting her. Although law enforcement officials later found a Bible and a peach on her kitchen table, no evidence existed at the time—or any time afterward during the whole investigation—that either Pearl or Edward Vance was ever in the home that evening.

Still others reported Pearl had been away visiting a "sick friend" earlier that evening and had just been driven home in the automobile of Elmer Carpenter, a brother of a friend. Reporters suggested that Pearl had just stepped from the vehicle when she was chased by a man, or men, and was cornered and shot at the back door of the Moore home, immediately across the street to the east from Pearl's home. These accounts also suggested a man, or men, then ran either down the alley behind the Moore home, ran north up the side street, or ran south toward the river. These accounts also stated the most likely main perpetrator of the violence was Edward Vance.

When all the accounts were sorted through by law enforcement officials, one thing came to the surface: There was absolutely no evidence to show Pearl ever made it back to her house after being dropped off by Elmer Carpenter. The stories of Edward hiding in the house, as it turned out, were likely created by the reporters.

It should be noted that at that time many reporters were paid either by the word or the story, rather than being on regular salary by the newspapers, so it would have been in their financial interest to come up with the best tale possible to keep the reading public buying newspapers. This writer is not suggesting the reporters lied on purpose. What I am suggesting is that, perhaps, the reporters were quick to run with information that had not yet been checked out for accuracy, and they did so in as many words as possible.

Eyewitness Accounts:

The initial eyewitness accounts also turned out to be little more than theories suggested by those living in the immediate neighborhood. Still, news reporters were quick to publish what must have been nearly every word that came out of the neighbors' mouths.

One neighbor, John Mangels, said he saw shadows struggling mightily on the back porch of the Moore home—and then saw the flash of a gunshot and a body fall. He also said he heard Pearl shout something that sounded like "Car" or "Carl" or "Char" before she died. Another neighbor, Marshal Rauch, said he ran out of his house and found Pearl facedown on the sidewalk out near the street behind the Moore house.

Still another neighbor, Arthur Bossen, who lived a block away, said he heard the shot, looked out his window, and saw figures run past.

Initially, when prompted by the reporters, many were certain they saw Edward Vance leaving the scene. However, later, under oath, all recanted this. At the same time, just as the reporters had suggested in their accounts, othre witnesses saw men running in three different directions after the shot—down an alley, up the side street, and down toward the river. Still others said two men could be seen running from the scene, although these witnesses could not provide specific descriptions or additional details. In criminal investigations it's fairly common for witnesses to a crime to give different accounts and descriptions. However, even taking that into consideration doesn't explain the witnesses seeing men run in three different directions—and at least two seemingly reliable witnesses stating there were two men running from the scene. Based upon the collective body of evidence, it is entirely possible as many as three men were involved.

The physical descriptions of persons running from the scene provided by other witnesses also did not match, which may be understandable, but not one of these descriptions came close to matching the physical appearance of Edward Vance. When questioned, many of the eyewitnesses stated the man they saw running from the scene was approximately 5'5" tall and "squat." Edward Vance was tall and thin of frame.

In the end, none of the witnesses could say they actually saw Edward Vance leaving the scene of the crime. The witnesses could not agree on the physical description or number of those involved. They could not even agree on the spot where Pearl's body was found. This was particularly odd because the coroner later determined that the shot would have been almost immediately fatal; therefore, it would have been extremely difficult, if not impossible, for Pearl to have moved from the initial location.

Still, in spite of all the conflicting eyewitness accounts, the news stories continued to suggest Edward had been responsible for the crime.

The Manhunt:

Immediately following these first news stories, additional information appeared that further inflamed the speculation that Pearl's ex-husband was the murderer—and created a climate of fear throughout the region. A story in *The Daily Times* warned that Edward Vance would likely return to town soon, and when he did, his return "...will result in one or more killings." The story went on to describe the townspeople's reaction: "Since the murder, everybody in the little town has gone about armed. Citizens are patrolling the streets armed with shotguns and revolvers. Day and night the watch is being maintained."

This characterization of the town's climate helped spur an immediate manhunt. Several groups of armed men did, in fact, then take to the streets. Most were extra deputies assigned to the case; others were local citizens whipped into a frenzy of fear. Even the Governor was drawn in; on May 12, he posted a $500 reward for information leading to the capture of Edward Vance.

The manhunt continued for over two weeks. During this period, there were numerous alleged sightings of Edward Vance.

He was reportedly seen everywhere from just outside the city limits of Buffalo near an abandoned mine to Keokuk, Iowa, to St. Louis, Missouri. One sighting in particular called for close scrutiny, at least for a little while. A taxi driver in Keokuk, Iowa, positively identified as Edward Vance the man he had driven part way to St. Louis on the evening of May 3—several days after the murder. The driver stated Edward had a small suitcase with him and appeared quite determined they waste no time in getting farther down that direction. The taxi driver made a positive identification and swore to it under oath. Once the authorities were made aware of this, the manhunt shifted south.

During this period two other individuals came forth to provide information that initially seemed plausible. A shop owner in Rock Island, Illinois, reported that Edward Vance purchased a small caliber handgun from him just a day or two before the murder. A taxi driver, also from Rock Island, came forth to say he had driven Edward Vance to Buffalo's town limits and dropped him off there the night of the crime. Later, when both were asked to testify under oath, they did not; they both returned to Rock Island. Still, their stories made for good reading in the papers.

At the same time, Edward Vance's mental state was also a frequent area of discussion in the news accounts. The fact that he had been hospitalized several times for what was described as "erratic" behavior drew the most attention and scrutiny. When it was suggested Edward had frequently made threats against the local citizens, none could be found to substantiate this claim. No matter, he was portrayed as a madman out to seek revenge upon the innocent residents of Buffalo. The fact that he had never harmed anyone, let alone made any threats, was dismissed.

A Body Found:

On the early morning of Sunday, May 18, an engineer at a local quarry discovered a body floating in the Mississippi River about a quarter of a mile west of Buffalo. The body was badly decomposed and bloated from its time in the water. The body was that of a man, but it was dressed in women's clothing. Reports at the time said the clothes consisted of a black silk dress, a red hat trimmed in pink, and new silk stockings. Rolled up under the dress was a pair of man's pants. Later reports stated that two shots had been fired into the mouth of the body—either of which would have proved fatal. The man who discovered the body was well aware of the reward being offered for information related to the whereabouts or capture of Edward Vance, so he immediately contacted legal authorities to say he had found Vance.

The body was so badly decomposed positive identification initially was not made. It was only after a member of the group sent to collect the body noticed a slight gap between two teeth, similar to a gap some said was known to exist in Edward's teeth, that the body was determined to be Edward Vance. The investigation into the possibility of Edward Vance making his escape to St. Louis was called off by Keokuk police after they were informed a body had been found believed to be that of Edward Vance.

Edward's father, Daniel Vance, was brought to see the body. He could not identify it as his son, but after he was informed it was Edward's body, he reportedly broke down and wept—then left to tell his wife. Shortly thereafter, and while still clinging to the hope of their son's innocence, his parent's held a brief funeral service at their home before the body was buried in the family plot in Rosedale Cemetery in Buffalo.

Just why a man's body was found in women's clothing was a popular subject for debate in both the media and within the citizenry of Buffalo. If the body really was that of Edward Vance, then most theorized he had probably killed his wife, snuck off to a place where he had hidden the clothing, quickly changed his clothes, and then hoped to escape by assuming the visage of a woman. However, as others questioned, if that were the case, why would he then kill himself before trying to make good his getaway? And how did he fire a fatal shot into his mouth—and then fire a second fatal shot into the same location? Furthermore, it was never determined the bullets were of .32 caliber.

From all accounts, both law enforcement and the local citizens were so ready for closure to the case that these questions were ignored, very little investigation took place after the body was found, and no formal inquest related to Edward Vance's death was conducted. Most significantly, it was never determined beyond a shadow of a doubt the body was that of Edward Vance.

Coroner's Report:

The Coroner's Report was concise, direct, and specific. Coroner J. D. Cantwell reported that a .32 caliber bullet entered Pearl's right breast, had taken a diagonal course through the heart, and then lodged just below the left shoulder blade.

This information was clear enough. However, for the bullet to travel in this manner, Pearl would have had to be positioned in one of two ways. One possibility would have had her prone, lying on the ground when the shot was fired. However, this scenario did not match any of the "eyewitness" accounts of the crime. The second possibility would have had Pearl standing, with the perpetrator kneeling below her, at the time the bullet entered her body. The existing evidence also didn't seem to support this theory. Given that both scenarios didn't seem to go along with the evidence, the authorities became more confused than ever, and this point of the investigation was never resolved.

However, whether Pearl was below or above the assailant when the shot was fired, the trajectory of the bullet indicated the shooter was left-handed. Edward Vance was right-handed. This point was not addressed in the investigation.

Coroner's Inquest:

While the Coroner's Report had been a very clinical representation of the immediate cause of death, the Coroner's Inquest was a long session of questioning of those who allegedly had information about both the causes leading up to the crime—and information about the crime itself. Most of the witnesses who had earlier provided details to the newspapers were questioned, this time under oath. Once under oath, they quickly changed their stories. Their "positive" identifications were no longer positive. Their physical positions in the neighborhood also came under close scrutiny; some who said they had a direct line of sight to the events turned out not to have had such a vantage point.

Twelve individuals were questioned during the inquest. After the questioning, it was determined there was not one piece of hard evidence to link Edward Vance to the murder. Therefore, an "open verdict" was issued by Coroner J. D. Cantwell. His official opinion was "Cause of death from hands of a party unknown to the jury."

My Speculation:

Not a single piece of hard evidence exists to link Edward Vance to the murder. If he didn't commit the crime, then who could have? Consider these possibilities.

At least two credible witnesses at the time of the crime reported two men, and possibly a third, fleeing from the scene. So many were immediately convinced Edward Vance was guilty that this line of inquiry was not pursued. In addition, with the large group of neighbors appearing almost as soon as the shot was fired, it is possible one or more of these individuals might later have been thought by onlookers to have been involved in the crime. However, and with that said, it is the belief of this writer, after studying every document I could find related to this case, that two men were, in fact, responsible for Pearl's death—and neither was Edward Vance.

Right before Pearl died, she was heard to say "Car," "Carp," or "Char." Just before being shot, she was dropped off near her home by Elmer *Carp*enter. Might she have been calling his name—to indicate he had been her attacker? According to the legal evidence, supposedly the last person to see Pearl alive was Charles Moore, her neighbor across the street who had said he witnessed Pearl leaving the vehicle that dropped her off that night. Might she have been saying *"Charles"*—to indicate he had been her attacker? Pearl was much older than both, but it had been rumored that both men had something of a "crush" on her. Might that have played into the events?

Another scenario—one I suggest in the book itself—is more likely. It was known in the months before the murder that Pearl had been contacted and asked to help, once again, with labor concerns involving several unions. Pearl spoke often of her desire to get back into the fight for the rights of workers. The strong union she had once helped form in Muscatine had lost effective leadership and was on the verge of collapse, leaving very little in the way of protection for the workers. She was aware they needed her help—badly. Representatives of other unions had also contacted her. The period of the "Roaring 20's" was a tumultuous time for unions, and having a person of Pearl's talents stand with them would have been a godsend for them. Pearl loved teaching, and she was a teacher beloved by all in Buffalo. Still, she yearned to get back to the good fight. Whether she would have actually left teaching to help the unions will never be known—because of the bullet that ended her life on the night of April 30, 1924.

I believe, because some of Pearl's former friends and acquaintances from her days in union activity had recently been murdered (see the beginning of this book), Pearl was "assassinated" by those who feared her potential reinvolvement in union activity. My theory is based on the research conducted in the writing of this book. Until proven otherwise, this seems to me the most plausible conclusion. However, the case, to this day, is still "officially open," and I welcome the comments and views of others on this matter.

In the end, the life and legacy of Pearl McGill demonstrates the power of the human spirit. Her determination to follow what she believed to be right can continue to inspire those today and in the future who strive for safety and justice in the workplace.

—JSC

ACKNOWLEDGMENTS

THIS BOOK COULD NOT HAVE been written without the generous assistance of many wonderful people, all of whom gave freely of their time and knowledge:

First and foremost, I'd like to thank Mrs. Jean Burns, niece of Pearl Mcgill, for a treasure-trove of artifacts and information. Mrs. Burns provided everything from original letters, photographs, and documents—to family histories and stories from the time period involved. However, her gracious hospitality and sincere encouragement will always be remembered most of all.

Kristin McHugh-Johnston, former Executive Director of the Muscatine History and Industry Center (Home of the Pearl Button Museum), provided invaluable Muscatine history and specifics of the button manufacturing process of the era. Her book, *Muscatine (Images of America Series)*, also provided much needed visual representation of the town of Muscatine of that time period. I'd also like to thank her for putting up with, and helping provide answers to, the dozens upon dozens of questions I posed to her.

I would also like to thank the following individuals for their contributions:

Mrs. Dorothy Boepple-LeVallee, granddaughter of John Frederick Boepple (founder of the Muscatine pearl button industry), for family history and biographical information.

Dr. Kate Rousmaniere, Professor and Chair, Department of Educational Leadership, Miami University, for invaluable information related to Pearl McGill's life and union activity. (Dr. Rousmaniere's writings were an inspiration to me, especially her article, "The Muscatine Button Workers' Strike of 1911-12: An Iowa Community in Conflict" (*The Annals of Iowa*, Volume 46, No. 4).)

Ron Deiss, professional archeologist, Moline, Illinois, for geographical information about, and historical film footage of, the pearl button industry.

Jon Duyvejonck, Mississippi River Biologist, for detailed information about the button manufacturing process (and, for visual illustration, gave to me samples of the many different types and styles of buttons manufactured in and around Muscatine at the time of the events of this story).

Phyllis Holmes, owner of "Pearl's Unique," in Newport, Arkansas, for history of the clamming industry in that region of the country in the early part of the Twentieth Century.

Anne Thompson, Archivist, Earlham College Archives, for help with vital records research.

Jason Stratman, Research Specialist, Missouri History Museum Library and Research Center, for helping source historical information and newspaper accounts of the era.

Margaret Blain, of Isles of Scilly, England, for sharing with me original booklets from the "American Pearl Button Company." These documents were valuable sources of information about the manufacturing process.

Ms. Jo Burgess, Iowa State Button Society, for sharing with me her vast knowledge of buttons and button manufacturing; she also provided me with many samples of the different styles of buttons created in the era described.

Madeleine Eagle, Vice President of the McKee Button Company, Muscatine, Iowa, for special assistance with architectural and structural information related to the original button factories (and gave a wonderful tour of the current McKee facility); her father, Theodore McKee also provided historical information involving the union activity during the button workers' strike of 1911.

Sheila Chaudoin, Photo Archivist and Local Historian at the Musser Public Library, Muscatine, Iowa, for her wonderful assistance with photo selection, especially within the Oscar Grossheim Collection—and permission for use of the photos.

Michele Arends, Cedar Falls, Iowa, for help with manuscript preparation and photo imaging.

Douglas and Judith Hartley, for providing photography for the book and historical artifacts.

Crystal and Cory Ford (daughter and son-in-law) and Jack and Donna Copeland (my parents)—for their love and support.

For providing historical and legal records, I'd also like to thank the following individuals from offices in Buffalo, Iowa and Davenport, Iowa: Christine Carson of the Buffalo Historical Society Museum; Kim Kauffman, CPP, Deputy Clerk, City of Buffalo; Patricia Richardson, Special Collections, Davenport Public Library; Sue Brewer, Operations Manager, Scott County Recorder's Office; Lynn Ann DeSmet, Supervisor, Scott County Courthouse. I'd also like to add a special thanks to the Scott County Coroner's Office and the Scott County Sheriff's Office for their kind assistance with medical and legal records research.

For their help in securing educational and historical records, I'd like to recognize the following individuals from the University of Northern Iowa: Philip Patton, UNI Registrar; Irene Elbert, Office Coordinator, UNI Registrar's Office; Stan Lyle, Research Librarian; Gerald Peterson, Archivist, Special Collections Library; Linda Berneking, Interlibrary Loan Specialist; Jim Davis, Professor of English Education. In addition, I'd like to thank Amanda Miller and T. Matteson Toenjes for technical support; Dana Peiffer, Technology Support Specialist, for providing the full range of technology support services; Kelsey Erenberger, for photo technology support and restoration.

While she is no longer with us, I'd like to give special recognition to my grandmother, Ocie Lee Dunavant, for always sharing with me her love of sewing and storytelling, both of which ended up having a great influence upon my telling of this story.

I'd also like to offer special gratitude to my wife, Linda, for her assistance all through the project—and for tolerating the mounds of books and research documents stacked all over the house—*and* for her support and encouragement during the large number of trips made to gather research for the project.

And, finally, I'd like to thank Rosemary Yokoi, the best editor and friend a writer ever had!

Thank you, and bless you all!

Photo Section

Pearl and fellow workers at the button factory where she worked in Muscatine. Pearl is on top row, far right.
(Photo courtesy of Jean Burns)

View down Second Street just to the east of Chestnut Street in downtown Muscatine. Pearl would have had a very similar view from her lodgings. (Photo courtesy of Musser Public Library, Graham Collection)

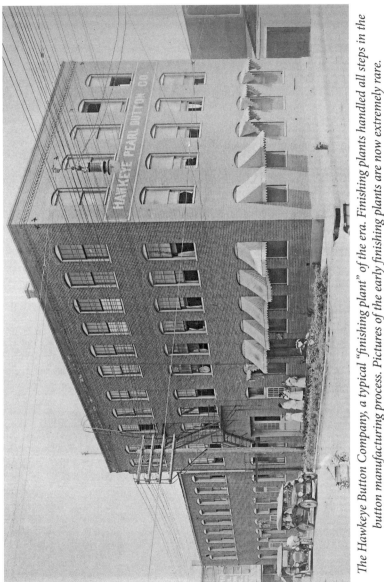

The Hawkeye Button Company, a typical "finishing plant" of the era. Finishing plants handled all steps in the button manufacturing process. Pictures of the early finishing plants are now extremely rare.
(Photo courtesy of Musser Public Library, Oscar Grossheim Collection)

Button blank cutting factory in Grandview, Iowa, owned and operated by Pearl's uncle, Sam Henry McGill. (Photo courtesy of Jean Burns)

Shells with holes denoting where button blanks were drilled out. Finished pearl buttons are piled below. (Copeland Collection)

Pearl (on left) and Mattie Flynn during their days with the Button Workers'
Protective Union in Muscatine. (Photo courtesy of Jean Burns)

The State Militia was ordered to Muscatine during the lockout/strike of 1911. They were charged with enforcing martial law until the violence subsided. (Photo courtesy of Musser Public Library, Oscar Grossheim Collection)

Weed Park (1911), Muscatine, Iowa, location of many meetings and rallies in support of the new Button Workers' Protective Union. Pearl gave her first public speech here. (Photo courtesy of Musser Public Library, Oscar Grossheim Collection)

Clammers and their clamming boats lined up along the Mississippi River at Muscatine. Note clams hanging from lines in the boats.
(Photo courtesy of Musser Public Library, Oscar Grossheim Collection)

Typical section of a clamming camp of the time period in the story. This particular photo is of the Miller family, long-time clammers in and around Muscatine. (Photo courtesy of Musser Public Library, Arnold Miller Collection)

"Mississippi Harvest," a bronze sculpture of a clam fisherman standing in a clam-filled boat with clamming forks over his head in Muscatine. (Photo courtesy of Douglas Hartley)

*Pearl while travelling to rally support for the workers in the button factories of
Muscatine. (Photo courtesy of Jean Burns)*

Pearl (circa 1915) in her teaching days, following her work with the unions.
(Photo courtesy of Jean Burns)

Pearl McGill-Vance (bottom right) with husband Edward Vance (standing to the right behind Pearl). Edward's brother is in the center.
(Photo courtesy of Jean Burns)